Succeeding in a Transition Economy:
Survival Strategies in Eastern Germany

AALBORG **UNIVERSITY PRESS**

Succeeding in a Transition Economy:
Survival Strategies in Eastern Germany

Erik A. Borg

Frank-Michael Kirsch

Renate Åkerhielm

Succeeding in a Transition Economy:
Survival Strategies in Eastern Germany
Erik A. Borg, Frank-Michael Kirsch, Renate Åkerhielm

© Aalborg University Press, 2010

Cover painting: Johanna Borg Bruchfeld
Layout and cover: Pernille Guldbæk Jensen, Guldbæk Grafisk
Printed by Silkeborg Bogtryk A/S, 2010
ISBN: 978-87-7307-980-5

Distribution:
Aalborg University Press
Niels Jernes Vej 6B
9220 Aalborg
Denmark
Phone: (+45) 99 40 71 40, Fax: (+45) 96 35 00 76
E-mail: aauf@forlag.aau.dk
www.forlag.aau.dk

All rights reserved. No part of this book may be reprinted or reproduced or utilized in any form or by any electronic, mechanical, or other means, now known or hereafter invented, including photocopying and recording, or in any information storage or retrieval system, without permission in writing from the publishers, except for reviews and short excerpts in scholarly publications.

Acknowledgments

We would like to acknowledge the financial support from the Baltic Sea Foundation for the research presented in this book. We would also like to thank the two reviewers for constructive remarks on the research in connection with the publication. Supportive comments also emerged during research conferences, and from reviewers of academic journals, where essential parts of this research have been presented.

We would furthermore like to acknowledge the contribution made by Donald Hughes who has translated the chapters 3 and 6 and the case studies on Rotkäppchen, Rhönbrauerei Dittmar, ASS Altenburger, Hedwig Bollhagen, Halloren, Kathi and Jenapharm, from German to English.

Stockholm in December, 2009
Erik A. Borg, Frank-Michael Kirsch, Renate Åkerhielm

Chapter outline

1. Introduction	7
Case study: Rotkäppchen - Strategies to eliminate prejudice	15
2. Survival strategies	27
Case study: Schott – finding the right partner	39
Case study: Rhönbrauerei Dittmar – A beer needs its home	43
3. In safe hands?	
Socio-Economical Experiences on the Road to a Market Economy	49
Case study: ASS Altenburger - The cards are being shuffled anew	84
4. Access to Investments and Intellectual Capital	91
Case study: Jenoptik – mitigating the "brain drain"	100
Case study: Freiberger Compound Materials – attracting new investments	105
5. Creating customer value	109
Case study: MIFA - Surviving by rapidly increasing productivity	115
Case study: Hedwig Bollhagen (HB) – "For me, rethinking wasn't necessary"	119
6. The safe anchor of Ostalgia	129
Case study: Halloren - Taking Ostalgia to the stock market	158
7. Attractive product design: Opportunities and obstacles	165
Case study: Meissen - Survival by design management	176

8. Developing competitive brands in a global economy 187
   Case study: Kathi does it step-by-step 192

9. Crisis management 207
   Case study: Jenapharm - A Partisan-Strategy for
   confronting an external disaster and an internal crisis at a time 210

10. Understanding survival 219

1. Introduction

This is a book about survival. How do companies survive when the basic conditions for their existence change overnight? The question has a newly revived and essential actuality as a result of the recent world economic crisis.

The fall of the Berlin Wall on November 9, 1989 and the launch of the German Economic, Monetary and Social Union on July 1, 1990 radically changed economic conditions for more than 8,000 previously state-, municipal- or party-owned companies in the former German Democratic Republic (GDR). Overnight, most East German manufacturing plants had been devalued, after having been able to survive for decades thanks to a protected market in the East—which also collapsed, along with the East German domestic market. For East German companies, the monetary union meant "the introduction of a social market economy without a market", as Birgit Breuel, president of the world's largest holding company, the Treuhand agency, described it.[1] In a move without historical precedent and under considerable political pressure, Treuhand privatised 15,000 companies and liquidated 4,000 others in less than five years.

Many of these 15,000 companies did not survive. But for several hundred medium-sized and small businesses the market economy provided a real upturn, and for about one hundred companies it opened doors to previously unimaginable opportunities. Today, several of these firms are brand or market leaders in Germany or even globally.

How did these companies succeed? For an answer, we visited 15 of these companies in about ten industries and evaluated the strategies they used to survive or, more importantly, become dominant players. What did they do differently from the companies that failed? Our starting point for the research project "East German Enterprises after Transition", which was financed by the Swedish foundation *Östersjöstiftelsen*, was six working hypotheses:[2]

---

[1] Birgit Breuel in Birgit Breuel, Michael C Burda (Hrsg.): *Ohne historisches Vorbild. Die Treuhandanstalt 1990-1994. Eine kritische Würdigung.* Bostelmann & Siebenhaar, Berlin 2005, p. 16.
[2] See: Erik A. Borg, Frank-Michael Kirsch, Renate Åkerhielm: Survivors in the Market Economy: East German Companies after Transition. *The Business Review*, Cambridge, Vol. 7, 2/2007.

- Access to investments and intellectual capital made it possible for East German companies to survive the introduction of the market economy.
- The companies were able to create customer value in relation to their products and services.
- Companies that survived an initial period of hostility towards East German products had a better chance of surviving.
- Nostalgic attitudes among consumers, so-called *ostalgia*, ensured a continuing market for East German products.
- Companies with more attractive product designs than what was common in eastern Germany made their products marketable in the West.
- East German companies that were able to sustain competitive brands after unification were able to succeed.

Unsurprisingly, the reality of the transition seemed more complicated than the hypotheses could express. We confronted these realities directly in an attempt to understand them, and during the process found similarities in successive companies' attitudes towards the market economy and the new political, economical and socio-cultural conditions in Germany. Our empirical studies and theoretical perspectives allowed us to generate conclusions that could be transferred to this reality, and be used by companies that must manage previously unforeseen (and unforeseeable) situations. The survival strategies we identified shall serve as inspiration and guidance for businesses coping with exceptional circumstances.

Central research perspectives

This book represents the outcome of research into the corporate transformation that took place after market economy reforms were instituted in the former German Democratic Republic (GDR), or East Germany. An appropriate focus for such a study is the type of change that can benefit organisational performance and increase a company's chances of survival (Haveman 1992). We conducted detailed case studies of companies that survived the transition. The research is predominantly qualitative, and adopts methodology that is recognised in this area (Denzin and Lincoln 1998; Berg 2001; Flick, von Kadorff and Steinke 2004).

The corporate transformation examined here can be studied with reference to consistent theoretical frameworks. Corporate transformation has previously been approached from several different angles (Bjelland and Wood 2008), notably holism (Kotter 1996; Kilmann 1995), ambidextrous forms of corporate transformation (O'Reilly and Tushman 2004), transformation through acquisition and restructuring (Collins 2001), and improvisational transformation (Wood 2007). Our study of corporate transformation is most clearly associated with the improvisational transformation perspective. Many changes seen in the studied companies seemed to occur as a result of ad hoc improvisations rather than systematic strategies. That is not to say that strategies, as such, were not adopted; rather, the ad hoc survival strategies put into place are closely related to the concrete actions taken to ensure short- and long-term survival. Consequently, strategic change leadership can be viewed as a primary task for management (Graetz 2000).

Strategies have been seen as vital to the survival of companies (Chebat 1999; Noble 1999). Mintzberg (1987) distinguishes five different definitions of corporate strategies, which can be viewed as plans, ploys, patterns, positions, and perspectives. A strategy can be intended or unintended, deliberate or inadvertent, emergent or realised. As a plan, a strategy represents a consciously intended course of action. When strategy is defined as a pattern, however, it represents a stream of actions. As a perspective, a strategy represents an integrated way of seeing the world (Mintzberg 1987). The strategies we describe in our case studies primarily represent patterns or streams of action taken in reaction to the transition to a market economy in the GDR. Strategic actions are not always deliberate, and not all strategies are realised. In our case, a survival strategy can be defined as the strategic actions taken to achieve transformation in a turbulent market. The focus of such a strategy was to ensure the survival of the company after market transition. Our contribution to strategy research is to describe how survival strategies were developed and executed in a particularly turbulent business environment.

In an improvisational approach to corporate transformation, it is essential to recognise a crisis and the need for radical transformation. Companies that survived the transition to a market economy recognised a need for change, and expressed a willingness to transform themselves in accordance with new market demands. Another aspect of improvisational transformation is the creation of inspiring but vague goals and the lack of clear, unbending principles for innovation. Furthermore, there is a need to start the transformation process without clear principles for guiding the change. Finally, in an improvisational transformation, it is essential to learn from the initial innovation (Wood 2007). The transition to a market economy did not resemble anything that managers of East German companies had previously experienced, so an ability to improvise can be viewed as having been essential to survival in their context.

The East German transformation process – a special and privileged one?

One director of the Treuhand agency describes the situation of East German companies during the transformation as follows:

"As a result of economic and monetary union on 1 July 1990, East German companies were confronted with international competition from one day to the next. The companies were not prepared for such a change in terms of the operational and cost structure of their products. They no longer received any price subsidies, any help from advantageous exchange rates, nor benefits from artificially low wages; they received no protection from imports and no special export promotion, and for political reasons were not granted any structural adjustment measures in order to ease the transition into the Common Market (as Great Britain, Denmark, Spain, Greece and Portugal had previously received). The East German Economy was left without any markets. Even its domestic market had disappeared. Eastern European markets provided no hope and western markets were beyond reach" (Vehse 1994).

But wasn't the East German transformation process a "privileged special case"? (Wiesenthal 1999).

The question is worth discussing. Unlike other transition economies in Eastern Europe, the transition of the former GDR was facilitated by considerable monetary assistance from western Germany. The introduction of the Deutschmark made the consumption of goods manufactured in the West possible to a degree that widely exceeded the level of production in the former East Germany. More than one-third of this consumption was effectively subsidised by western Germany. Unlike in the other post-socialist economies, many of these consumer goods were not manufactured under the East Germans' own power and on their own territory, but were produced in the West. For western Germany, where production capacity utilisation averaged only 65%, the crisis in the East was a golden opportunity to increase production levels and break into new markets—something that shaped politics towards eastern Germany from the beginning of 1990 (Luft 1992; Büttner 1995; Roesler 2005; Breuel 2005). In general, the "big brother has turned out to be not quite as generous and selfless as it at first seemed to be. The big brother insisted on the restitution of his old property rights, he demanded the right to buy his little brother's assets, and he effectively protected himself against his little brother's low-wage competition" (Sinn and Sinn 1992). This approach caused considerable damage over the longer term, and undermined the image of being "privileged".

The results from recent research in the field emphasises more of the similarities than the differences between the East German transformation process and that of other post-socialist economies. Despite considerable differences in productivity levels, the starting points were quite similar. These countries were highly dependent on Soviet raw materials and supplies, creating political and economic dependency and a protected market that was increasingly sheltered from western-style market thinking and technology.

Walter and Quitzau (2005) claim that Schumpeter's theory of "creative destruction" is inadequate for describing the East European transformation. Schumpeter's theory applies to changes made within a prevailing economic system. The transformation that took place in the former GDR and in other Eastern European countries was not about changes within a given structure, but rather changes to *the structure itself*. This created a new dimension for destruction and construction, and consequently, a wildly different initial situation.

What distinguished the transformation in eastern Germany from those of other East European countries was the course of the transition. With regard to the GDR, two economies that had been part of diametrically-opposed political systems for over 40 years were suddenly linked together under difficult political circumstances. As a result, the welfare gains seen in eastern Germany were achieve earlier than in other post-socialist countries. On the other hand, while the loss of social security and employment came later in eastern Germany, it was more protracted (Busch 2005). Unlike the former GDR, countries such as Hungary, Poland, the Czech Republic, Slovakia, Lithuania, Latvia, and Estonia suffered severe economic hardship during the first years of transition.

However, the results these countries achieved show considerable similarities.

For a majority of East Germans, the Deutschmark, which Helmut Kohl famously called West Germany's "strongest economic asset", was the most convincing argument for immediate German unity. The Deutschmark myth was

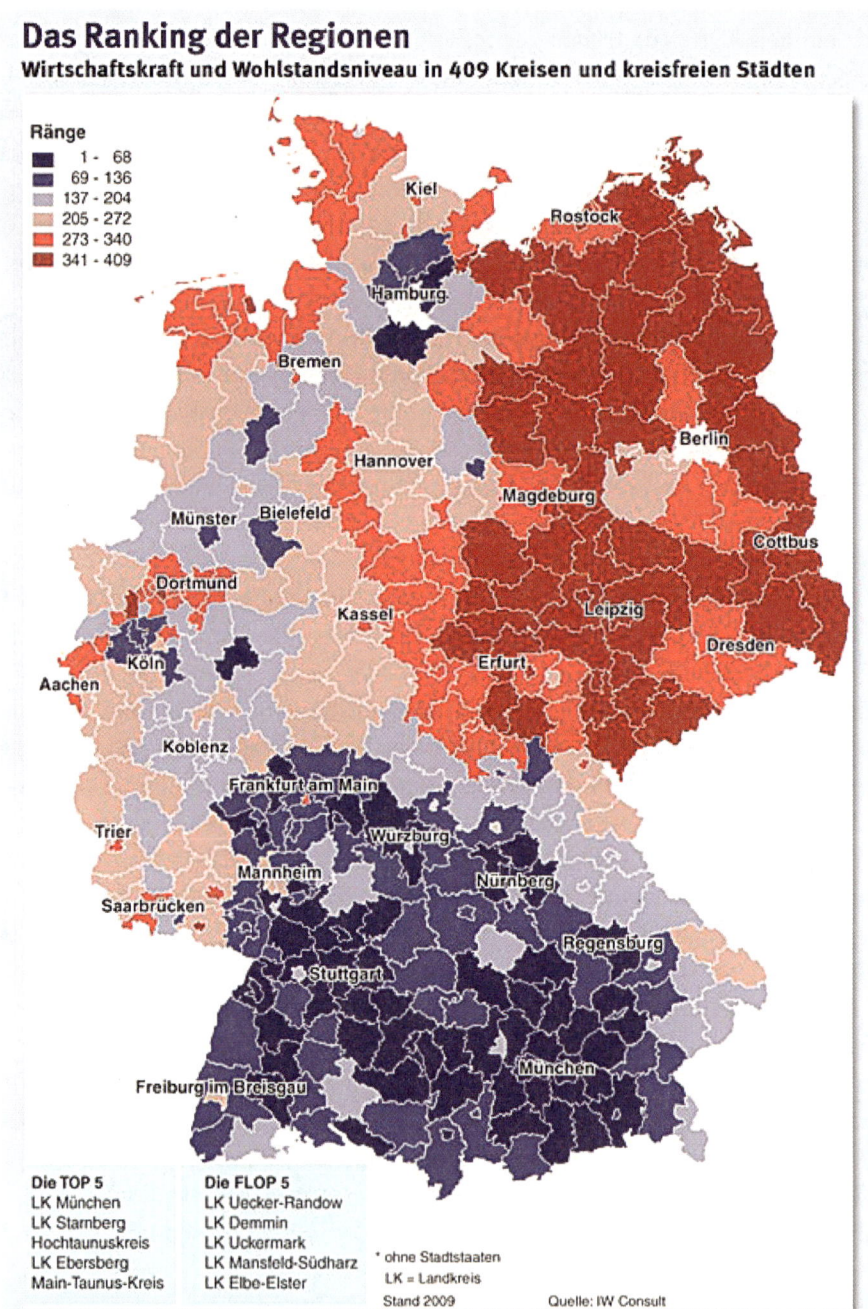

Figure: Ranking of the economic strength of German regions
Source: INSM - Initiative Neue Soziale Marktwirtschaft, Cologne.

hurried introduction of the Deutschmark turned out to be a poison chalice. No economy, no matter how strong, can absorb a 300-400 per cent revaluation of its currency. As the West German daily *Handelsblatt* wrote: "If, in 1948, the Federal Republic of Germany had entered into monetary union with the USA and at a rate of 1:1 between the D-Mark and the US dollar, a state that befell the GDR in relation to the D-Mark, then the Morgenthau Plan, which aimed for the obliteration of Germany, would have actually been realized" (Handelsblatt 1992,06,02).

When most of the East European economies had recovered from their difficult initial transitions, they reached a balanced level of growth that, for a part of the 1990s and beyond, exceeded 10 per cent. This rate of growth only occurred in East Germany in 1993 and 1994. Since 1997, eastern Germany's annual year-over-year growth rate has been under 2 per cent; the 0.1 per cent in 2001 even showed a negative growth (Seibel 2005). By 1997, eight years after unification, eastern Germany had not even achieved half of the industrial production generated during the last year of the GDR's existence in 1989 (Steinitz 1998). Even today, "the cutback East" ("Abbau Ost") has a deleterious effect on German industry and Germany's economic stability as a whole, as funding of about EUR 80 billion flows from west to east each year. The split in economic strength between eastern and western Germany is clear, as the figure above shows. Economic strength and levels of welfare give the impression that Germany remains divided. Although higher-growth areas around Dresden, Leipzig, Potsdam, Jena and Erfurt are more prosperous, per capita economic growth even in the leading Saxony region is 30% lower than the western German average. Unemployment in the eastern part of Germany is still more than twice as high as in the western part.

Even migration from eastern Germany has reached dramatic levels. More than three million people have left the new federal Länder since 1990, most notably qualified 18- to 29-year old adults, and young women in particular. A more than 25 per cent deficit of women in structurally weak regions is unparalleled in Europe, and has accelerated the economic and social process of erosion in the region (Kröhnert and Klingholz 2007).

Theory and practice

Under these conditions, how could companies in different industries succeed in developing products that can compete in the world market? Our analysis is based on theoretical premises in the field of corporate transformation and change in a transition economy, although we equally refer to the lessons learned by the companies themselves. The privatisation of state-owned economies in 1989–1990 was without historical precedent—both practically and even theoretically. Only when these actions are analysed by considering the national and international context at the time, and by understanding the conflicts between political and economic decisions and between the special interests of groups and individuals, the conclusions can be helpful for other protagonists. The more profound the political and socio-cultural environment that is studied, the more precisely one can assess whether abstractions can possibly be made from it. That, in turn, makes it easier to decide whether to pursue a similar approach under the actual circumstances or, in being aware of the potential risks, to take a different approach.

The third chapter deals with the experiences of privatisation during the transition to a market economy in eastern Germany. This transition was met with a number of obstacles created by political decisions that made it difficult for Treuhand to fulfil its duties, privatisation being just one of them. In our study we assess the work of Treuhand using criteria similar to those used in analysing the companies: which strategies are reusable, and which ones have turned out to be mistakes?

At the very least, we try to answer a question of similar relevance: what impact did Treuhand's operations have on the companies chosen by us? Would their strategies for survival have been more successful with or without or in conflict with Treuhand?

For a better understanding of the transition process we decided to give the reader some impressions of East German command policy in the field of economics before transition, both in the cases and in the chapters about Treuhand and the phenomenon *(n)ostalgia*. We explain its dependencies from East as well as from West, the system of state subsidies and several of the most absurd disproportions it caused, and even some of the consequences the socialist economy had for people in Eastern Germany. But we carefully distinguish between the political system (which led to stagnation) and the East German peoples' never-ending common sense, civil courage and spirit to overcome obstacles. In doing so, we avoid one of the principal mistakes of the German unification process.

What does it take to survive turbulent times? The transition forced East German companies to change and transform themselves just to continue to exist; our focus in this book is on corporate transformation via the implementation of survival strategies. Such strategies are not viewed merely as theoretical constructs formulated to accommodate complex hypothetical situations, but rather as practice and action. We strongly believe that our findings will help build a better understanding of change management. The recent turbulence in global markets illustrates the need for managers to find ways of coping not simply with change *within* a structure but with change *of* the structure itself. We describe different aspects of change and of ad hoc responses to new market conditions, all investigated from a common underlying perspective. The cases presented here provide context for the central message of this book, which demonstrates how corporations transform themselves by using successful strategies; our contribution is simply to interpret the desire to survive and the success of the survivors.

Case study: Rotkäppchen - Strategies to eliminate prejudice

How the GDR's favorite sparkling wine brand survived and its producer became market leader in Germany

Thirteen years after the fall of the Berlin Wall, the company *Rotkäppchen-Mumm Sektkellereien GmbH* Freyburg succeeded in becoming market leader in Germany. At least every other bottle of sparkling wine opened in Eastern Germany is of the Rotkäppchen brand, and every seventh bottle in the West. At its cellar locations Freyburg an der Unstrut, Hochheim am Main and Eltville and Breisach am Rhein, the business, with a turnover of 139.4 million bottles of sparkling wine and total sales of EUR 740.9 M[3], achieved a national market share for sparkling wine of 43.3 percent.[4] „In sparkling wine, we are the Federal market leader, a driving force in spirits and participants in the branded wine market", is the assessment of the company president.[5] Since 2002, Rotkäppchen has been annually selected as the *Most Trusted Brand* for sparkling wine

---

[3] Including spirits and wine.
[4] Press release from Rotkäppchen-Mumm-Sektkellereien on April 22, 2009.
[5] Rotkäppchen-Mumm in Sektlaune. AHGZ. The news portal for the hotel and catering industry. April 22, 2009.

in the Pegasus *Award European Most Trusted Brands* presented by *Readers Digest*; in 2002 with 21, but in 2007 with 50 percent of the votes in competition with 100 other sparkling wine brands. In the comprehensive industry survey *Best Brands,* Rotkäppchen Sekt came ninth out of all product brands in Germany in 2007.[6] The selection of Rotkäppchen Sekt as *sales hit of the year* by the industry magazine *Getränke Zeitung* and the naming of *Rotkäppchen Sekt Rosé Trocken* as Newcomer of the year, Product of the Year and Bestseller of the Year in 2006[7] are examples of the joint German and international recognition of an unprecedented achievement.[8] "Rotkäppchen is broadly regarded as the most successful business in the new Federal states ", comments the Chairman of the Gesellschaft für Unternehmensgeschichte at its 2004 Annual General Meeting, held in Freyburg, making it the first to be held in the East.[9] The business from Sachsen-Anhalt was transformed „from a restructuring case to the largest sparkling wine producer in the world after Freixenet".[10]

It is a success that today seems not only logical, but almost self-evident. But the never-ending praise from politicians of different persuasions is proof alone that this is an exception to the rule. Looking back at the time immediately following the fall of the Berlin Wall, it is clear that in 1991 or 1992, the history of the company founded in 1856 and steeped in tradition, could have come to an end. Instability and lack of orientation in the circumstances, in which the East German bureaucracy remained and that of the old Federal states was already there, made nearly every decision a balancing act with unknown consequences. In no way does the "Rotkäppchen success story" constitute a miracle, nor is it the stuff of the Brothers Grimm fairytale "Little Red Riding Hood" from which it gets its name, although certain media constantly claim this. Gunter Heise is the director and spokesperson for the management of the Rotkäppchen-Mumm Sektkellereien. Following studies in process technology at the Technical Uni-

---

[6] Survey by Werbeagentur Serviceplan and the Gesellschaft für Konsumforschung (society for consumer research).

[7] In the German trade journal *Getränke Zeitung, Lebensmittelpraxis* and *Rundschau für den Lebensmittelhandel.*

[8] In Sweden through, for example, an article in the largest national daily *Dagens Nyheter* on April 22, 2003: Östtyskt bubbel blev succé i väst.

[9] Naumburger Tageblatt, April 29, 2004.

[10] Christian Geinitz, Rotkäppchen und der scheue Wolf. *Frankfurter Allgemeine Zeitung*, December 29/30, 2007.

versity in Dresden, graduating in engineering, he assumed work at the "VEB Rotkäppchen Sektkellerei" in 1973 and from 1978, he worked as Technical Director. In a speech made in 2006 in conjunction with the company's 150th anniversary, in the presence of Federal Chancellor Dr. Merkel and the employees of all of the cellar locations owned by the company in East and West[11], Heise quotes from his diary from January 1990 through July 1991. Much of what gave him sleepless nights at the time has now been forgotten:

Two months after he stepped down as Deputy President in January 1990, Heise composed a discussion paper that "caused much discomfort and pressure on the management." It said:

"The sparkling wine market in the FRG has been fought, there is a glut. To capture this market for our own products requires comprehensive advertising activities. Following monetary union, our market will be supplied by the FRG. Sales are clearly a priority over production. /.../ The management and administrative structure cannot be compared with ours. The absolute numbers of staff in relation to production volume are about 70 percent lower than in our case. /.../ We need partners who have the capital, experience of company management and marketing experience. The development of the company into a sustainable sparkling wine business in the market is connected with radical cutbacks and consequences."

"On June 1, 1990", according to Heise, one month before the Economic, Monetary and Social Union, "we told the workforce at a heated workforce meeting, that they had to be cut by 50 percent." He himself considers his career alternatives and, at the celebrations, quotes from a text by the Mayor of his hometown from June 7, 1990: "At the main committee meeting of June 5, 1990, permission was granted to Herr Gunter Heise for the operation of the business – mobile trading in food and beverages. Business premises are not required." Heise explains to the guests present: "Back then, I regarded it as a short-term opportunity for me to operate a kiosk at Laucha swimming pool with my neighbor. At the time, I was unsure what would happen to me and Rotkäppchen. The irony of the story: the swimming pool, and thereby also the kiosk, will close this year."

---

[11] Speech by Gunter Heise on May 17, 2006. In: Press release from *Rotkäppchen-Mumm Sektkellereien GmbH*.

In 1990, *Rotkäppchen* is actually facing its final curtain. At the end of the 80s, 15 million bottles were produced and sold annually, making one bottle per GDR citizen. As a result of East German interest in Western products, sales plummet to 10 percent, 1.5 million bottles, after the fall of the Berlin Wall.[12] "We had hardly any hope," says Heise, looking back. At that time, he, as Technical Director, also sold sparkling wine on the market square.[13]

Of the former 350 employees in GDR times, a whole 70 could be kept on.[14] The blood-letting among the employees is the worst memory for Heise of the months after the Turnaround. Entire families, who had worked for Rotkäppchen for generations, lost the basis for the existence. In the town of Freyburg, with its 5,000 citizens, a walk through the streets became a case of running the gauntlet for Heise.[15]

What to do? First of all, there are contractual commitments to meet that were finalized under different social and economic conditions. Heise cites the example of an agreement between the state-run foreign trade companies of the GDR with the company Krones AG in the Federal Republic for the delivery of a sparkling wine bottling line. As a result of the Turnaround, the following situation emerged:

"The machines were being prepared, the buyer – the foreign trade companies – no longer existed and we had no money."

The situation seemed to be hopeless; they were "treading water". Finally, "we received an appointment in Neutraubling" at Krones AG and returned home "with a two-page agreement on the delivery of the sparkling wine bottling line. It was agreed that payment would be made three months after delivery.

'But where would we get the money from?' we wondered on our return.

Finally – four months later – we received the guarantee from the Treuhand Agency for this investment. The facility was then already up and running in Freyburg. In the small print on the guarantee certificate, it stated:

---

[12] Erfolgsstory aus dem Saale-Unstrut-Gebiet: Rotkäppchen will "das deutsche Sekthaus" werden. *Volksstimme* Magdeburg, September 19, 2001.
[13] Rotkäppchens zahmer Wolf. Gunter Heise machte Freyburg zur ersten Sektadresse in Deutschland. *Volksstimme* Magdeburg, March 23, 2002.
[14] Der Sekt zum Liebhaben. *Das Magazin*, Berlin 9/1995.
[15] Rotkäppchens zahmer Wolf, ibid.

"However, you are assigned to negotiate credit with the banks such that an own risk of 20-30 percent is accepted by the banks.'

Once I had familiarized myself with the subject of "own risk," we started from scratch again with the banks. The result of negotiations: We had to secure the own risk using a mortgage. Easier said than done…"[16]

Through negotiations with the Treuhand Agency, the Deutsche Bank and Krones AG the transaction finally goes through. Other decisions that Heise describes proceed faster:

"On June 27, I went with my predecessor, Herr Worch, to the Personnel Department of the Treuhand Agency in Berlin. I was given two days of thinking time. On August 1, I was the sole manager."[17]

Rotkäppchen is put up for sale by the Treuhand. The visions of prospective owners are seen "with horror:""to bottle other sparkling wines in Freyburg and put a lid on tradition". There are also numerous prospective buyers from outside the industry and most "also want additional money for Rotkäppchen".[18] The first round of privatization fails because the interested parties do not believe in the brand, "including West German sparkling wine producers, smart advisers, nobility. One of these commented: ‚With that name, we can at most put on performances of fairytales.'"[19] Four long-term employees decide to break with the dominating atmosphere of fear and worry at the company, prepare a concept and take over Rotkäppchen. The management buy-out gains the agreement of the Treuhand, which makes the allocation on March 4, 1993. The Eckes Family from Niederolm, known for their production of liqueur and fruit juices, is brought in as minority owner.[20] On the subject of the "later and current partners" of Rotkäppchen, Harald Eckes-Chantré, Heise says in his anniversary speech: "I wish many businesses in the new Federal Länder could have had partners like them."

Doubts remain about the decision, to which large responsibility is attached. Visits to the large wine producer in Rheingau raise the question of whether there was any meaning in having Freyburg. Only when Heise has also viewed

---

[16] Speech by Gunter Heise on May 17, 2006. Ibid.
[17] Ibid.
[18] Der Sekt zum Liebhaben, ibid.
[19] Geinitz, ibid.
[20] Der Sekt zum Liebhaben, ibid.

the small wine production of the competition does he regain his hope: "Their production looked no different to ours."[21]

The company builds on the degree of recognition amount the East German buyers that are slowly returning to the Rotkäppchen brand. They associate it with pleasant memories of nice everyday experiences or parties and celebrations. The name and red tops are retained. The bottles are given a modern look, but are still recognizable. The concept proves successful and generates the money for necessary investments. Already in 1991, 2.9 million bottles are sold once again; in 1992, 5.7 million; in 1993, 10 million.[22] At the time of the brand centenary in 1994, every fourth bottle of sparkling wine consumed in the east of Germany originates from *Rotkäppchen*.

In the old Federal Länder, the concept does not make a breakthrough. Five years after German unity, in 1995, market share there is at 0.3 percent. In the West, there are no East German memories while enjoying a bottle of Rotkäppchen. There, this sparkling wine is "something from the GDR"[23], the name reminds West German consumers of the grape juice *Rotbäckchen* and, with its red outfit, it confirms the prejudice that it is "too sweet."[24] The Freyburger are insulted by another prejudice: that it is "a sweet fizzy soda with no tradition".[25]

Nothing could be further from the truth. This company has survived one and a half centuries of varied German history with the Franco-Prussian War, the time of the kaisers, the Weimar Republic, inflation, two world wars, two dictatorships, nationalization and plan economy, giving it the confidence to survive the road back into the market economy. Its own history dates from 1856 with the establishment of a wine trading company at the heart of Germany's northernmost wine area. The founders, brothers Moritz and Julius Kloss and their friend Carl Foerster, quickly realized that it was possible to produce a sparkling wine full of promise from the Saale-Unstrut wines by way of a second fermentation. In 1858, the first bottles produced according to the original Champagne method left the *Freyburger Champagner-Fabrik-Gesellschaft*. In 1894, the company loses the dispute with a Champagne producer in Reims and is forced

---

[21] Rotkäppchens zahmer Wolf, ibid.
[22] Press release from Rotkäppchen-Mumm Sektkellereien GmbH from April 17, 2006.
[23] Rotkäppchens zahmer Wolf, ibid.
[24] Der Sekt zum Liebhaben, ibid.
[25] Rotkäppchens zahmer Wolf, ibid.

to rename its strongest-selling brand "Monopol." In relation to the red bottle cap associated with the brand, colloquially known in German as a "Kappe", the name *Rotkäppchen* (Little Red Riding Hood) is chosen.

Already in the 19th century, the brand's quality led to national Prussian and Saxonian prizes and various titles as royal court suppliers. Emperor Wilhelm II, during imperial maneuvers in Freyburg in 1903, is said to have introduced Rotkäppchen sparkling wines to several officers' casinos due to their appreciated digestibility.[26]

There were massive sales losses during the period of inflation. In October 1923, a bottle of Rotkäppchen cost 1,928,000 Marks. In the thirties, Rotkäppchen flourished anew, with sales, as previously, concentrated in the east and north German provinces.[27] Only in 1944 did production break down and armaments production moves into the basement.[28]

After the end of the Second World War, the business came under the President of the Province of Saxony in the Soviet occupation zone. In 1949, it became a nationally owned company. In the years 1956-57 and 1973-75, considerable investments are made. Only a short time before the fall of the Berlin Wall, the bottling, equipment and packaging plant is renewed.[29] To this extent, Rotkäppchen is a company in need of urgent investments to face the new market challenges, but it is not like other companies with ailing production facilities.

Double-digit growth rates in the East strengthen Rotkäppchen's position in the German sparkling wine market in the 1990s. In the area of the former GDR, three to four times as many bottles of Rotkäppchen are consumed annually compared with the GDR period, with the business continuing to grow and bucking the prevailing trend at the time of decreasing sales and falling turnover. In 2000, the company has a 57-percent market share in the East, but this remains at 3.1 percent in the West, despite extensive advertising campaigns and cost-intensive attempts to get a foot in the door of the large food chains.[30] With a fivefold increase in sales since privatization in 1993, Rotkäppchen is the most successful German sparkling wine brand at the end of the century.[31] The low

---

[26] Press release from April 17, 2006, ibid.
[27] Ibid.
[28] Der Sekt zum Liebhaben, ibid.
[29] Press release form April 17, 2006, ibid.
[30] Erfolgsstory aus dem Saale-Unstrut-Gebiet, ibid.
[31] Rotkäppchen schluckt Wolf. Wirtschaftsstandort Sachsen-Anhalt. http./www.wirtschaftsspiegel.com/archiv/archiv01/oktober/texte/wirtschaftsachs.htm

market share in the West is a conspicuous contrast. How can this imbalance be adjusted? After all, the Rotkäppchen brand has almost exhausted its growth potential in the East and it hardly seems possible to increase consumption there.

Using clever strategic moves, Rotkäppchen conquers the shelves of the old Federal retail chains. In September 2001, has its bid accepted for the purchase of the established Western brands *Mumm, Jules Mumm* and *MM,* outcompeting prominent fellow applicant *Henkell & Söhnlein*. Industry experts estimate the purchase price for the brands and property at DEM 270 M, that is, approximately EUR 140 M.[32] In January 2002, the brands are released from the Seagram *Portfolio* by the US cartel authorities. The sale is thus perfect and is accompanied by an unprecedented media echo, which creates attention for not only the brands acquired, but also the buyer, Rotkäppchen. In January 2003, the *Rotkäppchen-Mumm Sektkellereien GmbH*, as it is now called, expands again: the *Geldermann Privatsektkellerei* in Breisach, in Baden, is taken over.

The presence now achieved in the West proceeds with quantative growth, but above all a diversified brand assortment. Accompanying the *Rotkäppchen* brand, with 45.5 million bottles sold in 2001, is the traditional brand of *Mumm* from Hochheim am Main, in Hessen, and its premium sparkling wines and sales of 21 million bottles (2001). The fresh, fruity *Jules Mumm* from the same company, is targeted at a young, urbane and, above all, female group, with a turnover of 5.5 million bottles (2001). In the lower price segment among traditional branded sparkling wines, there is *MM Extra,* with 19.4 million bottles sold (2001). *MM* is produced in Eltville am Rhein and is one of the best known sparkling wine brands in Germany, particularly because of its market leadership in the 0.2-liter small bottle segment ("MMchen"). The superior brand, *Geldermann* from Breisach am Rhein, completes the offering at the top end. Geldermann sparkling wines are produced exclusively using the traditional bottle fermentation process. From this high-class cuvee, there was a turnover of three million bottles at the time of the takeover.[33]

In a multistage work process with various teams, comprising experts from all locations on equal terms, the merging of the Group of businesses is undertaken. Quality-management certification in accordance with DIN ISO 9001

---

32 Ost schluckt West. manager-magazin.de, September 18, 2001.
33 Press release on the takeover of Geldermann Privatsektkellerei from January 28, 2003.

follows on from the certification according to the International Food Standard (IFS) gained in 2004. This is successfully implemented in all four production locations.[34]

At the same time, a marketing and sales offensive is begun, which is designed for the specific characteristics of the individual brands. In this, the communications spectrum stretches from the constantly varied key image in TV and press ads of the "young lady in a red dress with a bottle of Rotkäppchen sparkling wine hidden behind her back" to action slogans designed to reflect the spirit of the times: "Deutschland braucht Mumm" ("Germany needs courage") or "Nicht reden, Mumm haben" ("Don't talk, have courage"). An interesting feature is the nostalgic play on advertising motifs from the 1980s for *MM extra,* resulting in recognition of the popular advertising spots of the time. Resonance for this was "far in excess of the already high expectations".[35] In contrast to this is the campaign entirely in black and white in selected lifestyle magazines, "Geldermann. Vive la différence." The *Geldermann Privatsektkellerei* presents itself as a connoisseur of a sophisticated sense of style and sponsors the cultural program "Aspekte" in the Second German Television channel.

Also worth mentioning are the tourist attractions and cultural events at the wine-producing locations. Both of these are windows on the region and deepen the customer's relationship with the brand. This applies to the historical vaulted cellar of Geldermann in Breisach, in Baden, as well as the courtyard of the historical Freyburg sparkling wine producer– one of the oldest listed production halls in Germany. In addition, a five-meter, handmade, wooden vat, corresponding to 1,600 baths filled with sparkling wine, attracts more than 125,000 visitors each year. "Germany's sparkling wine producer", was the wording in the commendation for the "Innovation Award of the Social Democratic Party of Germany (SPD) and the Working Committee of Self-employed of the SPD," is "in many respects an exemplary enterprise. The sensitive management of the employees, the cellars, the products go hand in hand with the attention paid to the business environment."[36]

---

[34] Press kit for the Bilanz press conference on April 26, 2005.
[35] Ibid.
[36] Commendation on the presentation of Dipl.-Ing. Gunter Heise with the Innovation Award of the SPD and AGS 2003. The award is presented annually to entrepreneurs who conduct business in an exemplary fashion for innovation, enterprise initiative and ecological and social commitment.

"The revenge of the East," mocked *Der Spiegel* when the companies in the old Federal Länder were taken over by Rotkäppchen and made fun of the "semi-dry candy mixture from Freyburg," of which the East Germans had once again found that it "didn't taste that bad to them."[37] Views of this nature have now been silenced. Instead, media reports continually state that the companies in the ownership of the Rotkäppchen-Mumm Sektkellereien are performing indisputably well. The Rotkäppchen has lost nothing in the East as a result. Quite the opposite: At 71 percent, a record market share was achieved in one month in 2005.[38] But more remarkable is the trend in western Germany. From 2005 to 2006, market share increased by a quarter there to 10.8 percent.[39] The total German market share for the Rotkäppchen brand was raised to 29 percent in 2008.[40]

Rotkäppchen-Mumm makes a decisive contribution to the fact that German sparkling wine, after years of stagnation, is again making gains in volume and quality. The share of German sparkling wines in the total German market is now an impressive 76.4 percent.[41]

In view of these figures, further growth in sparkling wine seems less likely. Accordingly, Rotkäppchen-Mumm acquired the German operations of *Eckes Spirituosen & Wein GmbH* in Niederolm, near Mainz, at the end of 2006. With the purchase of the producer of such famous brands as *Chantré*, *Eckes Edelkirsch* and *Echter Nordhäuser,* with an annual turnover of EUR 250 M, the market leader for sparkling wine has catapulted straight to the top of the spirits market. Eckes market share is 10 percent.[42]

In the anniversary year of 2006, a new product line was tested in addition to *Rotkäppchen Qualitätswein*. In selected stores in eastern Germany, only Germany quality wines were presented as a trial. The extensive recognition of *Rotkäppchen Sekt* provided support for sales: Within seven weeks, 500,000 bottles had been sold.[43] Subsequently, the company management agreed a cooperation with the wine-growers' cooperative *Deutsches Weintor* in Ilbesheim

---

[37] Die Rache des Ostens. *Der Spiegel* 8/2002, p. 87.
[38] Rotkäppchen will nach Rekordjahr Preise erhöhen. *Frankfurter Allgemeine Zeitung*, April 26, 2006.
[39] Press release from Rotkäppchen-Mumm Sektkellereien from April 24, 2007.
[40] Rotkäppchen-Mumm blickt "recht optimistisch" nach vorn. *Volksstimme* Magdeburg, April 22, 2009.
[41] Rotkäppchen legt weiter zu. *Volksstimme* Magdeburg, April 25, 2007.
[42] Auf Sekt und Wein folgt nun Schnaps. *Volksstimme* Magdeburg, November 9, 2006.
[43] Press release from April 24, 2007, ibid.

(Rheinland-Pfalz) for the bottling of four quality wines under the brand name of Rotkäppchen.

It is not only in Freyburg that innovation rests on a solid foundation of tradition. The various brands of the *Rotkäppchen-Mumm Sektkellereien* trace their long history in the locations of Hochheim, Eltville, Breisach and Freyburg back to the years 1811, 1827, 1838 and 1856. The traditional sparkling wine brands of the founders of the Freyburg wine producer *Kloss & Foerster* did not remain in Freyburg after the Second World War, but were produced in Rüdesheim am Rhein. For the 150th anniversary of the company, they acquired the companies and brought them back to the Unstrut – an "emotional decision, not an entrepreneurial one," according to Gunter Heise.[44] He greeted the successors of the Kloss Family at the celebrations with the words: "And so that grows together, to use one of the most convincing expressions of the time after the Turnaround, which belongs together."[45]

---

44 Geinitz, ibid.
45 Rede Gunter Heise, ibid.

2. Survival strategies

Strategy has become a major research area in the management and marketing fields, and is seen as a critical determinant of corporate success and survival (Graetz 2000; Chebat 1999; Noble 1999; Mintzberg 1987). One may distinguish between the strategy formulation and strategy implementation processes (Thorpe and Morgan 2007), the former being crucial to the latter. Establishing network relationships (Stokes 2006), developing dominant technology or design (Suárez and Utterback 1995), and establishing competitive brands (Urde 1994) have all been held to be important factors influencing the successful implementation of survival strategies. In this book, we identify four types of survival strategies: defensive non-interactive, offensive non-interactive, defensive interactive, and offensive interactive strategies. Each strategy has its advantages when it comes to ensuring enterprise survival.

Defensive strategies involve the salvaging of competence and intellectual capital. A defensive strategic move would be for a company to find out what it is good at and to defend the knowledge and information base necessary for this competence. Defensive strategies also involve the company rationalization. A large company may harbour within it a smaller, more competitive company: rationalizing the company and removing its least efficient parts can ensure survival. Survival involves focusing on the most effective parts of the company.

A defensive strategy can also involve the enterprise interacting with its environment. Finding partners and subcontracting parts of production can be defensive ways of ensuring survival. Communicating with customers can provide crucial information about future demand, so two-way marketing communication can be essential in gaining knowledge of market requirements. Attracting investment can also ensure survival – companies may sometimes need a "white knight" to remain in operation.

Survival strategies may also be *offensive*. Research and development can be classified as an offensive survival strategy. The company may have to reinvent itself to stay competitive in the market. Reinvention – also an offensive adaptation – can create a new enterprise out of one that can no longer survive. A threat of closure can be temporary and a bridging strategy may be appropriate; a company may have to make drastic changes that preserve it through a difficult period.

Finally, offensive strategies can also be interactive. A company may take an offensive approach to interacting with its business environment. An offensive interactive strategy could include an offensive branding strategy and Internet strategy. By developing its image, a company can further improve its positioning in the market. Event marketing can be used to gather customers around a winning concept that can ensure survival.

Strategy as formulating and implementing activities

There has been discussion in strategy research focusing on strategy formulation and implementation. Some feel that it is not what managers *say* they will do (i.e., formulation) that is important, but what they actually do (i.e., implementation). We take the stand here that both aspects of strategy are essential. Articulating and formulating future strategies are important in ensuring the necessary turnaround that is needed for company survival in turbulent markets. Fitting words to a difficult situation a company is in and communicating these throughout the organization can be a first step to ensuring survival.

Successfully implementing a well-conceived survival strategy can be necessary to company survival. Strategy is about taking the right action, and looking to the future when taking immediate action. For survival when the business environment is changing rapidly, bold actions are necessary. Managers may be more comfortable with business activities they are used to performing. In the transition the former East Germany underwent, few ordinary business activities of the past were adequate to ensure company survival in the global market economy. New actions were necessary to ensure the future of companies.

Formulating a corporate strategy

A major change forced on East German companies was adapting to the new market orientation of the economy. With this shift, East German companies suddenly needed a market-driven strategy. Walker et al. (1992) have formulated several key issues that must be addressed when developing such a strategy, some of which are particularly important to companies undergoing a transition. First, a strategy should have scope, mission, and intent. Managers should ask themselves what business they are in and what segments of the market they should focus on. This has been a major difficulty for companies in eastern German: often an entirely new market must be found and the whole mission of the company has had to change.

Second, there is the need to develop company objectives, what the business focus should be, and what timeframes should be set for each objective. The studied companies had to move quickly to salvage what they could. Companies incurred huge losses as their former markets disappeared and they had to look for new ones to ensure positive cash flow. Some companies set ad hoc objectives in the interest of short-term survival, postponing total restructuring until new sources of investment were found.

Third, there is the concern for resource allocation. Companies have limited resources, and this particularly applied the companies of the former East Germany. After unification, there was initially a shortage of investment and capital. Companies had to consider how limited resources should be allocated across the organization to make the highest returns. Alternate strategies had to be developed to examine alternate ways of ensuring the most effective resource allocation.

Fourth, it is essential to find sources of synergy. Companies that gain access to global markets can find new ways of using their competencies and combining their knowledge base with those of others. Many eastern German companies joined forces with companies in the west to pool their resources and achieve better overall results. New networks were formed and companies were able to make use of the market information they gained from new customers. Companies became increasingly efficient as they used their resources better and found new ways of co-operating with others.

Market-driven strategy

A market-driven strategy can have several components (Cravens and Piercy 2006). Central to a stronger market orientation is a focus on the customer base, as it is only in relation to existing and potential customers that survival can be ensured. A strong customer focus can ensure that the company finds markets when its environment changes drastically. A market-oriented company can understand its customers' needs and preferences and how these evolve over time. Establishing strong relationships with key customers can ensure that essential information about customer needs and preferences reaches the areas of the company that can use it. A strong customer orientation also involves creating superior customer value. In a competitive market, customers will have alternatives from which to choose. One way of choosing between alternatives is to evaluate the value of the alternate offerings in the market. By providing superior value, the company increases its chances of being the chosen alternative and ensures its survival. Customers can estimate customer value in a broad sense and take this into consideration. Consideration of brand reputation and the preferred company to deliver a given product or service can make a difference. Establishing strong relationships with the customer can thus influence the perceived customer value, and customers may prefer products or services from companies with which they have market relationships.

A market orientation can also focus on the skills of the company. The best way a company can compete for a place in the market is to do what it is good at. Customers may not respond positively to companies that try to be something they are not. Market orientation concerns using the market-oriented skills of the company. Marketers who focus on their strengths may have a better chance than those attempting to achieve a position in the market not based on the company's actual strengths. Investigating and developing the skills of a company can be central to a renewed market orientation. Disclosing "the truth" about the company can be a means of establishing honest relationships with customers.

A market orientation can also involve increasing the company's product and service innovation. Customer preferences do not remain stable over time and may respond favourably to innovation and renewal. Seeing the market as a dynamic and ever changing entity can ensure that the company develops over time. Market interaction is essential to ensure market-oriented innovation. A clear understanding of the needs and wants of customers not only at present, but also in the future, is important. Innovation that takes place *together with* customers rather than *for* customers can create superior customer satisfaction.

The essential focus of market orientation is to create competitive advantage. The combination of company skills, innovation, and market orientation can create advantages in relation to competitors. The focus of a market-driven strategy is to gain advantages in the market. After the transition to the market economy, companies in eastern Germany had competitors – this was a new reality that these companies woke up to face. Many former East Germans wanted to try out western products that they knew from the TV ads they could see even during East German times. After a while, customers from eastern Germany came to find desirable qualities in local products as well. Some former East German companies managed to leverage the market of eastern Germany, where it understood the preferences of consumers, to whom could relate via known products and services. However, the competition from the west was fierce, and companies had to work hard to keep their past customers. On the other hand, new markets in the west were open and companies from the east could attempt to break into them. The experience of former East German survivors in the present market economy exemplifies the demands the market economy placed on companies and the appropriate responses to these market demands. The situation of East German companies is examined further in the chapter, which discusses the privatization of East German companies after unification and the role of the holding company Treuhand.

Competitive positioning

A product achieves a position in the market in line with how it is perceived in the eyes of consumers. Consumers relate to products and services and can enhance their self-image through how and what they consume. Choosing a particular product can be viewed as expressing a preference and confirming a worldview. After German unification, customers in eastern Germany were keen to express their new freedom of choice and new western orientation. Few wanted to be associated with the old eastern products that were viewed as remnants of the past. Former East German producers had an image problem, and were viewed as lagging behind the west. Survival meant changing rapidly to keep up with competitors, and appealing to the nostalgia of former East Germans that emerged after the novelty of unification had worn off. A combination of rapid change and being true to tradition seems to have been a feasible survival strategy for several former East German companies. Positioning themselves profitably in the market of eastern Germany was not, however, unproblematic.

There are four mistakes companies can make when positioning themselves in the market (Hooley et al. 2008, p. 210). The first is *under positioning*, in which consumers have only a vague idea about what the company has to offer. Most eastern German companies that wanted to market their products in the west were under positioned. Western consumers did not know what these companies, products, or brands were all about. Some exceptions existed, however. East German companies that had already exported to the West before unification, such as Kathi and Meissen, had relevant marketing experience. However, such companies were few and far between when East German companies first faced the rigours of the market economy.

Second, there is the mistake of being *over positioned*. An over positioned company is associated with just one or a few capabilities, products, or brands. Customers may have heard of a company such as Schott, but associate it with just one or two products. The company may thereby have difficulties marketing its products in other market segments where it is virtually unknown.

Third, there is the danger of *confused positioning*, which occurs when companies frequently change their positioning and convey mixed messages to their customers. In turbulent markets where company survival is threatened, there is the danger that such a company may not make a consistent impression on its customers. They may not know how to relate to such a company's product or brand if it is constantly changing. The East German companies that survived unification, though often making adaptive changes, still remained true to a consistent concept and vision. One example is the company Ankerstein, which has made the same toy building blocks for decades. Not confusing its customers by rapidly changing its core products served it well as a means of survival. The company has adapted and evolved by adding new designs but within the frame of the familiar building block product line.

Finally, there is the danger of *doubtful positioning*. Companies that make claims that are unrealistic and consequently not met may not be accepted by consumers. Overstated claims that a the product range is more comprehensive than it is or that the offered solutions address any and all problems will soon be exposed by customers. Confronting the market economy introduced a new kind of realism to former East German companies. From the beginning, potential customers were sceptical of these companies, which found it difficult to express any claims to the market at the outset. Doubtful positions were soon uncovered by customers, and those companies that survived had to deliver on their promises and position themselves realistically in the market.

Reinventing the company

In the face of market turmoil and a new business environment, an appropriate strategy can be to reinvent the company. Reinvention has become a buzzword in industries where companies have had to rethink their strategic positions. Reinvention relies on the existing competencies of the company while attempting to gain additional knowledge that is relevant to the new situation the company faces. Facing a competitive market for the first time can be a good reason for reinvention. New market knowledge is needed, and companies must ask themselves what they really are good at doing, to determine what kind of new knowledge would let them adapt to the new conditions. According to Matheson Connell (2004), a company must ask several questions when reinventing itself, including: Who are our customers, and what industry are we in? How does our firm make money, and what are our distinctive capabilities? Furthermore, how are these capabilities translated into competitive advantages, and what strategic assets does the company hold? Finally, in what markets are these capabilities valuable, and are there other markets it would pay to serve?

A company can reinvent itself around both existing and new market demands. When reappearing in the market in a new guise, the company must find new ways to satisfy customers. A reinvented company can have a new image and find a new position in the market. In eastern Germany, companies had to dust off the old images of state ownership and lack of competition. The image of state-owned companies was stale and company reinvention was necessary. Companies such as Rotkäppchen, which makes sparkling wine, bought western brands to gain access to a new market where the company's own brand had little appeal. The company loosened its ties to the old days of East Germany, reappearing in the western market as a reinvented company appealing to a broader and very competitive market.

Reinvention is a tool for making strategic changes to the company and involves a fundamental shift in company function. Primarily, reinvention is a strategic tool with which to meet challenges in the market and revamp old images that have proven ineffective in a competitive market. Central to reinvention is the market positioning of a company. Let us say that a company is positioned among low-price, low-quality brands – this was often true of former East German brands entering competitive western markets for the first time. Faced with sharply increasing production costs after entering currency union, these companies had to reinvent themselves and attain more favourable market positions. Improving product quality and design was one means of reinvention in this situation. Halloren, for example, Germany's oldest chocolate manufacturer, reinvented itself by launching new brands and improving its quality with access to better ingredients. This reinvention was necessary for the company to survive, and was combined with an appeal to the old habits of eastern Germany consumers who knew the company and its brands. Customers were willing to return to their old habits now that the old company had improved and could meet competition from western brands.

Reinvention can be constructed around those who have vested interests in the company. Investors who harbour doubts about a company may change their minds if the company shows willingness to reinvent itself, so a new beginning can be a means of attracting investment. Distributors also have vested interests in the company, and they may have to be on board to relay new messages and images to customers. Suppliers and employees may also have to be on board in order to secure successful reinvention. Companies may also have tainted reputations vis-à-vis government agencies and legislators. For example, a former polluter or rule breaker may have to reinvent itself to create a new reputation and image in the eyes of government agencies. The most important group on which to focus the reinvention, obviously, are the consumers, who may react favourably to a reinvented company. A sharp market focus on reinventing the company may provide a new start to a company that needs to gain access to a viable market in order to survive.

When reinventing themselves, East German companies had to identify their capabilities and determine which of them could be translated into value in a competitive market. The Schott company in Jena, for example, defined itself as a high-tech company with specific capabilities. It took a while for the company to come up with marketable products, but it managed by persistently reinventing itself around known capabilities. It stuck to the industry it was in and found ways to make money. Schott translated its capabilities into strategic advantages, and is now a leader in its field.

Adjusting to the international marketing environment

A central concern of a business strategy is to adjust to changes in the operating environment. With unification, companies in East Germany faced dramatic changes in their business environment. Central to strategy formulation in these companies was adjusting to a competitive and global market. Companies went from existing in a sheltered world with few or no competitors and a certain future in which the survival of the company was ensured through central planning. The market environment placed new demands on them, and in most markets there has been fierce competition.

Analysis of the business environment usually includes consideration of the economic, technological, socio–cultural, political, and legal environment surrounding the company (Doole and Lowe 2008; Palmer and Hartley 2002). An essential part of a corporate strategy making involves adjusting to the social context of the company (Post, Lawrence and Weber 2002). All these aspects of the business environment represent essential considerations when formulating and implementing a business strategy. The economic environment includes the level of economic development, the trading infrastructure, and the general economic development of the region. Eastern Germany lagged the west in several economic respects. Its marketing environment was not sufficiently developed to support modern marketing strategy. It took a few years to build up economic infrastructure in the east, and companies suffered from a lack of opportunities during this time after the market economy was introduced. Eastern Europe was considered an emerging market and experienced economic reform and significant opportunities in international markets.

The technological environment in East Germany differed from that of the West. Lack of competition and shortages of key resources led to the slower development of new technology. Comparisons of patents sought in western and eastern Germany showed that East German companies such as Carl Zeiss frequently sought patents and gradually developed technological competence. Between 1973 and 1990, the Zeiss company in Jena, East Germany, developed 1674 patents versus 724 patents for the western Zeiss in Oberkochen, West Germany, though outside Germany Zeiss Oberkochen sought more patents than did Zeiss Jena. The Zeiss company in Jena, however, was unable to innovate "by plan" (Kogut and Zander 2000) and did not benefit as much from its patents in terms of new innovation. Our interviews with Zeiss company personnel indicate that engineers in the East German part of the company in Jena were strongly encouraged, if not forced, to seek as many new patents as possible. They were, however, unable to *apply* many of these patents, which were obtained for their own sake and not for any innovative potential. Technologically, East Germany was many years behind its western counterpart and had to catch up to compete in international markets.

Survival can also be dependent on adjustment to the social and cultural environment. Companies that developed survival strategies after German unification faced social turmoil. There were vast numbers of bankruptcies and individual consumers held on to their few savings. In the post-socialist society, uncertainty and economic hardship emerged and held sway, though new opportunities were simultaneously opening. Culturally, the ideas embedded in the planned economy still prevailed early in the introduction of the market economy. Managers had to convince their employees to look for markets rather than hope for government support. Newly earned freedoms were discovered and gradually filtered through into the business culture.

Culture also influenced the buying behaviour of East German consumers, who now had a choice of new products entering their market. The companies of the east had to adapt quickly to new preferences that developed after unification. Some customers did not miss what they had been offered before, while others eventually grew – retrospectively – to accept and even miss some of their old products. Eastern-style products also found a small but growing niche market in the west.

Political environment is also an essential factor to take into consideration when developing a survival strategy. The former East Germany faced "Kohlonization" led by former Chancellor Helmut Kohl, as it had to adopt a West German-style liberal democracy with the rapid introduction of the market economy. It was thought that privatization would ensure economic restructuring, and that the market would make the selection. At the outset, the government thought it could sell companies for a profit. Restructuring eventually became costly, as few companies fetched high prices and many needed financial support from either the central or regional government.

Finally, does the legal business environment have an effect on companies carving out a future under turbulent economic conditions? Legally, the situation of East German assets was uncertain. The legal system in East Germany had been vastly different from that of the west. After unification, companies that had existed before the communist era could now face claims from previous owners. Privatization took time as legal uncertainties persisted, and several company failures can be attributed to the time lag between the decision to privatize and the emergence of the company as a private entity.

Using marketing intelligence

Marketing intelligence has attracted growing interest and is seen as a means of creative problem solving (Andersson and Vincze 2004). Companies need information about the market in order to develop business strategies. At the outset, former East German companies seemed ill informed about markets in the west. They had previously been sheltered from competition and did not have to adjust to market demand. However, we found that, after unification, companies soon attempted to gain information about their western counterparts in order to improve their productivity. Some companies soon became remarkably well informed about the technology being used by their new competitors. Once they gained access to investment capital, these companies were quickly able to make necessary changes.

Marketing intelligence relies on some form of qualitative or quantitative marketing research. Marketing research is a growing field and has made many contributions to general descriptions of the intelligence field (Malhotra and Birks 2007; Kent 2007; Parasuraman, Grewal and Krishnan 2004). Central to marketing intelligence is some form of problem recognition that relies on environmental analysis. Companies undergoing a transition to the market economy realize quickly that their business environment has changed and that "business as usual" is not a viable option. Recognizing the necessity of fundamental change is essential to survival. Turbulent markets, such as the rapidly changing former East German market, demanded a great deal from management. Changes had to be made swiftly and companies had to react appropriately to changes in their business environment.

The new market-oriented managers had to identify essential problems in their existing business models. At the time of transition, it was thought that the East European market would remain available to eastern German companies after transition: they thought they would do well there, since many of them had been market leaders in the Eastern Bloc. However, East European consumers quickly turned to western products and services and the former markets in the East were quickly lost. Quickly realizing that the old days of producing for East European markets were gone was essential to survival. The eastern market was lost, not least due to the introduction of the Deutschmark (DM), which drove up production costs by 400%. With this new cost structure, eastern German companies were unable to compete in the East European markets.

It was essential to generate alternate modes of action. Strategies identified as successful by our empirical study showed that survivors developed several alternatives to their former business models. One strategy, for example, was to appeal to the local market by offering a local alternative, while another was to reach out to the competitive western German market. Yet a third alternative was to attempt to penetrate international markets. Some companies joined forces with western companies through strategic alliances and mergers. Former East German companies were not only bought by companies from the west, some even bought companies in western Germany. This was the case with the Zeiss company in Jena, and the Rotkäppchen and Halloren companies in Halle. These companies made strategic acquisitions of companies in the west that provided access to new markets, useful insight, and business intelligence needed to survive in the market economy.

Successful companies had strategic alternatives and chose from different modes of action. Essential to business intelligence is evaluating the alternatives carefully and making the best choices. As the market was in turmoil after unification, it was difficult to evaluate the soundness of the available alternatives. An element of trial and error was evident in the transition companies. In the first years after transition, companies rapidly tried out various ways of surviving, and the companies that survived were those that made the best choices. Establishing connections and relationships with western markets seems to have been a good choice among the alternatives, though concentrating on the local market was also a viable option for many companies.

Successful survival strategies do not prove viable in theory, but in practice. It does not help to generate good strategies if they are not properly implemented. A central theme in the surviving companies was an emphasis on action and strategy implementation. Companies that waited for the government in order to privatize could easily miss opportunities to implement viable survival strategies. Many of the companies we studied saw what was happening and quickly found ways around the new bureaucracy that surrounded the privatization and transition of the former East German economy. Companies survived the market turmoil by taking strategic action at defining moments of their own market development.

An international strategy

A new form of internationalization was central to the survival of former East German companies. Not only have the surviving companies found new markets in the west, but perhaps more importantly, companies have been able to establish networks that include western companies. The surviving companies have gained access to new investment and new production methods. Management has replaced an East European outlook with a more global outlook on their business activities.

However, it is essential to point out that not everything about these companies changed. Companies combined new insight with a revitalized view of their own capabilities. They remained in their old businesses and were able to convince new business partners in the west that what they were doing could have market value in an international market. The studied companies underwent internationalization with a clear East German touch and remained true to some of their values and capabilities. Many of these companies predated East German establishment and were able to realign themselves with their former traditions.

Case study: Schott – finding the right partner

Historical background

In 1884, Otto Schott, Ernst Abbe, and Carl Zeiss and his son Roderich founded Glastechnisches Laboratorium Schott & Genossen (Schott and Genossen laboratory for glass technology), and over 1000 employees were working at the factory by the company's twenty-fifth anniversary in 1909. Dr. Otto Schott took a scientific approach to the development of optical glass and the melting of new types of technical glass. Technical laboratory glass was improved by the invention of borosilicate glass. A corporate information leaflet from Schott, edited by Jürgen Steiner, Dieter Kappler, and Hermann-Josef Berg (2003), provides the following insight into the history of the company.

At the Schott factory, melting and processing technologies were under continual development for use in optical, technical, chemical, pharmaceutical, electro–technical, and household applications. Schott products gained an international reputation, and over 50% of production was exported by 1900.

In 1927, Otto Schott's son Erich Schott succeeded his father as the manager of the company. After the Nazis came to power in 1933, it became a challenge for the company to retain as much independence from government influence as possible. Eric Schott together with a colleague intervened in the Berlin Ministry of Economics to remove a government commissioner installed by the Nazis. However, it was impossible for the Schott factory to avoid involvement in the German war effort. As a producer of military glass, the Schott glassworks were targeted by Allied bombing and suffered serious damage once in March 1945.

In April 1945, American troops entered Jena. Members of an army unit of 3000 men who inspected German factories after German capitulation came to the Schott factory. With them were representatives of the American company

Eastman Kodak and the English manufacturer of optical glass, Chance Brothers & Co. The reconnaissance troops took photographs, made sketches, and requisitioned many documents on glass composition, melt data, production processes, patent specifications, and factory layouts as well as drawings of machines and sample pieces of glass. Today, these reports are kept in a US archive in Washington.

In June 1945, Otto Schott was ordered by American troops to start the loading machinery and materials needed for relocating the factory onto 50 railroad cars. The Americans did not have time to relocate the whole factory and focused on an "intellectual dismantling program" involving relocation of the best minds in the factory. At the last minute, some of the people on the relocation list managed to avoid deportation. Forty-one people called the "41 glassmakers", including Erich Schott, were placed under temporary arrest and interrogated regarding their political and occupational activities. The glassmakers prepared to produce glass in Zwiesel in the American zone in western Germany where Schott had a subsidiary that was making glass. In 1950, the western part of the company was relocated to Mainz, and was to receive DM 15 million from the Marshall Plan.

As American troops left Jena in June 1945, the Red Army moved in. The new Russian commander of the Schott factory, Major Gantmann, ordered production to restart. Most of what was produced at the factory in Jena was taken to Russia as part of the war reparation payments. The factory was later to be dismantled and moved to Russia in 1946. In 1948, what remained of the factory in Jena was expropriated by the State of Thuringia without compensation.

The Schott glass factory in Jena became important to the German Democratic Republic, which was formed in 1949. The Schott manufacturing efforts were constantly trying to keep up with international standards. Changes in managerial structure as the company became a state-owned company made it difficult to run the company efficiently, and the technical expertise in the management was weakened. Experienced specialists and master craftsmen supervised production under East German rule. New experts were educated at the newly organized technical schools, and the glass specialists who had been deported to Russia were able to return to the factory in Jena.

The traditionalists, called "Schottians" and "Zeissians", who believed in traditional ways of running a factory inspired by the liberal ideas of the likes of Otto Schott and Ernst Abbe, were suspected of being reactionaries by the East German regime. The Communist Party wanted to become more powerful by replacing skilled managers with political appointees. In 1953, 24 managers were arrested one night and accused of consciously hindering the reconstruction of the East in order to promote reconstruction in the West. The state security police, the Stasi, conducted mentally and physically draining interrogations that in some cases lasted up to a year. The 24 managers were condemned to long sentences. Only one of the persecuted managers eluded capture, Dr. Wilhelm Schacht, who from 1942 led the legal department in Jena. Schacht and his family fled to the West shortly before the arrests took place. Unrest broke out in June 1953 as the workers went on strike; this unrest was quelled with the help of the Soviets.

In 1981, the legal dispute between Schott in the west and the east was settled. The simultaneous use of the same brand name in both the west and the east had caused confusion among customers. After 1981, the eastern part of the company was named Jenaer Glaswerk, and the Jena company was granted DM 4 million for giving up the rights to the Schott name. This remained the name of the company until the Schott corporate brand name returned to Jena in 1998, seven years after the unification of Germany.

After German unification

Shortly after the Berlin Wall came down in 1989, the management at Jenaer Glaswerk contacted Schott in Mainz. A delegation from Schott in western Germany visited the factory in Jena, as the western German management wanted to help the company in the east. Jenaer Glaswerk then had 4,300 employees and was technologically 10 to 15 years behind the west. The situation was summed up in the words of Helmut Fahlbusch, then chairman of the Schott Jenaer Glass Supervisory Board: "From a pure business point of view everything spoke against a commitment to Jena. What motivated us was our historical obligation to the place where Schott was founded and our moral obligation to the people there after the collapse of socialism".

In 1990, the two companies signed a letter of intent to join ranks in a Carl Zeiss Foundation after a transition period. That same year the company became a GmbH – a public limited company. The Treuhandanstalt, the holding company set up to privatize East German businesses, was initially the sole shareholder of the newly incorporated company. In 1990, the two companies entered into a contract on consultancy services, transfer of know-how, and patent utilization. Wolfgang Meyer, the Provisional Production and Technology Director in Jena, concluded the following: "We concluded quite soon after the fall of communism the only chance of survival the Jenaer Glaswerk had would be to be involved in co-operation with Schott in Mainz".

In 1991, Schott in Mainz took over 51% of the shares, the remaining 49% remaining the property of Treuhand until 1995, when it was sold to Schott. From the beginning of the privatization, EUR 12.75 million was invested in the company in Jena. The moneys were spent on improved production facilities, future-oriented technologies, improved efficiency, and environmental protection measures. To make the transition to the market economy possible, Treuhand made EUR 122.5 million and the State of Thuringia EUR 30.6 million available to the company in Jena, to finance worker benefits and cover losses. By 1995, sales revenues had already exceeded production costs and the company broke even, something that was unusual among East German companies at that time.

The survival of the company

Under the East German regime, everything at the Jena-based company had been politicized, and 80% of the export market was in the Soviet Union. When Eastern Germany changed over to the Deutschmark, however, Jenaer Glaswerk's Russian customers could no longer afford to buy its products. Turnover was reduced to a mere 10% of previous levels as the company's whole eastern market was lost. The question of how to survive was acute in Jena.

The company traditionally made all its products in-house and had few subcontractors. The company also was responsible for other functions in the local community, such as maintaining roads and swimming pools in the vicinity of the factory. In 1989, the company elected a new CEO by popular vote among the employees; shortly thereafter, three thousand employees were fired. There was initially a strong belief that managers from the west could save the company. Later, the notion spread in eastern companies that the best managers from the west did not come to the east. Moreover, western managers were often viewed as arrogant.

After unification, many of the ineffective former production processes were stopped, and all research and development moved the west (though some later returned to the Jena site). Each production line in Jena had to fight for its survival, and the company had to cope with overcapacity. In 1993, the company started a joint project with Asahi Glass to develop borosilicate float glass – Borofloat. In 1998, the company became a comprehensive supplier of optical materials and components for semiconductor manufacturing, and three years later entered into photovoltaic technology. These innovations represented technological turning points for the company, showing that it could stand on its own two feet and develop marketable products for the global market.

Two survival strategies of the company have been to let its customers determine what to produce and to provide good customer support. Tailor-made specialized float glass solutions today represent over half the company's turnover. The company works closely with its customers, the parent company in Mainz, and the local university in Jena. The company is trying to know its limitations and realize that it cannot do everything and must specialize in areas in which it has expertise; accordingly, the company is trying to find markets in these areas of competence. A dominant survival strategy is to have specialized knowledge and to use it in close co-operation with customers.

Case study: Rhönbrauerei Dittmar – A beer needs its home

How the long-established Rhönbrauerei Dittmar GmbH survived when collapse threatened

The Rhoen is a highland area at the heart of the border triangle between the German Länder of Bavaria, Hesse and Thuringia. The highest peak in the Rhoen is the 950-meter Wasserkuppe. It is on the Hesse side.

The brewery Rhönbrauerei Dittmar GmbH is located in the Thuringian town of Kaltennordheim, which has 1,800 inhabitants.

Thuringia was part of the GDR; Hesse belonged to the Federal Republic of Germany. But the Wasserkuppe graced the labels of the brewery that was private until 1963 and then semi-nationalized until 1972. Following full nationalization in 1972, this was no longer permitted. A nationally owned company represented by a symbol that was located in the West? An affront. The Hesse peak was replaced by two fir trees. It was impossible to see where they were located. Friedrich Dittmar, great grandson of the founder of the company, became technical manager of the nationalized company, one of many private owners who translates VEB, people's firm, with "Vaters ehemaliger Betrieb" - "father's former factory". This traditional business, founded in 1875, was now managed by others. The company became part of the Rennsteig beverages combine of companies. This name also includes significant connotations of "home." Rhoen beer was and remained popular. It was known and appreciated throughout the region, but also further afield.

"What was it like after the fall of the Wall?" we ask Senior Manager Friedrich Dittmar and his daughter Christel Reukauf, President and part owner of the brewery that was reprivatized in 1990. "Did your customers remain loyal to you?"

We find out that the interest in Western beer, which was known from TV commercials, but was so far away, was greater for a short time after the Wall fell. It could be now enjoyed "over there" – no wonder, with the border to the West suddenly open and only 15 kilometers away – or at home, you could pay four or five times the original amount in GDR Marks, which was replaced by the Deutschmark on July 1, 1990 as a result of the Economic, Monetary and Social Union. The beer from breweries in Bavaria, the Rhine area, Lower Saxony and Schleswig-Holstein was immediately available in the East following the fall of the Wall – the beer-laden trucks arrived continuously.

"And you continued to supply your beer to bars and restaurants?"

"We tried at least. We were well-known in the region, but also beyond. Already during GDR times, we produced quality and for this reason, we received the additional allowance for the so-called Delikat, which was a program for the production of higher quality food and drink. This enabled the purchase of better ingredients and the sale of our Rhoen beer throughout the district. In turn, this meant new customers and higher product quality. This was to our benefit after the 'turning point.' But initially, it was of no use. Breweries from Bavaria and Hesse made a run on local pubs and restaurants, supplying everything from beer and glasses to new bar equipment and even new furnishings. Who could resist gladly saying Yes to that, especially when you had had to wait years for new equipment?"

"But for you, this Yes was a No. In the race between the hare and the tortoise, you were the tortoise, but never dared to say: I am already here!"

"We did say so. And some things were still possible through contacts established over decades," reassures Senior Manager Dittmar. „But the overall situation was absurd. Almost daily, salesmen came to the brewery, wanting to sell us everything under the sun. Production equipment, distribution solutions, endless marketing ideas. And in our warehouse, the crates of beer mounted up. Hardly anyone wanted to have it and the sell-by date was drawing ever nearer."

When we ask how they overcame this situation, it is quiet for a while. Then Frau Reukauf says with a look that radiates dignity and at the same time has an air of the wistfulness with which this decision was made: "First of all, we opened a liquor store and sold the beer from the West." "What other option did we have?" adds the Senior Manager. We can sense what this must have cost him, this fifth-generation master brewer.

Already a month before the Economic, Monetary and Social Union, he is once again the owner of his family firm. With a large number of investments made in GDR times, which now proved obsolete, but were registered as assets by the Treuhand Agency and cost money when the firm was bought back. What was the value of a coal-fired boiler house erected for 1.5 million and operated by 19 employees, when it had to make way for oil drums for reasons of the environment and efficiency? What was to be done with the wooden beer crates and other equipment, which no longer met quality standards and had to be replaced by new ones?

Our interviewees say that, at the time, they were still "rather blue-eyed" in their negotiations with the Treuhand. New West German owners, often with well-performing businesses behind them, brought in their lawyers, who prevented payment for earlier investments that were no longer effective. The Dittmars did not have the experience or money for such solutions. "In some cases, we were able to correct matters later with the successor organization to the Treuhand," explains Frau Reukauf, "in that we were referred to other people for different decisions. But back then, we were simply steamrollered by the situation and acted accordingly. With the benefit of hindsight, we would have done many things very differently."

The most difficult aspect was dismissal of employees, who had been employed by the firm for decades. The staff reductions from 160 to a final number of 45 meant that any walk through the town, where everybody knows everybody, was running the gauntlet. This experience left its mark and is forever associated with the memory of the turning point and the time immediately after. At the same time, the Dittmar and Reukauf families enjoyed new freedom. "We looked around in Hesse, in particular, to find out how comparable businesses worked, had many talks with people in the same industry. Before we had the money available, we knew which investments were most urgent and when we had the money, we did not put off any time in equipping the company. Meanwhile, most people here had also understood how much it costs if you spurn your own products. And Rhoen beer was well-known, had a good reputation not only, but particularly, from the GDR time. Our logo was from 1934; we were able to prove to the Patents Office in Munich why it had disappeared in 1972, and virtually bought it back."

"'... und dein Tag wird Rhöner' [Eng. 'and your day has a touch of the Rhoen'] is the motto on the bottles and crates. This *Rhöner* sounds a bit like *schöner* [Eng. prettier] and *röter* [Eng. redder], at least for those not familiar with the Rhoen."

"Yes, it reminds our customers of their home, the Rhoen. Beer needs a home. And this home, the Rhoen, also has the advantage that you cannot tell whether it is in the East or the West. With the prejudices against eastern products that still exist in the West, it is no bad thing that the customer there does not know exactly where Rhönbier comes from. In terms of quality, we can truly keep up."

"The Wasserkuppe in Hesse as your logo thus fulfills an entirely new purpose. With this, you can avoid anything that might look like Ostalgie, the nostalgia for East Germany?"

"Yes, in the West. That would be detrimental to business. But here, we still drive around with our Trabant Kombi with its integrated beer-serving device, when friends of our company have parties. It is as well-loved as our bright red fire truck thirst-quencher of the Borgward trademark, which was built in 1958.«

"And you are also using advertising again, which is equally well received in East and West. I can just imagine the media outcry in Sweden, if the state liquor store Systembolaget were to use the slogan you use here 'Doppelbock macht doppelt Bock' [Eng. Doppelbock makes you twice as horny]. This cheeky statement would immediately be banned, regardless of the fact that the Swedish state has already prohibited the advertising of alcohol anyway. And Systembolaget does not carry any Bock beer."

It is actually fascinating to see the marketing strategies used by the Rhönbrauerei Dittmar to secure the loyalty of customers, particularly in the brewery's home area, while it also attracts the many tourists who visit the Rhoen Reserve European Biosphere, which is under UNESCO protection. There are such events as Beer Day in April, the Doppelbockanstich in the autumn and the three-day brewery festival in the summer, all traditional and much-loved highlights in the calendar that bring together producer and customers. The contracted restaurants of the Rhönbrauerei, now numbering 250, are promoted at the same time at their own initiative. In addition, there are the lotteries and samplings in all listed drink markets within a radius of up to 120 kilometers, organized by creative event management.[46] Using incentives, individual groups are targeted. The launch of the "Feuertaufe" beer, for example, brought together 250 firefighters from the entire region. Growing numbers of activities aimed at more specific customer profiles are complemented by merchandise and a presence on the Internet, which places heavy emphasis on the connection with the region.

During a tour of the company, led by Senior Manager Dittmar, we see evidence of the systematic transition to high-tech that has taken place since 1990. Stainless steel tanks in the fermenting basement, a fully automated mash-house and a fully automatic bottling facility make a strong impression. At the same time, machines and kegs come to our attention as reminders that provide visitors with the context of tradition and innovation. The history of brewing technique since the foundation of this family business in 1875 becomes even clearer in the museum that is part of the company, which also serves as a meeting place for visitors, associations and institutions.

The Rhönbrauerei Dittmar now produces Rhöner Pils, Rhöner Landpremium, Rhöner Edel Export Spezial and three types of wheat beer in accordance with the German purity requirements. To this can be added mixed beer drinks according to the taste of the day and such seasonal beers as Rhöner Bock, Doppelbock and Christmas beer. The "Original Rhöner Urtyp Dunkel" received the CMA quality label from the German Agriculture and Nutrition Economic Society ten years in succession.

The Rhönbrauerei was one of the first midsize breweries to introduce a quality and environmental management system. In 2002, it gained DIN EN ISO 9001:2000 and VO Nr. 761/2001 certification. The Thuringian Ministry of Agriculture, Conservation and the Environment has also awarded the firm, annually to date, the quality label "Proven quality from Thuringia." The criteria for this are an explicit relationship to the home area and customer proximity, the practice of environmental protection through short transport routes and reus-

---

[46] Cf. Guy Nufer-Kellermann, Brauwelt No. 34-35/2007.

able packaging, predominant use of regional raw materials, the creation and securing of work and training positions in the home region, as well as quality, taste and variety of products.

The Rhönbrauerei Dittmar is one of seven Thuringian companies that want to profile themselves under the umbrella trademark of Rhoen as a quality region. The approximately 100 other companies come from Bavaria and Hesse.

3. In safe hands?

Socio-Economical Experiences on the Road to a Market Economy

In spring 2008, German dailies reported the success of the estate agent Bernd F. Lunkewitz before the Federal Supreme Court, the highest German court. In 1991, Lunkewitz had acquired the best-known book publisher in the GDR, the Aufbau-Verlag, from the Treuhand and turned it into a competitive enterprise in the German publishing world. It transpired that the Treuhand did not own this publishing company and, accordingly, was not entitled to sell it (Spiegel 2008).

A decade and a half after the disbandment of the Treuhand Agency, its decisions are still making headlines. They are as polarizing as they always were. While the President of the Institute of Economic Research in Munich, Hans Werner Sinn states: "German industry has not yet recovered from the cutting knife that was wielded under the ownership of the Treuhand, when three quarters of industrial jobs were lost" (Sinn 2005, p. 25), the national economist Michael C. Burda calls "the successful privatization of eastern Germany" an "unparalleled feat in economic history" (Burda 2005, p. 185). "With the virtually total privatization of a complete national economy," explains former Federal Minister of Finance, Theodor Waigel, "the Treuhand did outstanding work" (Waigel 2005, p. 71). Others are less enthusiastic. Lunkewitz, publisher mentioned above, accuses the Treuhand of "behaving like a criminal association in certain respects." The Treuhand brings charges, but later withdraws them when the publisher insists on going to court, where he could provide evidence to support his claims (Spiegel 2008). "The Treuhand's privatization campaign," wrote *Stern*, "left behind worse desolation than the dismantlement by the Russians after the Second World War" (Jaenecke 2001). Otto Köhler goes further in "The Great Dispossession. How the Treuhand liquidated a national economy." Using a reference from the historian Ernst Nolte, he describes the business approach of the Main Trusteeship Office East (HTO), established in 1939 in occupied Poland using unmistakably recognizable features of present history (Köhler 1994).

In the following, three issues are addressed.

The first issue addresses the Treuhand Agency (trusteeship agency) as an institution. What led to its establishment, how was its function composed and how were these functions put into practice?

The second issue investigates the positive and negative experiences that were made in the transformation of the East German planned economy into a market economy. Which of these deserve to be retained: due to their exemplary innovative powers that stretched beyond the special circumstances or because of their discouraging, counterproductive effects. The specific political and socio-cultural conditions in which the Treuhand's work was embedded, will be discussed on a case by case basis.

The third issue addresses alternatives to the Treuhand itself and its assignment.

Treuhand – a child of the Turning Point

The foundation of the Treuhand Agency dates back to the time of The Turning Point in the GDR. The idea was made public in February 1990 by the citizens' movement "Democracy Now" at the Round Table discussions. Its supporters were aware that a change in conditions of ownership was imminent. In the process of the formation of market-economy structures, state ownership should not be lost by the East Germans. At the same time, "wild privatization" by some combine leaders and company directors had to be brought under control.

The term "social property" did not exist in Federal German law. In the GDR, it meant state and municipal ownership. In 1989, social property comprised an estimated 96 percent of industry and productive trade (Luft 1992, p. 35). In 1972, 11,800 companies that were privately or semi-state-owned were dispossessed under Honecker and became social property.[47] This was the death knell for the middle tier of business in the GDR and signaled further prevention of individual profitable initiatives. Perhaps more than the cooperative ownership that also existed, the social property remained strangely distant from its owner, the people. This overall abstract and artificial-like form of ownership of the

---

[47] Figures from Harry Meier: Mittelstand in den neuen Bundesländern, Flensburg 1997, Pages 24.

means of production restricted the scope of the producer and the consumer. Another restriction was the command economy on which it was based. In all of this, the People's ownership represented an economic and legal value that belonged to all East Germans. Accordingly, the "Government of National Responsibility" under Prime Minister Modrow established in law: "To safeguard social property, the Agency for Trusteeship of Social Property will be established effective March 1, 1990" (Gesetzblatt der DDR 1990). However, this did not mean that barriers were being put up against imminent privatization. On the same day, the "Ordinance for the Conversion of Combines etc. into Companies" was published: "Companies are to be transformed into limited liability companies or stock companies" (Gesetzblatt der DDR 1990). This step became possible because in the GDR, German commercial law was legally valid. In fact, in the extremely brief period from March 1 through to the end of June 1990, 8,500 limited liability or stock companies were formed (Treuhand intern 1993, p. 30). There was also consensus in the Modrow government regarding the provision of ownership rights or share certificates for state-owned wealth to East German citizens, but not regarding the procedure of issue and the related preparation work.

In the period of the Modrow government, the Enterprise Act of March 7, 1990 was passed, which declared the dispossession of 1972 unfair and paved the way for the first wave of reprivatization through the Treuhand Agency. Prior to German unification, 1,565 enterprises were returned to their original owners (press release from the GDR Ministry of Economy 1990). In addition, virtually 3,500 small businesses and restaurants were transferred to the private sphere (Waigel 2005, p. 62).

Modification of the Treuhand assignment

The Volkskammer parliamentary election of March 18, 1990 was the first and last free election during the existence of the GDR. With a turnout of 94 percent, the highest in German history, there was a clear mandate for immediate unification with the Federal Republic. The victor was the "Allianz für Deutschland," a conservative electoral alliance. Prime Minister Lothar de Maizière (CDU) formed a coalition of the Allianz, SPD and the Liberals. His government endeavors to achieve the goal of the accession of the GDR to the Federal Republic in accordance with Article 23 of the Basic Constitutional Law, thereby securing the rights of GDR citizens through binding agreements. With the "Adoption of the Economic and Social Legal system of the Federal Republic" as declared in the government's manifesto, this corresponded to the decision made by the Kohl cabinet in February 1990, whereby "the GDR /.../ (must) complete the transition from the socialist planned economy to a market economy rapidly and consistently." (Roesler 2005, p. 94).

The assignment and orientation of the Treuhand are modified. The monetary union that is in progress deepens the fear of significant liquidity difficulties in East German businesses. The de Maizière government negotiates with the West German banks regarding the terms and conditions of credit provision. As a result, "the representatives of the banks make /.../ a credit provision to the Treuhand Agency dependent on an unequivocal orientation of its assignment position in favor of the privatization of state-owned companies, including property, and the provision of corresponding securities." (Treuhand intern 1993, p. 41).

The new Treuhand Law passed by the Volkskammer on June 17, 1990 provides support for these terms. The goal is no longer the "trusteeship of social property", but "the entrepreneurial activity of the state in completing a return to privatization as rapidly and extensively as possible": "The social wealth must be privatized." Furthermore, "the competitiveness of many companies is to be promoted where possible and thereby jobs are to be secured and new jobs created" and "property is to be provided for economic purposes." There is mention of "the possibility" that "provision may be made at a later date for the investors to obtain a guaranteed share in social wealth in the case of a GDR Mark/Deutschmark overall reduction by 2:1. The Treuhand Agency is assigned "to promptly, not later than two months after this law comes into effect, establish trusteeship stock companies in the line of capital establishment" (Law on Privatization and Reorganization of State-owned Property 1990).

However, Treuhand stock companies are never created. The Treuhand President, Detlev Carsten Rohwedder, apologizes succinctly before the East German Parliament after the decision is made as it involves a clear breach of the law. His argument was the foreseeable coordination problems between the Treuhand Agency and the Treuhand stock companies, difficulties of a personnel nature and lack of time (Volkskammer der DDR 1990). Along with this, there is a further softening of the legal assignment: the prescribed fulfillment of the Treuhand assignments "in a decentralized organizational structure" (Treuhand Act, Section 7, Paragraph 1 1990).

Structure and responsibilities

In reality, the organizational structure of the Treuhand is anything but decentralized. "Nowhere else," notes Wolfgang Seibel in the most thorough and convincing presentation of the history of the Treuhand to date, "had the dominance of the West German Federal Republic in relation to the absorbed GDR been so quickly and so rigorously implemented, but curiously enough, using organizational means that were borrowed from the state structure of the East German dictatorship that fell in 1989" (Seibel 2005, p. 153). In rigid hierarchical style, 15 branch offices in the capitals of the GDR counties were placed under the jurisdiction of the central Berlin office. Quite appropriately, Seidel calls this "the resurrected legacy of the central planned economy" (Seibel 2005, p. 140). The organizational and technical chaos of the first few weeks, graphically described in the diary published by Birgit Breuel, "Treuhand intern" (Treuhand intern 1993), contrasted with a hegemonistic bureaucratic solution, which remained as the chaos subsided little by little. Rohwedder compares the Treuhand Agency with a galleon. You could get on board voluntarily, but you also had to let yourself be chained voluntarily and row in time (Seibel 2005, p. 173). He states categorically: "We are already kicking the issues in the right direction" (Treuhand intern 1993, p. 170). The external offices did have a certain latitude in making decisions, but only to the extent that this related to the fulfillment of goals established from above. This had nothing to do with decentralization. The branch managers described their position in retrospect, "in metaphorical oriental, feudal conditions", as "little king, guru, oriental potentate" (Seibel 2005, p. 144).

The Administrative Council (Verwaltungsrat) of the Treuhand that had comprised 23 members since the German unification on October 3, 1990 was composed of West German industrialists and bankers, a Belgian industrialist with long experience of management and board activities in the Federal Republic, the prime ministers of the East German Länder, two representatives of the Federation and four (all West German) trade unionists. The Administrative Council appoints the management team of the Treuhand.

The Treuhand as "an institution of public law with direct Federal responsibility" answers to the Federal Ministry of Finance, but possesses far-reaching freedoms in its own approach and decision-making. As an independent administrative unit, it is separate from the Federation and can determine its own budget. It has the right of self-refinancing in relation to the capital market. In 1990 and 1991, it is also relieved of liability for gross negligence on the part of leading Treuhand employees. In the event of damages to enterprises, for example through erroneous contracts, the employee involved is not to be held accountable according to law. Breuel speaks of "revolutionary management" of legislation. Whenever the hopelessly inefficient combines, which become "dinosaurs of the plan economy" (Rohwedder), cannot be sold, they are split up and offered to interested parties in portions, without the approval of the legislators. Only when the Division Act is passed in April 1991 is the legality of the practice that has been going on for six months finally confirmed.[48]

Another example of an approach that has no clear legal status is the tension between the economic independence of the enterprises and the legal duty to interfere assigned to the Treuhand Agency (Ingerenzpflicht). "Is it an organization that ultimately answers for all of the commitments and errors of the enterprises? This cannot be the aim, but only in 1992 do the legislators provide clarity: The Treuhand Agency is no ruling enterprise in terms of the group law" (Treuhand intern 1993, p. 60). But with the two-year limbo, the Treuhand enterprises have greater difficulties to bear than the Treuhand, since they have had their entrepreneurial responsibility removed and are paralyzed and unable to operate in the market.

The dimension of the task facing the Treuhand is huge: Under its jurisdiction, there are more than 8,000 enterprises, with around four million workers and 32,000 premises. The property wealth comprises approximately 57 percent of the area of the GDR: 25 billion square meters of land. The number of workers in the 8,000 enterprises alone exceeds the total number of employees in the 25 largest listed companies in the US. "A Holding of this kind, which is the product of a transitional phase, had never been seen in the Western world" (Treuhand intern 1993, p. 229).

Prioritization and timetables for the completion of individual assignments are dependent on political approval. In turn, these are dominated by pressure from ongoing developments in the East, with excessive expectations from the population, election campaign profiles of the parties and narrow deadlines, all of which demands priority for individual measures and sidelines everything else. Foreign political issues must also be brought into the equation. Abroad,

---

[48] Retrieval, split-up and new establishment account for the number of enterprises on offer for sale through the Treuhand, which grew by more than 4,000: from about 8,000 to 12,354.

the path to German unity is followed with fascination, but is also accompanied by suspicion and fear of the power of a new Germany. There is a requirement for the German-German economic and financial transaction to comply with the rules of the EU.

Restructuring before privatization or privatization before restructuring?

July 1, 1990: this is the date that, like no other, determines the work of the Treuhand and its consequences are still felt today. This day marks the start of the economic, monetary and social union, and is also the date of the introduction of the Deutschmark in the GDR. The Treuhand assumes responsibility for preparing businesses for this shift. It provides credit guarantees on application if the liquidity status for the second half of 1990 can be guaranteed. In the month of July alone, 7,600 applications are received. Breuel speaks of an emergency solution, with unreasonable spatial and technical conditions for the Treuhand employees (Treuhand intern 1993, p. 65). In subsequent months, other processes for liquidity preparation are agreed with the banks. On the part of businesses, the credit applications must now be accompanied by a specific restructuring and business concept. At the end of the third quarter of 1990, the THA had provided liquidity credit guarantees for DEM 25.4 billion (Treuhand intern 1993, p. 67) – the means to pay salaries and wages and of settling other running expenses. These funds are not intended for investment in capital. On this subject, Rohwedder states on November 22, 1990: "The Treuhand Agency is not permitted, not willing and not in the position to take care of the restructuring concept in a gentle manner. The enterprises will only be granted enough money by us that they will be down on their uppers, but able to keep their heads above water" (Treuhand intern 1993, p. 170).

On the matter of restructuring, the first West German Chairman of the Treuhand, the former IBM Manager and head of the Bundesbahn, Reiner Maria Gohlke, had a different opinion compared with his successors Rohwedder and Breuel. After 35 days, "following differences of opinion with the head of the Administrative Council (Rohwedder) and his deputy", he relinquishes his position. He explains in writing: "To me, there is no doubt that the restructuring of the GDR economy is one of the greatest challenges of our time. I remain of the opinion that this economy has major opportunities because of its resources, particularly the supply of engineers and technicians. /.../ It will be the task of the Treuhand Agency, to channel its contacts with the many interested parties and the contracts ready for signing in such a manner that these are beneficial to the economy in general and do not become a general sell-out" (Köhler 1994, p. 73).

Restructuring before privatization, as supported publicly by Gohlke, is not an option for Rohwedder. "Privatization is the most effective restructuring", is the principle established in the so-called Easter letter, written five days prior to his murder by RAF terrorists. The letter commences with the formulation "Rapid privatization – resolute restructuring – cautious closure", whereby the resolute restructuring should be undertaken where possible by whoever has already bought an enterprise. Because maintaining jobs, which "(have) lost their competitiveness /.../ is expensive in all respects and slows down the desired remodeling of the national economy" (Treuhand intern 1993, p. 224).

The noble intention of „cautious" closure has its reasons. State-owned companies in the GDR, particularly the combines, fulfilled distinguished social, state and municipal purposes. They supported company nurseries, day and weekly crèches, company clinics, cultural centers, company holiday homes and children's holiday camps. Along with the loss of jobs when a company was closed, the workers lost trusted services that affected private lives deeply. Market economy structures do not envisage such tasks and responsibilities for companies. Faced by privatization, they are a cost issue to be eliminated and are a negative feature in the competition to find investors. At the same time, radical elimination of social services that fall under the responsibility of companies opens the door for potential, unpredictable conflict. Anyone accustomed to services of this kind for 40 years, supports their continuation. Conversely, western restructuring agents were hardly of the mind to accept structures that contradicted their view of the market economy.

Discrete bargaining

As of the second quarter of 1991, the Treuhand conducts privatization at almost any price and opts for "discrete bargaining", meaning direct sale following informal negotiations with selected external interested parties. The branch managers and senior employees from the head office are rewarded with premiums corresponding to a bonus system, the more and the faster they implement privatization. Billions in subsidies from state funds are helpful in disposing of individual large companies. The search for foreign investors only increases when it becomes obvious that West German companies are only moderately interested in investment in East Germany. Management buy-outs are now also permitted after initial applications are delayed by bureaucracy and dogged by distrust. In contrast to the other former socialist countries, East Germans, as associates of companies, have no priority in MBOs, a priority that is assigned to West German and foreign investors (Roesler 2005, p. 101).

The cautious interest in companies in the East from the beginning onwards, particularly from major companies in the West, had various explanations. Breuel names two of these, which are worth analyzing: "The West German companies had enough capacity at their disposal to allow them to additionally provide for the new Federal States and often had little interest in having their own facilities or competing companies in the East" (Breuel 2005, p. 25).

At a utilization rate of 65 percent of West German production capacity in 1990 (Roesler 2005, p. 98), it was easier to supply the east than to make investments there. The latter was an uncertain business, due to unstable conditions, deficient infrastructure and disappearing eastern markets, while the former was profitable: "The boom in demand from the new Länder contributed to the increase in the financial wealth of West German companies in an amount of more than DEM 300 billion from 1989 to 1991" (Luft 1992, p. 221) – and this was, it should be noted, at a time of worldwide recession. The real growth of GDP in West Germany of 4.5 percent in 1990 was the highest since 1976 and in 1991, it remained at 3.2 percent. Fifty percent of this alone was attributable to the market in East Germany (Büttner 1995, p. 121).

In September 1990, during the so-called Chancellor's Round in the Upturn East campaign, Rohwedder convinced Federal Chancellor Kohl to call on German business to put high-profile managers and specialists of all disciplines at the immediate disposal of the Treuhand Agency on a supply basis. The approximately 300 industrial and banking experts were certainly of invaluable help in accelerating the work capacity of the Treuhand (Treuhand intern 1993, p. 85).

However, the fact is that the free access that these experts enjoyed to the disposal of enterprises in the East provided their West German mother companies with unexpected and competition-distorting advantages and reined in East German competition. The mere mention by interested parties to the Treuhand of the intention to acquire a business was sufficient to gain the forced disclosure and price information from in-house sources. "For the employees of East German companies, from the worker at the bench to the management /.../ this all remained inscrutable, why one by one, representatives of a West German company, with the permission of the THA, demanded to see all the business documentation" (Roesler 2005, p. 100). After viewing files pertaining to personnel, new development, markets and customer information, it was decided whether an acquisition would be the most profitable solution. Armed with the necessary information, it was also possible to make the argument to the THA for liquidation rather than letting the business go to a third party (Härtel et. al. 1991, p. 13). If it came to out-competing an East German party making an offer, the privileged knowledge also made this easier. Frequently, East German markets were subsequently taken over by West German companies. Even in the diary "Treuhand intern" published by Birgit Breuel, it is stated that "the German industrial leaders are playing Monopoly", "able to play hard to get initially", before suddenly wanting to "take the leading role", when interested parties from abroad make offers (Treuhand intern 1993, p. 390).

The "discrete bargaining" gave foreign interests in the appropriate industries, such as banking, insurance, energy, media and lucrative hotels, little chance, but it was "in all respects, the best sales process for keeping things cozy. Some of the sales that gave rise to concerns after their announcement would have been impossible without the favoritism contained in 'discrete bargaining'. Rohwedder was, for example, a director of Allianz, which grabbed the East German insurance sector 'in one piece', and also of Ruhrgas-AG, which succeeded in taking over the East German district gas network. But the biggest corruption cases of the Treuhand story – associated with the company names Leuna/Elf Aquitaine and Bremer Vulkan/Baltic Shipyards – were at least alleviated by the THA's preferred sales process." Already in September 1990, the three largest West German energy groups had secured three quarters of the East German energy market with the help of the Treuhand (Roesler 2005, p. 99); the consequences of this decision are still discernable today.

Why was it that "discrete bargaining" was assigned priority in most of the cases? The answer lies mainly in the preferential treatment given to West German industrial and banking capital. Burdensome East German competition was not permitted to come to the fore. That more than four fifths of the privatized East German business wealth ended up in West German hands speaks for itself.[49] Walter and Quitzau discuss Vickrey Auctions[50] and Asset Stripping as possible alternatives, but support the opinion that these economic and socio-political goals were harmful (Walter, Quitzau 2005, p. 166). Suggestions, made before the monetary union and taking into account specifically East German experiences, were at the time dismissed as "market economy crimes." These included the most varied forms of barter, which ultimately, after valuable time had been lost, were also acceptable to the Federation of German Industries and the German Chambers of Industry and Commerce. The practice of many years of compensation trading with West European countries was also rejected by the Federal Government, Industrial Associations and supporters of pure market economic theory as a "relic of the natural economy", as East German companies used this know-how in business with eastern partners (Luft 1992, p. 258). Measures in support of East European export markets to rescue East German businesses and jobs (Köhler 1994, p. 78), which the former Treuhand head Gohlke and others had suggested, were rejected likewise. In particular, this applies to such models as Gerlinde and Hans-Werner Sinn's participation model, but it demands the fulfillment of „the task of the Treuhand set out in Article 25 of the Unification Treaty and in the preamble to the Second Trusteeship Law /.../ to give East German savers claims on the former public property to compensate them for having part of their savings converted at 2:1" (Sinn and Sinn 1992, p. 84). In this context, pointing out who actually owned the property that was for sale had already become almost politically incorrect in August 1991.[51]

Total privatization

It has to be asked whether the heave-ho privatization of an entire national eco-

---

[49] See Page 19.
[50] Offers are submitted concealed; the highest offer wins at the price of the second-highest offer.
[51] On this subject, it is stated in Jumpstart: "The property being sold belongs to a people who had the misfortune to live in the Soviet occupation zone, who had to write off much of their human capital with the introduction of the market economy, and who suffered a severe financial loss from the currency conversion and the restitution policy. These considerations alone should rule out trying to hasten the upswing by selling off the East German economy, especially since the likelihood of success is slender. /.../ A selloff would be in keeping neither with the principle of equality embodied in the German Constitution nor with the need to establish a sound basis for a prosperous common future" (Sinn and Sinn 1992, p. 85).

nomy, which "was thrown into the market simultaneously," (Betz 2000, p. 17) was actually necessary. There were and are sufficient serious arguments against this: it is an economic statement of the obvious that an excess supply of a product when there is reduced demand must have a price-lowering effect: "The principle that price falls when supply increases remains valid even when what is being sold is firms" (Sinn and Sinn 1992, p. 85). For such a comprehensive supply as this, there was neither a national or international market at hand. On the contrary, entire industries were saturated and the production capacity was not being utilized: "The current policy is based on the unrealistic assumption that there is a 'market for firms' on which a whole economy can be sold in a very short time. A market that can absorb such a large supply of firms so quickly just does not exist. Nonetheless, if all these firms are offered for sale at the same time, the prices will fall to ridiculous levels and what is legally a sale will become nothing more than an outright gift in economic terms" (Sinn and Sinn 1992, p. 84). This was exactly what happened. The Treuhand's chosen strategy of total privatization was "an embarrassing professional blunder by educated market economists" (Maier 1991, p. 6).

Where, above all, was the fulfillment of the legal assignment mentioned above, "to generate the competitiveness of as many enterprises as possible, thereby securing jobs and creating new ones"? And why did the Rohwedder Formula "Privatization is the most effective restructuring" become the general line of the Treuhand? In itself, this formula, as Seibel writes, was "a prognosis justified by nothing" (Seibel 2005, p. 165). The answer is not difficult to deduce from the practical behavior of the Treuhand, but also from the behavior of certain Bonn ministries: The Federal government did not make decisions according to a political or economic concept – there was none available – but on the basis of the threat of the loss of political prestige. It feared the political and social responsibility for a restructuring of East German companies at the hands of the state. Seibel cites fiscal grounds, due to which "it was ruled out after the currency shock of July 1, 1990, that the Federation, with its industrial state ownership in East Germany, should do what it had always done in West Germany and should also have done in the 1990s, namely to restructure Federal businesses prior to their divestment to achieve as high a sales prices as possible and to hinder any negative effects on the regional economic structure" (Seibel 2005, p. 363). However, there is no sign of a structural policy on the part of the Kohl government. "Structural policy considerations could only be applied by the Federation /.../ in exceptional cases relating to the 'industrial core' and to filter in a reluctant Treuhand into business policy. Anything else would have led to extensive state restructuring holdings and uncountable fiscal risks – quite apart from the fact that the FRG would also have to carry the *political* cost of each restructuring solution" (Seibel 2005, p. 363).

With total privatization, a consequence was a devaluation of the offering in its entirety and of its somewhat lucrative segments, and not only because of the increased capital market rates and record discount. There is a rumor that, in the sale of the enterprises on offer, it is a question of valueless goods left out on the rain. The leveling – Rohwedder speaks of "the entire salad" (Köhler 1994, p. 86) – affects experienced export businesses with full order books just as much as enterprises with future-oriented new development and is especially unsettling for interested foreign parties. The Treuhand does not necessarily do much to dispel the rumor. A journalist from the conservative, national German daily *Die Welt* asked Rohwedder, whether it would be meaningful, "to give away, dump the entire junk in the East as quickly as possible regardless of the cost, maybe even adding financial incentives?" The Treuhand President makes a gentle protest against the expression "regardless of the cost" – in this respect the Treuhand would have "make a bit of effort" and differentiate. But otherwise, "we need to quickly push back the state". He expressly confirms the statement, "that it is a matter of shells with not a great deal of content" (Treuhand intern 1993, p. 196).

Monetary union with consequences

A striking argument for the GDR to join the Federal Republic was the establishment of equal living conditions for all Germans in the Basic Constitutional Law. The economy demonstrated that fulfillment of the promises made by the politicians supporting rapid state unity immediately and unequivocally was impossible. In 1994, the formulation of Article 72 Section 2 Basic Law "Maintenance of uniformity in living conditions" was replaced by "creation of equivalent living conditions".

However, the consequences of the hurried monetary union for the businesses in the East could not be eliminated at the stroke of a pen. July 1, 1990, the day on which the D-Mark arrived, sealed German unity in advance. The significance for the Federal Republic of Germany, according to Chancellor Kohl, was "that we bring our strongest economic asset: the German Mark. In this way, we will involve the people of the GDR immediately and directly in what the citizens of the Federal Republic have built up and achieved over decades of persistent work" (Deutscher Bundestag, February 15, 1990).

Subjectively, many East Germans actually perceived the new currency as a sort of gift. The D-Mark myth was even stronger in the East than in the West. The wealth and abundance of the offerings that could be seen on Federal TV, growing time and money demands in overcoming the results of economy of scarcity and rising black market prices for obtaining "second currency" D-Marks, made this a fascination that promised solutions for various everyday problems.

Similar conditions applied in the economic sphere. In 1980, the GDR Ministry for Foreign Trade gained DEM 42 for goods valued at 100 GDR Marks, while this was only DEM 35 in 1985, DEM 28 in 1986 and all of DEM 23 in 1989 (Sinn and Sinn 1992, p. 59). This meant that in 1989, 4.40 GDR Marks had to be used to obtain one DM. Naturally, it cannot be deduced from this that DM 1 had a corresponding value of 4.40 GDR Marks – even if the black market rate was even higher. The GDR only conducted slightly less than a quarter of its trade with Western countries and thereby in convertible currency. Nearly two thirds was conducted with countries in the Council for Mutual Economic Assistance (COMECON) on the basis of the conversion ruble, which had the status of an internal currency. As an internal currency, the GDR Mark was even superior to the D-Mark. According to calculations by the Statistisches Bundesamt in 1990, the East-West basket of goods was such that 100 East Marks corresponded to DEM 108. Using the Eastern goods basket as a basis, this was as much as DEM 132, while with the Western goods basket, it was DEM 88 (Sinn and Sinn 1992, p. 54). Highly state-subsidized rents, leases, basic consumer goods, childcare and children's clothing, medical services, energy costs, etc., in the GDR made their impact here.

Through the monetary union, which was completed entirely over accounts, children under 15 received up to DM 2,000, Adults under 60 up to DM 4,000 and over 60, up to DM 6,000 at an exchange rate of 1:1 for their GDR Marks; money in excess of these amounts was exchanged at a rate of two GDR Marks to one DM. The wealth of private households was thus reduced from 193.4 billion GDR Marks to DEM 129.1 billion.[52] Current transactions, such as salaries,

---

[52] In comparison, the *annual growth rate* (!) among West German savers was DEM 220 billion in 1988 (R. Schröder 2005, p. 43).

wages, rents and leases were converted at a rate of 1:1, debts and obligations at a rate of 2:1.

As Birgit Breuel describes, for the East German companies, the monetary union meant „the introduction of a social market economy without a market" (Breuel 2005, p. 16). The fact that 4.40 GDR Marks were needed to generate DEM 1 remained unchanged because productivity was still at about a third of the rate of that in the old Federal Länder. But no recipient paid the GDR exporter DEM 400 instead of the DEM 100 to date for the same product. Karl Otto Pöhl, the head of the Federal Central Bank who had resigned because of the rushed implementation of the monetary union, told the Treuhand investigative committee of the Bundestag that it was "as if you were to introduce the DEM in Austria today and convert the Schilling at a rate of 1:1" (Köhler 1994, p. 151).

A revaluation of the currency of between 300 and 400 percent overburdened the East German economy. It lost its markets, which had been turned into hard-currency markets overnight, including the GDR's domestic market. The President of the Bund der Deutschen Industrie at the time, Tyll Necker, summarized the situation in a comparison: "I am definitely in favor of competition, but with an approximate distribution of chances that is fair. You can't put old sailing boats and modern yachts into a regatta and then blame the crews of the old boats when they lose. Only a temporary, declining and staggered adjustment of the disadvantages can provide the good crew of the old boat the chance to prove its skills" (Luft 1992, p. 177). The *Handelsblatt* daily wrote: "If, in 1948, the Federal Republic of Germany had entered into monetary union with the USA and at a rate of 1:1 between the D-Mark and the US dollar, a state that befell the GDR in relation to the D-Mark, then the Morgenthau-Plan, which supported the obliteration of Germany, would have actually been realized."[53]

In hindsight, the blame for the "disaster", as Pöhl described the monetary union (Köhler 1994, p. 154), was directed at the excessively favorable exchange rate for the East Germans and the unions with their wage demands in the East. Such a view rather conceals the real reasons.

For the East German companies, the exchange rate was actually impossible to bear. "High wages destroy a large part of an industry; only those firms that are

---

[53] „Das westdeutsche Wirtschaftswunder von 1948 läßt sich im Osten nicht wiederholen". Handelsblatt, Düsseldorf, June 2, 1992. Quoted from Luft 1992, p. 255.

productive enough to be able to afford them can survive" (Sinn and Sinn 1992, p. 144). But what are "high wages"? The collective bargaining parties, whose representatives all came from the old Federal Länder, had "no interest from an employer or employee perspective to allow low-wage competition to emerge in East Germany. The Treuhand, in exercising its employer function, which had be based on strict containment of payroll expenses, had no chance of asserting itself against this cartel of interests, even if its representatives had wanted to do so" (Seibel 2005, p. 161). In terms of wages, salaries and pensions, a conversion rate of anything other than 1:1 would have created a potential for conflict that it would have been impossible to impede politically. The average wage of a skilled worker in the GDR comprised 48 percent of a skilled worker in West Germany, the basic pension was 270 GDR Marks. At a conversion rate of 1:4, the result would have been a pension of DEM 68 for anyone on basic pension and about DEM 270 for the skilled worker (R. Schröder 2005, p. 43). "Even at a one-to-one adjustment of this wage, the average monthly wage of an East German industrial worker would be close to the level of entitlement for social welfare in West Germany" (von Dohnanyi 2005, p. 323). "I am convinced", said the Federal Minister of Labor and Social Affairs, Norbert Blüm, in a letter to the Federal Chancellor on March 27, 1990, "that a conversion rate below the rate of 1:1 would lead to deep social alienation and destabilizing political consequences" (Seibel 2005, p. 91).

The destabilizing consequences now had to be borne by the existing enterprises under Treuhand ownership, whose productivity did not correspond to wage levels and who did not have a market for their – too expensive products. This made them and their employees dependent on transfer payments. Lothar Späth, responsible for restructuring Jenoptik, describes the situation thus: "Since many of our products had no market, our motto was: Anything but production! /.../ In any case, we had fixed costs and if the workers also came to the plant, we would have automatically driven the costs for materials and energy through the roof. So we told them: You'll get your money only if you stay at home" (Späth 2005, p. 104).

In all of this, the question remains of whether the disastrous results for the enterprises had not been foreseen, or at least sensed, by the designers of the monetary union.

The answer to this is an unequivocal yes.

The directorate of the Bundesbank was openly critical. The President of the Bundesbank warned of a "premature monetary union at unrealistic conversion rates".[54] A special report by the Expert Council on the Assessment of Overall Economic Development from January 20, 1990 urged a *gradual* creation of a monetary union and stated in a letter to the Federal Chancellor on February 9, 1990 "Reservations against a rushed monetary policy integration". The letter said: "The nominal wages will then rise in excess of the increase in productivity. This will be done at the cost of the GDR's manufacturing base and there will be no influx of capital from the West, which is urgently required. The pressure on the Federal Republic would grow /.../. There would be an enormous burden on public finances, not only would considerable tax increases be required, much more public funding would be tied up in consumption use and would thus be unavailable for the financing of measures to improve infrastructure."[55]

The consequence assessments that were provided not only by referees from official advisory bodies, but also by renowned experts, and warnings about the risks of an overhasty monetary union and the presentation of alternative models and suggestions for improvements, are entirely rejected by coalition politicians. To Kohl, the economists remain "gurus, who, to crown it all, are also highly paid" (Betz 2000, p. 18). While in January, Federal Finance Minister Waigel described the proposal by the SPD Member of Parliament Matthäus-Maier for the abandonment of a gradually introduced monetary union as "breakneck", in a debate in the Bundestag on February 15, 1990, he argued in support of this: "In particular, the people of the GDR, no longer see any promise of success in a gradual plan. They now want a clear promise of sustainable political and economic freedom. /.../ They want to have their lives in their own hands, politically and economically – in the GDR or in the Federal Republic. It must be our goal that they do so in their homeland, the GDR" (Deutscher Bundestag, February 15, 1990).

The illusion aroused in the GDR of a rapid alignment of living conditions paid off in the Volkskammer elections in March. As a result of the monetary union, the fact remains "that in the unification process, institutional integration and assimilation of the East with the West in the political order were prioritized over economic development. The collapse of production in the GDR as a result of the introduction of the D-Mark, the col-

---

[54] Deutsche Bundesbank, Extracts from press articles, February 12, 1990. Quoted from Seibel 2005, p. 86.
[55] Expert Advisory Board, Annual Report 1990/1991 (Sondergutachten). Quoted from Seibel 2005, p. 86.

lapse of the domestic market and, subsequently, the export markets in Central and Eastern Europe, and their takeover by West German companies, all of this was accepted and approved by the politicians responsible. /.../ Politics made do with financially absorbing and alleviating the worst social consequences. This route was expensive and painful. However, for the Western economy, it promised increases in sales, market share and fast profits. In the East, it was to create the conditions for investment, modern technology and new structures. That is why it was chosen." (Busch 2005, p. 77).

Following the monetary union, the value of the wealth administered by the Treuhand – apart from property – crashed dramatically. To its functions was added that of stopgap for adventurous political shifts with far-reaching consequences not only for the East, but also for West Germany.

Return before compensation

No other issue in the process of German unification caused so much dissatisfaction as the prioritization of return over the possibility of compensation to dispossessed and qualified former owners of land and buildings or their heirs. First recorded in the joint declaration by the governments of the FRG and the GDR on the settlement of open property issues on June 15, 1990, the principle was brought into law by the Volkskammer of the GDR on September 23, 1990 and became part of German Basic Law through inclusion in the Unification Treaty. Due to the subsequent submission of 2.17 million property claims, the principal of "return before compensation" caused fear and panic among hundreds of thousands of East German house-owners, who had bought or leased the land for their homes in good faith from the East German state. "When a qualified former owner from the West suddenly stood at their door, the constitutional state took on characteristics of human disdain" (Schmidt 1993, p. 117). The entire legal profession found itself subjected to general judgments and condemnation, in particular, because, in the lucrative market areas, property speculators had gained the right to make claims by purchasing properties and were now claiming their right of "return".[56]

---

[56] According to Helmut Schmidt: „During my lifetime, I have made much fun of my own guild of economists and their predictions. Today, my preference is to wish that the guild of German lawyers could be sent to purgatory. Or, even better, to Stralsund, to visit the Mayor, to the land registry office in Potsdam, to the Chairman of Jenoptik or the President of the Treuhand Agency, where they would understand, what they have done and continue to do through their wealth settlement" (H. Schmidt 1993, p. 115).

That stumbling block – or rather: that road of stumbling blocks – on the way to German unity, became a bureaucratic process of putting out fires to limit the damage. Thomas G. Betz, to whom we owe the bluntest and most coherent presentation of the principal of "return before compensation", highlights "legal chaos" and "a compendium of absurdities" merely by listing some of the laws and ordinances passed between 1991 and 1994: the Obstacle-Removal Law, the Enterprise Return Ordinance, the Law on Changes to Property Rights, the Register Procedure Acceleration Law, the Land Sequestration, Property Law Settlement, Settlement Attainment, Compensation and GDR Debt Register Settlement Law, the Property Market, Mortgage Transfer Fee and Treuhand Agency Renaming Ordinance, and finally, the Declaration on the Powerlessness of Reichsmark Securities (Betz 2005, p. 113). It was of little use. The unsettled ownership status of a good third of the former "people's firms" formed an obstacle to massive privatization, restructuring and investment.

The citizens affected blamed the Treuhand Agency, but the Agency was simply the implementing body for hasty political decisions. The decisions became the nightmare of the Treuhand employees, making a permanent encroachment into their daily work. "You are the conveyors" was what they were told by an official from the Justice Ministry, who had been invited to explain the legislation (Treuhand intern 1993, p. 247). Rohwedder described the consequences of the principle of "return before compensation" within the Treuhand: "You have to imagine that at some point in time, everything that was later owned by the people and then assigned to the Treuhand, had belonged to someone. And in principle, according to the Unification Treaty, the former owners were to get back whatever had once belonged to them. That means that, at least in theory, every piece of land and every business has parties qualified to make claims. It could be a Jewish family, forced out of Germany in 1936 and now resident in New Zealand. It could be farmers who want to have their farmland returned. It could be small to medium-size entrepreneurs, who had lost their business in the final wave of nationalization in 1972. All of these people want to have their property back /.../ If an interested party wants to buy part of a former industrial combine and says that he will create 1,000 jobs there, the Treuhand Agency cannot hand over the business to him today if at the same time, there is somewhere a set of heirs saying that the business belonged to our grandfather, we want it back, but we have no plans to run it as a business. This cannot go on forever" (Treuhand intern 1993, p. 199). According to Rohwedder, there is only one inroad and this comprises the Rule of Precedence for investors who create jobs, invest and do something for the environment. The owners are then given compensation (Treuhand intern 1993, p. 170).

The authorities toiled on this Rule of Precedence for investors. The principle could no longer be reversed because, in the meantime, there were also claims from abroad and the threat of complications in foreign relations.

The principle of "return before compensation" was not repealed, but defused in terms of its devastating effect through settlement payments to qualified parties and time-consuming processing of cases. Now investors also had the opportunity to buy enterprises in competition with the former owners, if their investment concept was better than that of the former owners. If this was the case, the investors received a certificate of priority for investment.

The cost of the administrative chaos that was created had to be borne by the taxpayer. At the beginning of the 1990s, according to an estimate by the German Council of Industry and Commerce, investments in the range of DEM 200 billion were being hindered by unsettled property issues alone: "For a long time, investors, and also presumably qualified reprivatizers /.../ could not be sure that the disputed properties definitely belonged to them, and that they would be allowed to keep them, which meant that they held back on restructuring. Banks were hesitant to provide credit as long as the property could not be mortgaged /.../. Such resources as time and money – instead of being used for the economic restructuring process – were invested in legal battles, which is senseless from the point of view of national economy because it creates no value" (Betz 2005, p. 116).

Thomas G. Betz's analysis is insightful, particularly in light of his practical experience, gained from his employment at the Treuhand. If the entitlement to the return of an enterprise was confirmed, the claimant received on application a "compensatory payment due to significant reduction in wealth", as long as businesses remaining in operation were in debt. In addition, they were entitled to payments for the reinstatement of competitive capacity, called "compensatory payment due to significant reduction in profit status". These "were often of more significant value than the net value of the property to be returned, some of them even exceeding these values many times over and thus advanced to become 'objects of desire' (Betz 2005, p. 113). Payment was applied as a standard calculation, and „the people at the Treuhand made up the happy rhyme: With paper and pen, it's easy you see, to multiply by three" (Betz 2005, p. 115).

However, the involuntary peak of absurdity was reached with the legal interpretation that only permitted the business operations of a company to be resumed in the industry in which it was originally active. This meant that "a former producer of trousers, in conjunction with the return of his former dispossessed business, was only allowed to produce trousers in future and not high-tech goods, even if he were highly suited to the latter. In this manner, through 'return before compensation,' Germany invested not in an industrial future but in its past and in obsolete industries, for which the emerging countries had become responsible in terms of international work distribution" (Betz 2005, p. 116).

The implementation of "return before compensation" was, apart from the Czech Republic, an international novelty. It "degraded (East Germans) to the position of extras in the struggle over division of their own livelihood" (Baale 2008, p. 79). The highly praised market, which was supposed to guide matters in a neoliberal manner, was abandoned and decision-making power placed in the hands of a hopelessly over-extended authority. It was left to the authority's employees to cut their way through a jungle of laws.

Balance sheet 1994

"It was a time of *learning by doing* in its purest form", is the opening statement of a balance sheet of the Treuhand activities written by Birgit Breuel (Breuel 2005, p. 24). At the time of the "half-hearted dissolution of the Treuhand Agency" (Breuel) on December 31, 1994 and the transfer of unresolved cases to the "the Federal Agency for Special Tasks relating to Unification," the Treuhand had undertaken 15,102 privatizations, reprivatized 4,358 businesses, returned to the former owners or their heirs, handed over 310 firms to municipalities or placed them under the responsibility of the local authorities, and phased out and discontinued 3,718 businesses following part-privatization and outsourcing.[57] Approximately 25,000 small businesses, shops, restaurants and pharmacies were transferred to new owners. The Treuhand estate agency (TLG) had sold 36,800 properties, while the Treuhand itself had sold 9,700. During the Treuhand's nearly five years of operation, a total of about 85,000 individual

---

[57] According to Roesler, 3,940 enterprises (Roesler 2005, p.105).

privatization contracts were signed, comprising all areas and sizes of business – from pubs to land for development of apartment properties or establishment of industry to an integrated steelworks (Breuel 2005, p. 24).

Other figures are less impressive.

85 percent of the business property privatized by the Treuhand is now West German, 10 percent foreign and only 5 percent East German property (Betz 2000, p. 17). According to current estimates, EUR 250 billion in wealth was transformed into a loss of EUR 150 billion (Roesler 2005, p. 105). Three quarters of all jobs in the Treuhand area were lost (Priewe 2001, p. 20). "In the industrial sector, combined employment in THA and privatised firms had fallen from 3.2 million in 1989 to less than 800,000 by the end of 1992, a clear indication of the extent of deindustrialisation" (Priewe 1993, p. 343).

In Eastern Germany, industrial production in 1991 and 1992 fell to a level of 30 to 32 percent of the industrial production of the GDR in 1989 (Drost 1993, p. 457).[58] In 1994, production was only at 48 percent of the 1989 level; the gross domestic product (GDP) generated per inhabitant was 57.4 percent of the level of the old Federal Länder (Roesler 2005, p. 105). In 1997, not even 90 percent of the overall economic performance and less than half of the industrial production of the final year of the GDR, 1989, had been achieved (Steinitz 1998).

According to Sinn and Sinn (1992) "the severity of the depression in East Germany is without parallel in modern economic history. Not even the Great Depression of 1928-1933 was as bad. Then, the downturn was spread over a much longer period and, even so, the relative fall in output was smaller. Industrial output in Germany fell by 40 percent and gross domestic product (GDP) by 24 percent; in the United States the corresponding figures were 35 percent and 30 percent" (Sinn and Sinn 1992, p. 29). "The former German Democratic Republic (GDR) has been reduced to a structure of a developing country. Research and development have dwindled to almost Zero" (Krysmanski 1994, p. 4).

---

[58] Similar information from the Expert Council on the Assessment of Overall Economic Development, 1992. Annual Expert Report 1992/3, Wiesbaden: "Total industrial production in East Germany decreased by more than 70 percent between 1989 and 1992, reaching a trough in mid-1992" (Priewe 1993, p. 343).

Today's balance sheet

Twenty years after the fall of the wall, the German east remains a transfer economy that is still unable to stand on its own two feet. Economic performance does not even meet 70 percent of total consumption. Some 850,000 jobs are transfer-dependent. The annual funding of about EUR 80 billion that flows from West to East corresponds in total to the overall German national deficit. Despite there being some growth regions that give hope, such as Dresden, Leipzig, Potsdam, Jena and Erfurt, the per-head economic performance in the exemplary East German state of Saxony is still 30 percent below the German average. In 31 of 34 labor agency districts, the number of jobless is at least 30 percent more than the Federal average. The tax-coverage rate is less than 50 percent. The gap, according to Christian Geinitz in the daily *Frankfurter Allgemeine Zeitung*, will remain (Geinitz, *FAZ*, April 5 and October 2, 2007).

A consequence of the sustained disproportion in unified Germany is the dramatic process of migration from the East. The net loss from 1989 through 2006 totaled 1.74 million people, with approximately three million migrating and emigrating. In particular, qualified 18-29-year-old adults are leaving the new Federal Länder, according to study by the Institute for Economic Research in Halle (Schmidt 2008). A primary devastating factor is the migration of young, well-educated women. A more than 25 percent deficit of women in structurally weak regions is unparalleled in Europe and accelerates the economic and social process of erosion (Kröhnert, Klingholz 2007).

Without historical precedent

Asked to assess the work of the Treuhand ten years on, Belgian André Leysen, a member of the Treuhand Administrative Council at the time, quotes the Polish politician Bronislaw Geremek. It is easy to make fish soup from the fish found in an aquarium, but it is difficult to turn the fish soup back into an aquarium full of fish. It can be understood from this imagery that the assignments given to the Treuhand were really unfeasible "managed illusions" (Seidel). "Many may say", Leysen freely admits, "that the Treuhand Agency did everything wrong" (Leysen 2005, p. 58). This honestly acknowledged self-doubt is in refreshing contrast to success-heavy tenor of the book "Without historical precedent", which peaks in the accusation by Waigel that all of those who expressed radical criticism of the economic implementation of the reunification were ex-post know-alls (Waigel 2005, p. 70).

Only when the measures and decisions of the time are scientifically analyzed can they be of help to other users. This includes consideration of the historical conditions, the uncertainties of the time, conflicts between political and economic decisions, the implementation of claims to power, group and individual interests. The more profound and detailed the political and socio-cultural environment is studied, the more precisely it can be assessed whether abstractions can be made from this, to consider or discourage similar behavior under other circumstances. For example, inasmuch as the contribution of Lothar Späth, former Minister-President of Baden-Württemberg and later responsible for the restructuring of Jenoptik, to "Without Historical Precedent" is of considerable importance, he gives an authentic and ruthless description of the situation at the time and also puts himself in the position of those affected by the decisions (Späth 2005, p. 97).

Foreign interest in the work of the Treuhand Agency was unusually high from the very outset. This was primarily attributable to the media impact of German unification. The question of how a transformation process could be tackled, with a political change of regime and socio-economic upheaval taking place at the same time, was put to the Treuhand by numerous delegations, mainly from Eastern Europe. The request for the sharing of experience of privatization of a state-run economy topped the agenda (Treuhand intern 1993, p. 169; Breuel 2005, p. 28).

What experiences of this process – positive and negative – are worth highlighting?

The Minister of Economy from the Modrow Government, Christa Luft, admitted in 1992: "Most companies in the new Federal Länder were hardly viable in their initial form and, accordingly, difficult or impossible to sell." She bases her assessment on four factors (Luft 1992, p. 179):

Industry-specific company sizes that were unusually large by West European standards. Machine-construction companies with more than 1,000 employees serve as an example. In West Germany these comprised only 3 percent of the total, while in East Germany the figure was 22 percent. But in the East, there were fewer mid-size companies, whereby businesses with up to 200 employees comprised 31 percent in the GDR and 80 percent in the West.

The range of production of an enterprise that is unnecessary under market-economy conditions. This was a result of the economy of scarcity, which, in particular, forced combines to be their own suppliers and to produce preliminary products themselves at great cost. To this was added the development and production of noncore products as assigned by the state, which continuously tried to react to the shortages of "a thousand small items."

The inefficient cost structure. The proportion of costs for live work on turnover, meaning payroll and payroll-related costs, was, at an average of 25 percent, more than twice as high as in the old Federal Länder, where it was around 12 percent.

A range of products that was renewed too slowly and was often only marketable in East European markets. In 1990, slightly less than a quarter of all industrial products were in their introductory or growth phases of the product life cycle. But three quarters were in the stagnation and decline phase. Their availability in the Western markets also subsided. Facts of this kind were nothing new in the East or in the West. However, a new feature was the disclosure of the overall economic situation of the GDR. This was only possible after Honecker was ousted on October 18, 1989. Gerhard Schürer, at the time President of the state Planning Commission, disclosed the insolvency of the GDR to the Politburo in a classified document ten days before the fall of the Wall. Exports were only sufficiently to cover 35 percent of hard-currency expenses. Although the national debt of the GDR, at DEM 49 billion, was low in comparison with the Federal Republic[59], it meant that survival in the manner applied to date was impossible: „Suspension of the debt alone in 1990, would require a reduction in living standards of 25-30 percent and would make the GDR ungovernable " (Schürer 1992, p. 1119).

Self-criticism, 10 years on

To avoid a situation in which buyers of East German enterprises were only interested in the purchase of lucrative property and subsequently closed the companies, business concepts had to be presented. The Treuhand reviewed workplace and investment commitments and secured these contractually under threat of penalties. Further, an assessment was made to determine whether the

---

[59] The indebtedness of public households in the Federal Republic amounted to DEM 930 billion in 1989 and DEM 1,200 billion in 1990.

business concept guaranteed the continuation of the enterprise. The concept proved viable, particularly for interested small to medium-size entrepreneurs. These parties regularly brought forward their approved medium-term investments to enable them to produce marketable products at competitive cost in the shortest possible time (Treuhand intern 1993, p. 130).

The obligation for buyers to present a business concept is definitely an experience worth preserving, creating a legal basis to make phonies, cheats, charlatans and speculators face up to their legal responsibilities. Naturally, this was no guarantee for "clean" sales. "In many cases the THA gave contracts to incompetent and even fraudulent investors who lacked capital and pursued primarily speculative ends" (Priewe 1993, p. 345). A not insignificant share of the privatization – despite all measures of caution – was based on property speculation (Kurz 1993, p. 105). A transitional period such as that after the fall of the Wall, with its previously unforeseen opportunities, had a magical appeal for criminal elements. In contrast to the business concept, plans for research and development were absent. Birgit Breuel writes: "Even from the perspective of the time, it was a mistake not to demand a concept for research and development along with each business concept. From today's perspective, it was wrong not to make improvements in equity following the collapse of the CIS markets" (Breuel 2005, p. 26).

Both problems are related. Businesses in the sales pipeline were forced into drastic cost-cutting. They were no longer able to afford expensive research and development staff and even closed their R&D departments. In this manner, innovation potential was lost, which were lacking in the competition for new processes and products aimed at conquering new markets. Companies that had already been sold were generally used as extended workbenches for West German businesses. Apart from the exceptions that prove the rules, parts of the R&D areas were integrated into the West German parent companies or individual East German researchers were employed there. Usually, however, entire research departments were dissolved. The consequences of this approach appear in a survey of 260 East German companies that was conducted in January 1992 by the Institute for Economic Research in Halle. Within two years, from the beginning of 1990 to the beginning of 1992, R&D capacity in the companies still administered by the Treuhand was cut to a level of 36 percent. In the East German businesses that had already been privatized, it shrank to 27 percent (Luft 1992, p. 181).

In 1989, the number of researchers and developers as a proportion of the total population in the Federal Republic and the GDR was virtually identical. Within a period of only five years, this changed radically. In East German industrial research, the number of persons employed fell from 86,209 (1989) to 15,851 (1994) (Jordan 1999). In 1992, total expenditure per head for research and development in the economy in the new Federal Länder amounted to only a tenth of the comparable expenditure in the old Federal Länder, DEM 85 compared with DEM 840 (Steinitz 1998, p. 9). In the period from the fall of the Wall to the end of 1992 alone, 82 percent of all R&D jobs in the new Federal Länder were eliminated (Jordan 1999).

In 2009, the Annual Governmental Report on the state of the German Unity notices that "less than five percent of the industrial R&D investments in Germany are made in the new Bundesländer. In a world of fast technological change this can be a disadvantage for development" (Jahresbericht 2009, p. 6). A widely acknowledged locational advantage of East Germany – personnel with a good general educational level and proficient in science and technology – was lost as a result of the policy described above.

Western imports to the East

"A chance was missed for joint construction of the united Germany," writes Birgit Breuel, "when more than 200,000 paragraphs of West German legal system were transferred. It would have been better to remove the worst of the overflowing bureaucracy of the Federal Republic and adapt it to the new conditions. Thus, the incrustations of the West remained and were given to the East directly" (Breuel 2005, p. 26). This insight, expressed ten years after the disbandment of the Treuhand, applies not only to the export of West German bureaucracy to the East. The Treuhand was the embodiment of policy that only lent validity to the Western model and transposed it onto the East without understanding of the East or questioning the sense of the transfer. The Treuhand was the opposite concept to the words of Federal President Richard von Weizsäcker, which he expressed a year after German unification: "The unified Germany will not merely be an enlarged Federal Republic, but something new and shared. Both parts of Germany must contribute through their history and their life experience. It is only from this that inner unity can result" (Pinkert 1998, p. 31). A year later, he warned that "there is no such thing as the West Germans being the teachers and the East Germans their pupils" (Pinkert 1998, p. 32). The history and life experience of the East Germans bore no value for the Treuhand policy. Certainly, two thirds of the "oarsmen", in keeping with Rohwedder's galley image above, were East Germans, who, in his opinion, worked "like navvies" (Treuhand intern 1993, p. 172). But that was their lot. "Already in the autumn of 1990, the Treuhand elite had been almost completely replaced. Since the summer of 1992, there had not been a single East German among the management and directors of the Treuhand Agency. The professional experience, the local and regional knowledge, the biographical and everyday intricacies of the East German environment – none of these were represented among the staff at management level in a major organization that encroached drastically on the living conditions in East Germany on a daily basis. Parallels for this kind of replacement of a native elite are not easy to find – perhaps only, *horribile dictu*, under colonial regimes or occupational forces" (Seibel 2005, p. 153).

In all of the leading committees of the Treuhand Agency and among the heads of the regional offices, there was not a single representative of East German economic interests. When questioned about the reasons for this, Breuel responded three years after the closure of the Treuhand: "There was simply nobody that we could have used" (Marschall 1997). Of the department managers, approximately 19 percent were East Germans (Seibel 2005, p. 174).

The gender structure of the Treuhand Agency was just as unbalanced. The image of the leadership of the THA conveyed by its president, Frau Breuel, applied only to her. Among the 46 directors and the 15 heads of the regional offices of the Treuhand, there was not a single woman. On July 1, 1992, there were only 13 women among the 166 department managers, that is 8 percent" (Seibel 2005, p. 175).

"The sale of the people's property, not only in terms of content but also people, was something that West Germany negotiated with itself." Olaf Baale, who draws this conclusion, studied the behavior of Treuhand employees toward representatives of businesses that were to be sold or closed. He quotes one of the heads of the regional offices who could remember "a stable of young trainees," who conducted their work "as a continuation of their law seminars. To this day, I can understand that some of those affected from East and West, who had dealings with this awkward up-and-coming generation, had the feeling the Treuhand Agency was continuing the work of its predecessors." Baale writes: "If it were possible to recreate the tone used by these people toward former GDR citizens, some of them would be red with embarrassment. Nobody who had to experience it will ever forget how audacious Treuhand employees applied the total power of their authority and maltreated educated, experienced people with their incompetence and poor behavior" (Baale 2008, p. 93). This image corresponds to the fact mentioned by Birgit Breuel that, among the parties interested in companies to be given away, (there were) students, who wanted an Eastern company as an appropriate testing ground for them to cut their teeth on immediately after graduation" (Treuhand intern 1993, p. 322).

"The decision by the economic and political spheres in the old Federal Länder to make the West the measure of (nearly) all things, with no regard for any progressive achievements in the East, has sometimes generated new problems." This was Breuel's insight ten years on, her thesis exemplified using over-dimensioned water and wastewater companies (Breuel 2005, p. 26).

Criticism of the woman who was once Treuhand President is strongly understated. The exclusion of East Germans from all significant decisions, their downgrading to controlled executors of West German instructions not only hindered the much-lauded human unity, it was also, entirely unnecessarily, an obstacle on the road to economic prosperity. A demoralizing and destabilizing command structure had been the experience of 40 years. What came in its place required far greater individual effort to ensure a retained or improved livelihood. Accordingly, for most employees, the tone, tact and structure following the replacement of the elite was all too familiar. Subordination and adaptation, as so often in German history, seemed to be the order of the day – and not the feeling of being able to associate the hard-won freedom with the active freedom of involvement, with the active shaping of the new conditions. These conditions were once again predetermined and finalized. They pledged to those, who had briefly tested moral courage, grassroots democracy and codetermination after the fall of the Wall, dictation through new superiors.

The political rhetoric condemned the old system. But if profit could be made from the private sphere, the rules of the old system came to aid of the new system right on cue. No example illustrates this so vividly as the approach to old debts of East German companies.

East German economic law applied by West German private banks

The Treuhand graded the former nationally owned companies according to a school grading system of 1 to 6. Grade 1 was "Enterprise operates profitably. No further restructuring required. Rapidly implement privatization." In the allocation of Grade 5, it was noted: "Restructuring doubtful". Grade 6 meant: "Enterprise not viable for restructuring", and the decision was to be made between liquidation and complete closure (Baale 2008, p. 97). In the assessment of businesses, there was often discovery of old GDR credits, which the businesses had received from the East German state.

These credits had nothing in common with market-economy credit agreements. They were part of the plan economy and served as arbitrary steering and control instruments for plan fulfillment. In the words of constitutional law expert Rupert Scholz, the credits were "plan-economy instruments of force according to the principle of meager endowment and forced credit" (Schachtschneider 1996, p. 102). If the companies did not fulfill the plans set for them by the state, for example, because the equity assigned to them by the state was insufficient or the plan was illusionary due to supplies being unavailable, the state intervened using the credits described above. The risk of renewed failure was then borne by the state. Bankruptcy did not exist in the GDR; ultimately, the state bore responsibility for its enterprises. The people's property could not be insolvent or heavily in debt. In legal terms, there were neither creditors nor debtors. If a company were to have invested of its own accord to reduce its credit obligations, this would have been unlawful in relation to the plan targets. The assumption of debt, with the accompanying responsibility and ownership, was absent, as was the arbitrary attempt to pay off debts. Accordingly, the old GDR credits cannot be equated with debts in a market-economy sense. They only made sense in a command system, which had been abolished through the peaceful revolt in the GDR.

But already prior to October 3, 1990, the State Bank of the GDR had been given to West German private banks in a deal that will only be completely explained when through the opening of the related files in 10 to 15 years' time. These private banks now demanded that the East German companies pay back their debts to the East German state, but not at the East German rate of interest of 1.8 percent, but at the regular market rate of 10-12 percent.

The East German companies, which had to settle their debts at a conversion rate of 2:1 in DM, were mostly unable to pay. Instead, the Treuhand paid or deducted the old debts from the market value-based purchase price. In both instances, the taxpayer was required to cough up. "As a final consequence, old East German debts of around DEM 180 billion were up for negotiation and to that was added interest demands totaling DEM 40-50 billion at the time" (Baale 2008, p. 56). Hundreds of companies forfeited their ability to be restructured because of their old GDR debts and were closed down as a result.

Karl Albrecht Schachtschneider, holder of the Chair of Public Law at the University of Nurnberg-Erlangen, analyzes the debt problem in his publication, "Socialist debts after the revolution". He demonstrates that „the material force of the old-debt policy /.../ (is) in itself grossly unfair and /.../ (breaches) the equality principle in Art. 3 Section. 1 of the Basic Law (and) /.../ the freedom principle in Art. 2 Section 1 of the Basic Law" (Schachtschneider 1996, p. 195). In this context, he determines that the state "(may) not transfer claims to the private sphere, which it cannot enforce itself for political, even moral reasons. There is a difference if the Federal Republic enforces claims against /.../ businesses and pushes these to ruin or if the same is done by a private bank. /.../ Also in this respect, the fairness principle is disregarded in a manner that breaches the Basic Law" (Schachtschneider 1996, p. 185).

There is nothing, Schachtschneider argues, that justifies the revival of the socialist debts. "Such a measure would require the revival of the institutions of the plan economy of the GDR. Federal German policy rendered instruments of the socialist despotism retroactive. This was and is not only in breach of German Basic Law, but unfeasible in the absence of the revolutionary plan economy with its former idiosyncrasies" (Schachtschneider 1996, p. 154). "The breach of the legal ban on retroactivity is also a breach of the property guarantee because the laws that govern property must also comply with the rule of law" (Schachtschneider 1996, p. 160).

The absurdity of the decision becomes clear, when its consequences are considered: „If the (GDR- – FMK) Treaty Law and the Credit Ordinance /.../ continue to set the standard, the entire socialist economic system must remain in effect because these provisions can only have any possible meaning in a socialist plan economy. Without this economic system, they cannot be used; they have no function. The so-called credits would have to retain their socialist function in line with the "prevailing law" that had applied to date, that of planning, steering and control. Socialist ownership according to Art. 10 of the GDR constitution would need to be retained because the socialist economic law of the GDR was based consistently on this system-defining decision. There was no repayment obligation in a real sense. There was no threat of bankruptcy. The state had to approve the obligations" (Schachtschneider 1996, p. 147).

Consequently, Schachtschneider estimates the damages that occurred to the reunited Germany through the missed settlement as at least DEM 500 billion (Baale 2008, p. 61). The beneficiaries of the billion D-Mark redistribution of public property to the private sphere were the West German banks, who gained the profits without needing to take risks: "They had advantages in the debts, the interest, the fees. /.../ The damage to the general public is immeasurable, particularly in terms of the old debts, which /.../ were primarily borne by the people. The banks were not supported by any law that could justify the endurance of the socialist debts" (Schachtschneider 1996, p. 158).

But it was doable even without such a law. The policy on old debt of the Federal government and the Treuhand gives off warning signals. They prove what consequences an early sale of state-owned banks to private banks can have. Legally, the political decisions could no longer be reversed even if, as Schachtschneider and numerous other renowned lawyers demonstrate, they contravened scandalously the Basic Law and important principles of the rule of law and the free economy. However, the appeal to the Federal Constitutional Court ends in failure on April 8, 1997. After more than three years, the judges rule that there was no breach of the constitution. The question of whether the legislators had chosen the most practical solution in the Unification Treaty was not theirs to decide. "Nobody wanted to touch the wounds that had left behind, the economic cuts and dictation among the people. The entire Treuhand policy would have been rendered illegal if the Federal judges had declared the settlement of old debts as unconstitutional" (Baale 2008, p. 60).

Die Treuhand – authority without alternative?

The Treuhand was the most unpopular institution in Eastern Germany. Its decisions brought hundreds of thousands of citizens onto the street once again. The potash miners in the Thuringia town of Bischofferode, commenced a hunger strike, which triggered a wave of solidarity throughout East Germany in spring 1993.[60] Massive protests against company liquidation and mass layoffs had already been held earlier. There is an unusual example in Breuel's Treuhand di-

---

[60] The reason was the closure of the mine, planned for the end of 1993, in favor of the collieries in Hessen, whose potash was less competitive in the World market than that from Bischofferode. The slogan "Bischofferode is everywhere" became a signal for protests and resistance against the policy of deindustrialization.

ary. A mayor of three Thuringia communities had identical signs put up next to the town name signs with the wording "Warning! Employees of the Treuhand Agency enter this area /.../ at their own risk" (Treuhand intern 1993, p. 320). He was no longer willing to accept the sellout of municipal property.

But the Treuhand was also unpopular in the West. There, it was regarded as "gigantic capital-destruction machine". There was always criticism – if it didn't come from one side, it came from the other. „If the Treuhand was quick to privatize, it was breaking up productivity resources; if it carried out liquidation, it was destroying jobs, and when it provided financial support to ailing companies for the interim securing of liquidity, it was a money-waster, especially if the business ultimately had to be closed" (Betz 2000, p. 13).

"The Treuhand Agency was, in a certain sense, a paradoxical institution," notes the American Jutta E. Howard (Howard 2001, p. 157). On the one hand, equipped with an unparalleled degree of property and power, it was on the other "acceptable to admonish the Treuhand; it was safe, legitimate and a generally accepted practice. The agency became the most convenient instrument for expressing one's frustration – perhaps in this way, fulfilling an important social function at a time of enormous and painful social upheaval and economic transformation. /.../ From a political perspective the Treuhand was a clever invention because it had to take the beating for the decisions which were made in Bonn" (Howard 2001, p. 126).

But a state institution with nearly 5,000 employees, which cost DEM 820 M in a single year[61], should be judged by different criteria than its undoubtedly perceived function as the bogeyman of the nation and stopgap for the politicians responsible.[62] Associated with this is the matter of possible alternatives to the Treuhand.

An assessment of its work must take into account the overhasty and partly negligent political agenda, which restricted the scope of the Treuhand and prac-

---

[61] Amount for 1992, in which the THA "used DEM 460 M for advisory services as opposed to DEM 360 M for full-time employees. It was also not unusual for Treuhand employees to switch to advisory status." (Seibel 2005, p. 184).

[62] According to Thomas Betz, "Federal Finance Minister Waigel turns up (repeatedly) at the Berlin head office of the Treuhand Agency to give messages of support to the gathered employees, who were often subjected to personal attacks, and to provide assurance that Bonn stood steadfastly behind them. But this was not to be seen in any newspaper. Instead, the motto being passed around in the lobbies of the ministries is ‚Save Bonn, sacrifice the Treuhand!'" (Betz 2000, p. 13).

tically confronted it with new conditions from one day to the next. This applied to the monetary union in particular. The situation, entirely without historical precedent, of the transfer of a state-regulated planned economy into a market economy, with the accompanying change of regime, was a challenge for all those involved. But this must not lead to praise for lack of concept or even lack of thought in retrospect. And not everything proceeded without a plan, as the decision-makers of the time now claim. Ulrich Busch destroys this legend: "The Federal Government's decision at the beginning of 1990 to abandon the concept that had been favored till then of gradual unification and to tackle the incorporation of the GDR by expanding the monetary area, followed very closely – alongside tactical electoral motives – a well-conceived calculation, by which there was appropriate preparatory work and extensive strategic planning in the Chancellor's Office in Bonn, in the Research Advisory Council and in the Research Center for joint German economic and social issues." But this was not the only thing: "The stakeholders from German industry, banks, insurance companies and commercial groups had also been assigned due consideration in the concept of the monetary union, so there can be no question of unilateral political action" (Busch 2005, p. 77).[63]

It was absolutely correct to decide to separate the Treuhand Agency as an institution from ministerial bureaucracy and to provide it extensive freedom to make its own decisions. The value of this decision only becomes comprehensible in the cases. The official apparatus is too unwieldy in its actions; it is not capable of making quick decisions, as is the practice at the Treuhand. Of the abundance of examples, only the liquidation of the East German airline *Interflug* is mentioned here. Despite a large number of serious applicants in Germany and, in particular, abroad[64], there is a failure to sell due to the conflicting positions of the Federal Department of Transportation, the Federal Ministry of Economy and the Federal Cartel Office. The Treuhand was forced to take their demands into account. The case became extremely protracted until the running

---

[63] Busch refers in this context to the work of Karl Heinz Roth: Anschließen, angleichen, abwickeln. Die westdeutschen Planungen zur Übernahme der DDR 1952-1990, Konkret Literatur Verlag, Hamburg 2000.

[64] This was hardly about the "fuel-thirsty, personnel-intensive and loud" aircraft of Soviet manufacture, but was about the establishment in the East European market, Interflug's landing rights, its attractive location in Berlin and also the possibility to serve the German domestic market (Bothmann 1995, p. 189). The property wealth of Interflug amounted to DEM 1.2 billion (Treuhand intern 1993, p. 184).

costs only permitted closure. Deficit estimates for 1990 are ultimately based on annual losses of DEM 200 M (Bothmann 1995, p. 188). Breuel describes an "Interflug tragedy" and repeats the agency's assertion, "that there had never been so much intensive effort to find a solution" (Treuhand intern 1993, p. 180).

The collapse of "Interflug" makes it clear what the impact would have been of the Treuhand assignment being conducted by a federal ministry. "In that case," says Breuel, „work on legislation and provisions would have taken a long time, during which there should have been a need to keep the businesses going artificially. And there would have been a total dependence on politics so that many decisions made by the Treuhand, for example, in the case of closures, could never have been made" (Breuel 2005, p. 28). With these words, the former president of the Treuhand confirmed the agency's function as a pledged bulwark of politics. The agency did what the politicians responsible did not dare do themselves.

Naturally, the dependence on politics existed, even if it was in a way that was different to a ministry. The Treuhand answered to the Federal Minister of Finance, a decision indicating that the protagonists of German unity regarded the matter as primarily a problem of financial policy. The traditional separation of economic and finance policy in Germany played its part. Seibel mentions not least pragmatic and tactical coalition considerations. The Federal Ministry of Economy would have "found it more difficult to oppose the political pressure for justification for the actual economic effects of the Treuhand activities than the Finance Ministry that was traditionally limited to its fiscal tasks" (Seibel 2005, p. 120).

For Klaus von Dohnanyi, as for the numerous other protagonists of the direct unification process, "the immediate proximity of the Finance Ministry" was a weighty error. To him, the Treuhand would have "better suited to the Ministry for economics or a reconstruction ministry of its own" (von Dohnanyi 2005, p. 322). It was not for nothing that Minister for economics Hausmann and his successor Möllemann made the case for the Treuhand to be responsible to the Federal Ministry of Economy (Seibel 2005, p. 121).

Even tougher were the consequences of parliamentary control that had been neglected for years. Representatives of the governing coalition delayed the work of the investigative committees that were ultimately formed; The Federal Government denied insight into important documents. The debate in the Bundestag on the report by the second "Treuhandanstalt" investigative committee on

September 21, 1994 is a lesson in the subject of privatization practice, which seemed to have become immune to its responsibility before parliament.

On December 31, 1994, the Treuhand Agency was disbanded. Remaining work was transferred to the successor organization, the "Federal Agency for unification-derived Special Tasks." Media-consciously, Birgit Breuel removes a sign, originally hung hastily, with the writing "Treuhandanstalt" from the Detlev-Rohwedder Building in Berlin. "An institution that had become a negative symbol of time after the turnaround for many East Germans, had lost face to a certain extent. As much as the Federal Government had welcomed the scapegoat function of the Treuhand Agency since 1990 /.../, it was of little political interest for the Federation to maintain this institutional symbol of a kill-or-cure economic remedy after the monetary union, and the economic and social faults it caused, in the long term" (Seibel 2005, p. 370).

The Moor had done his duty, the Moor could go – in this case, he had to go.

Case Study: The cards are being shuffled anew

How *ASS Altenburger*, formerly *VEB Spielkarten*, became market leader in Germany

"How did we survive the Turnaround? With confidence in our cards, despite everything. The disruption in our sales was huge; who would want to play cards in times like those? Nonetheless, we had a feeling, rather than certainty, that our cards would once again be in demand. Because they had always been in demand! Why should that change?"[65]

Marketing Manager Gerd Matthes, who experienced the company as an employee in the final years of the GDR, speaks about his and his colleague's basic sense of trust in the Thuringian company's product, playing cards. The uncertainty that existed in other quarters regarding the value of the product hardly existed for this company. Tradition provided strength, the in-house expertise and know-how, the experience of export to the West, the practiced, tricky deal-

---

[65] Author's discussions with Gerd Matthes in Altenburg on April 18, 2007.

ings with GDR officials – often party functionaries, whose ideology was not tarnished by expertise.

But the fall of the Berlin Wall brought chaos in place of the strict party regime, and nobody knew how long it would last. An outmoded machine park, with two and a half processing machines, was conceivably a poor prerequisite for the 150 employees in their fight for survival under Western conditions. The fact that the Western market would now have the power was something that was clear several months prior to German unification. But it was not clear how a market would emerge from the chaos, in which the playing card factory would find its place.

"Sitting around and waiting was deadly. We had a well-filled warehouse, but because the wholesale offices were closed, this was not of any great help. We had a company meeting and discussed internally how we could now access our customers. We made tables in our own workshop and then went off in private vehicles to the local markets, but also to the large cities, such as Leipzig and Dresden. From morning to evening, we sold our playing cards, regardless of a person's position, management and workers alike. On some days, we had sales of DEM 10,000. This meant that we could at least pay wages. And more importantly, in these markets, we had direct customer contact that provided the confirmation of the demand for our products. That helped."

Such a situation was exceptional in the history of the playing card factory. To offset the gripping fears of the employees about their existence, there was a centuries-old, prestigious tradition that had put Altenburg at the heart of playing cards production in Germany.

As can be seen in the Altenburg Playing Cards Museum, there is evidence of the first card maker in the area in 1509. In 1664, Andreas Knoblauch from Zwickau applies to Duke Friedrich Wilhelm for permission to live in Altenburg and to make playing cards. In 1731, Christian Hoffmann receives the "Privileges with legal prohibition against several card-making companies in the said Principality." In 1813, the evening company of Hans Carl Leopold von der Gabelentz/Poschwitz played Skat for the first time. In 1832, the Bechstein brothers' *Herzogliche Sächsische Altenburgische Concessionierte Spielkartenfabrik* (Ducal Saxonian Altenburger Concession Playing Card Factory) opens its doors for the first time. In1898, this was merged with the first German playing card factory that was founded by Johann Caspar Kern in 1765 in Stralsund.

The *Vereinigte Altenburger und Stralsunder Spielkartenfabriken-AG*, called *ASS* from 1931, is the market leader in Germany until the end of the Second

World War, with products that are world-renowned. Having been disassembled in 1945/46 by the Russian victors, while production was in progress, the state of Thuringia immediately provides for re-establishment. At this time, replacement companies already exist in West Germany, which merge in 1950 to become *Vereinigte Altenburger und Stralsunder Spielkartenfabriken AG* in Stuttgart, later Leinfelden/Echterdingen.

At the time of the fall of the Berlin Wall, there is thus an Altenburger Spielkartenfabrik in the East and one in the West. Only in 1996 is this duplication ended in court with the defeat of the Altenburger Spielkartenfabrik in the dispute over the name ASS. The sustained brand awareness in East and West Germany is more than 60 percent. *ASS Altenburger* is by far the best-known brand of playing cards in Germany.[66]

This fact gives the basis for growth, but investments are needed for this and they cannot be raised by the company itself. A management buy-out fails. In 1991, the Treuhand Agency reprivatizes the former "Zentragbetrieb"[67] and offers it for sale. "The handling by the Treuhand," in Gerd Matthes' opinion, "was canny." They presented our advantages in every conceivable way and described us as the top business in the region. Seven companies competed for us."

The *Vereinigte Münchner Spielkartenfabriken GmbH & Co. KG F.X. Schmid* received the allocation, in particular because of its concept that contained social commitment. However, of 150 employees, only 75 kept their jobs.

Five years later, the games manufacturer *Ravensburger* takes over *F.X. Schmid,* thereby also acquiring the Altenburger Spielkartenfabrik. The total *F.X. Schmid* production range is integrated with the production in Altenburg. As a separate profit center, Altenburg is integrated into the successful marketing of the largest European games and puzzle manufacturer. The systematically expanded production location at the end of the 1990s is attributable to the high level of above-average professional experience and, at the time, still had a low

---

[66] ASS Altenburger. Eine echte Marke mit Herz. In: *Spielzeug international. Das unabhängige Fachmagazin für Spielwaren, Hobby, Geschenkartikel und Entertainment*. Ebermannstadt, 06-07/2007, p. 54.

[67] *Zentrag* was the abbreviation for the company founded in October 1945 in the Soviet occupation zone, Zentrale Druckerei-, Einkaufs- und Revisionsgesellschaft mbH. As *Vereinigung Organisationseigener Betriebe,* the *VOB Zentrag* in the GDR came under the Central Committee of the Socialist Unity Party of Germany and was led directly from a body of the Central Committee. With the more than 90 print companies, newspaper publishers and sales bodies under its control, the Socialist Unity Party had a monopoly over more than 90 percent of the printing capacity of the GDR.

wage level compared to the West, with a market based on Eastern Europe. "Despite everything, we were a profitable business from the time of the Turnaround onward," says Gerd Matthes, "we have never been in the red."

However, this is what happens to the parent company Ravensburger in 2001, upon which it plans to sell a subsidiary. The situation creates renewed uncertainty among production workers, but not at management level. With a goal-oriented approach, it succeeded in building Altenburg into one of the most important production locations for playing cards in Europe. Its traditional good reputation enjoyed in Germany, now radiates throughout Europe.

In 2002, the "Spielkarte" ("playing card"), as the business is known in Altenburg and the surrounding area, becomes the largest subsidiary of the Belgian Cartamundi Group, the world's largest playing cards group, with sales of EUR 141 M. Cartamundi continuously invests in processing, printing and storage technology. The new print hall alone, which was placed in operation in 2005, cost EUR 5 M; in 2006, EUR 1 M went to a fully automatic card-processing machine. In 2008, Cartamundi is named Company of the Year by *Ernst & Young* and the *Financial Times*. *ASS Altenburger*, with responsibility for the German and Austrian market, receives a high amount of praise from the jury for "Creativity, innovation and vision in relation to a traditional product."[68]

The ties to the growing parent companies led to new areas of business and viable product lines. Traditional playing cards for the games and stationery trade are now only one of at least three pillars. To this can be added license cards, cards for board games and advertising cards for businesses and private customers.

Continuous growth shows that there is a market for cards, which are designed based on themes for major events such as the premiere of a new James Bond movie or world and European soccer championships. "We are at the table with Bond and want to take part in the win," says Peter Warns, President of ASS Altenburger, referring to the premiere of *Casino Royale*.[69] For *ASS Altenburger* and the parent company *Cartamundi*, sales of poker cards increased tenfold because the companies used the trend reinforced by the media for its own market-

---

[68] Katrin Müller: Von Fußballbegeisterten und Kartenspielern. Press information from the Spielkartenfabrik Altenburg GmbH, January 8, 2009.

[69] *James Bond zockt mit Spielkarten aus Ostdeutschland. ASS Altenburger profitiert vom neuen Poker-Boom.* In: Frankfurter Allgemeine Zeitung, November 23, 2006, p. 24.

ing purposes. The *Gute Karten* (good cards) catalogue, with the complete playing cards range for 2007, has the historical editions of Skat, rummy, bridge and canasta at the start, demonstrating the strong links with tradition. At the same time, the games collections segment and children's and license cards dominate in terms of sheer quantity. New areas with high potential are pre-school and early learning games, which are being tested at Altenburg schools and pre-schools. The fact that the matter of balance between tradition and trends is one of the most important for the further development of the business is made clear by the president in an interview with the German daily *Frankfurter Allgemeine Zeitung*:

"He does not take a purely positive view of the future. With the huge expansion of television and cinema, the international, English-language presentation of playing cards is becoming increasingly dominant. For example, this applies to the letters in the corners of the pictorial cards, where there is "Q" (Queen) instead of "D" (Dame) or "J" (Jack) instead of "B" (Bauer, Bube). These designs are made by producers throughout the world and thereby penetrate the German market, which to date has been used to domestic products. "Our trump card has always been our own, protected card pictures. It was what people wanted and they received it only from us," says Warns. "We need to be careful that, in the joy of the poker boom, we don't cut the ground from under our feet.""[70]

Cutting the ground from under our feet and using our success for their own ends is something being tried not least by product pirates, primarily in China, India and Turkey. A medium-size company such as *ASS Altenburger*, which sold 45 million games in 2008 and made EUR 23 M, is particularly affected by the resulting financial damage. But even worse, explains Gerd Matthes, is the loss of image. In Germany, the customer has quality-awareness and plagiarized products printed on poor board are quickly recognized as such and are left lying. However, some Turkish copies are printed in good-quality board and irritation due to the bad purchase only arises after a short period of use, with the customer seldom able to discern the reasons for this. The Altenburger defend themselves with loud and publicly effective campaigns that the media are all too keen to pick up on, but it is an irritation that affects many industries, the discovery of which requires a criminal nose. Accordingly, the public cutting-

---

[70] Ibid.

up of 60,000 rummy games from China, turned into an event with huge press, radio and television coverage. The potential retail value of the seven-ton cargo amounted to EUR 100,000. Between 2004 and 2006, investigators foiled ten major cases of piracy valued at more than EUR 1 M. "But, naturally, the undetected figure is enormous," complains the President.[71]

In 2009, the city celebrates a major anniversary: 500 years of Altenburger Spielkarten. Today, *ASS Altenburger* is once again by far the market leader for playing cards in Germany and, with 159 employees, one of the most important employers in the structurally weak region. How did they manage after the lean period following the fall of the Berlin Wall? Matthes: "We always believed in our product, found the right investors, constantly surprised the market with new, constructive ideas, learned to find value for money in purchasing and knew to always provide our skilled employees with new motivation." And what did you carry with you from GDR times into the market economy? "Some skilled employees, a sense of solidarity, a connection with each other and to the region, and a generous portion of resourcefulness – 'Geht nicht gibts nicht' [there is no such thing as 'can't be done']. As a printing company, we were directly responsible to the Central Committee of the Socialist Unity Party, which meant that then massaging of figures in the six-month report to Berlin had to be well-founded to succeed in obtaining all the goods that were in short supply, such as printing, paper and machinery requirements. In particular our connections with the top tier kept some of the prestige-seeking small officials at bay. And through our exports to the non-socialist economic area, which was ideologically damned, but generated hard currency[72], we learned a little market economics. It wasn't all for nothing."

---

[71] Ibid.

[72] In the RBB television program "Pornography made in GDR," broadcast on September 13, 2007, Gerd Matthes spoke about an assignment from the Party, the production of playing cards with sexually explicit images for export to the West. Since the ownership and dissemination of pornographic images was punishable in the GDR and could lead to jail sentences of up to two years, such assignments carried certain risks, also or simply because the client and the legislator were one and the same. Accordingly, production and distribution were subject to rigorous security arrangements. Nobody in the territory of the GDR was to come into contact with this material. Nonetheless, not all of the cards ended up with enemies of the class struggle.

4. Access to Investments and Intellectual Capital

How companies transform knowledge and information into intellectual capital can be a significant factor in explaining their economic accomplishments and survival (Borg 2001). The term "intellectual capital", coined by John Kenneth Galbraith, can be defined as the intellectual material – i.e., knowledge, information, intellectual property, and experience – used in creating wealth (Stewart 1997). Our study of companies in emerging markets has demonstrated that developing and rescuing intellectual capital can be essential to ensuring survival in the market economy. By using their financial capital to develop the potentials of their intellectual capital, companies can improve their ability to produce market value and secure competitive advantage in a competitive and increasingly globalized market.

Several attempts have been made to measure intellectual capital. Knowledge assets are more difficult to measure than are ordinary assets (Bontis 2001). Intellectual capital is embedded in the organization and in the relationships between the organization and its environment. The knowledge and information used to produce products and services are unique to a company, and any measurements of them are not easy to report systematically and compare across organizations.

As innovation has become a major determinant of competitiveness, investment in knowledge and intangible assets, such as intellectual capital, has become essential (Petty and Guthrie 2000). Intellectual capital is arguably crucial to the long-term success of companies, and companies that manage their intellectual capital well outperform other companies (Bornemann et al. 1999). Intellectual capital has been regarded as playing a major role in creating sustainable competitive advantage (Kaplan and Norton 2004).

By developing intellectual capital, companies can improve their ability to compete in the global marketplace. We live in a knowledge-oriented society where companies must be innovative to survive global competition. Competitiveness is related to the ability to create innovations and incorporate them into products and services. A knowledge-oriented company must be organized around its intellectual capital. A learning organization will be able to develop intellectual capital and use its knowledge base to its own advantage. An appropriate intellectual capital strategy can identify the actual knowledge base of a company and its future research and development (R&D) needs. The company can then decide what can be accomplished internally and what external R&D resources are needed. Networking or joint venturing as well as acquisitions can be appropriate components of an intellectual capital strategy.

Financial and Intellectual Capital

Traditionally, financial capital alone has been valued by accounting in companies. Although financial capital is important and must be taken into account, intellectual capital has become increasingly important. While the role of financial capital is obvious and has received much attention, less attention has been paid to intellectual capital. In our increasingly knowledge- and research-oriented world, handling the intellectual development and processes of companies is gaining in importance. Financial capital includes all the company's physical and monetary assets, while intellectual capital comprises all the invisible, intangible processes and assets. Together, they constitute the total value of a company (Roos et al. 1997, p. 30).

The rest of this chapter will focus on intellectual capital while not ignoring financial value of companies. Several companies examined in our case studies were able to attract financial capital, and were able to deploy it effectively, since they also deployed their intellectual capital in a productive way, i.e., the intangible assets were managed in a way that optimized the use of financial capital. The two kinds of capital are clearly related and linked to each other. Without intellectual capital, financial capital cannot easily be deployed profitably, while intellectual capital is useless without the backing of tangible financial capital.

Research into intellectual capital is partly rooted in the study of intangible assets. Information-based capital has been described by Itami and Roehl (1987) as a type of invisible asset. Companies must manage the information that flows through them, as the unique information base that a company represents can be a long-term strategic asset to the organization. Invisible assets can even have a longer-lasting impact on the competitive advantage of a company than its financial assets.

Main Components of Intellectual Capital

We identify four main components of intellectual capital (Brooking 1997, p. 13). First, there are market assets. These market-related intangibles represent great potential to the organization, and include brands, customer loyalty, distribution channels, franchising, and licensing agreements. Market assets are essential because they provide competitive advantage in the marketplace. These assets ensure that customers know what the company represents and can relate to the company.

Second, there are human-centred assets, consisting of collective expertise, creative and problem solving abilities, leadership, and entrepreneurial and managerial skills. These intangibles are possessed by the employees of the company. Individuals are dynamic entities who fit into different jobs and are managed to ensure that the organization benefits from their individual skills. The company does not own human-centred assets, as people have the right to leave the company, so "brain drain" can be a problem for an organization unable to make its workplace attractive enough to individuals possessing skills essential to it.

Third, there are intellectual property assets, including expertise, trade secrets, copyright, patents, and various design rights. Countries possess various legal mechanisms that govern intellectual property rights. Some companies have elaborate intellectual property rights strategies and apply for hundreds of patents each year, of which the company uses only a few. Intellectual property rights can define the areas in which a company works and ensure that competitors have difficulties entering the same area at least for as long as applicable patents are valid. A company can protect its knowledge and information in the form of intellectual property rights in order to have a temporary monopoly in a particular area. The rights are put in place so the company can recoup the often-costly R&D investment in new products and services.

Fourth, there are infrastructural assets, represented by the technologies, methodologies, and processes that enable the company to function. Such asserts include corporate culture, risk assessment methodologies, sales-force management methods, financial structure, market and customer information databases, and communication systems such as e-mail and the Internet. The company needs an infrastructure to function properly and investments in infrastructural assets have a strong intangible component. The company must be capable of managing its infrastructure and must constantly develop its infrastructural assets.

Core competence

The study of the core competence of a company takes a narrower approach to the intangible assets of the company than does the study of intellectual capital. Core competence, part of a company's knowledge base, has been described by Hamel and Heene (1994) as the bundle of characteristic skills and technologies of a company that creates disproportionate value for customers; this translates into competitive advantage. A core competence differentiates its owner from competitors, facilitating entrance into new markets. Furthermore, core competence is not an asset, but an activity and an accumulation of learning and is thus a source of competitive advantage. Finally, a core competence usually results in more than one product or service, and a single product can be can be the result of multiple competencies.

To survive in turbulent times, a company may have to focus on its core competence. The managers of those companies that survived privatization and the introduction of the market economy in eastern Germany were all acutely aware that their companies were good at *something*. The essential factor was turning these core competencies into marketable products or services, since it is only in the marketplace that competitive advantage can be found. Focusing on their core competencies improved the studied companies' likelihood of creating market value for their products.

Intellectual capital indicators

To identify the attention paid to and use of intellectual capital in a company, Brooking (1997) developed an intellectual capital indicator comprising 20 questions managers could ask themselves about their the company's use of intangible assets. These questions can be useful in the analysis of intellectual capital and provide a practical instrument to managers in developing the human resources of a company. These 20 indicator questions ask whether a company:

1. ensures that all employees know what their jobs are and how they contribute to corporate goals
2. ensures that every employee is treated as a valuable asset, and that management strives to match each employee with the optimal job
3. ensures that every employee has the opportunity to create a career plan with the company
4. evaluates the return on investment (ROI) for R&D

5. identifies the expertise generated by R&D
6. knows who its repeat customers are
7. evaluates the ROI of the distribution channel
8. has a proactive intellectual property strategy
9. audits all its licensing deals
10. ensures there is synergy between employee learning programmes and corporate goals
11. ensures its position in the mind of the prospect is the same as the one it promotes
12. knows the value of its brands
13. ensures every staff scientist and engineer understands the rudiments of patent protection
14. generates new intellectual capital through business collaboration
15. ensures its management processes make it strong
16. possesses the infrastructure needed to help employees do a good job
17. possesses a mechanism to capture employee recommendations to improve any aspects of the business
18. ensures its employees are quickly rewarded for helping the company achieve its corporate goals
19. understands the innovation process and encourages all employees to participate in it
20. possesses a corporate culture that is one of its greatest strengths

The list touches on a wide range of issues related to intellectual capital (Brooking 1997) and can be used both as a practical checklist and to probe issues relating to intellectual capital. As a tool for research into the use of intellectual capital in particular companies, it examines issues mainly concerning how management deals with the company's intangible capital, such as the amount of attention paid to intellectual capital and whether intellectual capital plays a prominent role in management. The list can also be used in case studies to gather information about the context in which intellectual capital is handled.

Developing an Intellectual Capital Strategy

No business is so well organized that it cannot be reinvented into something better. Intellectual capital is dynamic and in constant change, so management must constantly reinvent its organization to make use of the latest intellectual capital. One way of doing this is to find flaws in the present organization and correct them. Some trends underline this need to find flaws. The direction of the power relationship in markets is reversing as more power shifts to customers. Corporations are unbundling and rebundling their competencies as new organizational forms emerge. Industry boundaries are eroding and reforming as business crosses industry boundaries and new industries emerge. Companies are also liberating under-used assets and finding new uses for the intellectual capital they possess.

An intellectual capital strategy can be divided into four elements (Stewart 2001, p. 53). First, the strategy should find the knowledge business of the company, which can be identified and evaluated in terms of input, process, and output. Questions that help in identifying the knowledge business include: How knowledge intensive is the business? Who gets paid for what knowledge? Is this a good knowledge business? Does whoever owns the knowledge also create the most value? These questions may also help to identify the revenues generated by intellectual capital.

Second, an intellectual capital strategy must identify the knowledge assets of the company, i.e., its particular expertise, capabilities, brands, intellectual properties, and processes. The company's knowledge assets transform raw material into something more valuable. Companies have all kinds of useless knowledge, including some that they think is valuable but that is not needed or appreciated by customers. An intellectual capital strategy can help identify the real knowledge assets of the company. As part of this strategy, management should ask itself who sells what, who buys what, and who profits and by how much.

Third, a strategy to develop intellectual capital is concerned with investing in and exploiting the company's knowledge assets, which represent various options that can be exploited. Knowledge assets differ from other assets, as they build on the fundamentals of the knowledge economy and the growing knowledge intensity of products, services, and jobs. Companies should exploit markets for more knowledge-intensive goods and services. In addition to knowledge-intensity strategies, companies should also manage their asset strategies. An asset strategy exploits knowledge assets by increasing the return on physical and financial wealth: knowledge becomes a means of making tangible, "hard" assets work harder.

Fourth, companies should manage their knowledge business by improving the efficiency of their knowledge work and workers. Companies often manage knowledge poorly. Knowledge management has recently become an issue, prompting companies to learn a wider range of management skills to better manage intellectual capital and improve productivity (Stewart 2001). The marriage of computing and communication is proving to be useful in improving knowledge management.

A Survey on Intellectual Capital

In 1998, the accounting and consultancy firm Arthur Andersen conducted an international survey measuring intellectual capital as a strategic performance measurement (Andersen 1998). Several interesting aspects of intellectual capital were identified by this groundbreaking survey (Bontis 2001). Most respondents believed that organizations would increasingly report intellectual capital, and about three-quarters of respondents were already tracking two or more non-financial measurements.

Most respondents to the Arthur Anderson survey agreed that knowledge measurement would improve organizational performance. About half the respondents believed that what was learned from the *process* of measuring intellectual capital was as important as the information received from the measurements themselves. The process of measuring was, in other words, perceived as being as significant as the actual figures produced by the measurement process.

Finally, the Arthur Anderson researchers believed that the sample of companies responding to the survey may have been biased, in that the respondents were likely more pro-intellectual property than the average company. Intellectual property is unlikely to be included in all financial balance sheets in the near future. External reporting of intellectual property is likely to be done voluntarily. Intellectual property measurements are more likely to become an internal management tool rather than a metric communicated to shareholders and investors.

The Strategies Involved in Intellectual Capital Management

Intellectual capital management can be divided into five different knowledge-centred strategies as identified by Wiig (1997b):

- Knowledge strategy as business strategy
- Intellectual asset management strategy
- Personal knowledge strategy
- Knowledge creation strategy
- Knowledge transfer strategy

Knowledge strategy, which can be viewed as part of the business strategy, emphasizes knowledge – its creation, capture, organization, renewal, sharing, and use. Knowledge strategy impinges on all the plans and operations of a company. Intellectual capital management can be implemented via intellectual asset management strategy, which involves enterprise-level management of knowledge assets such as patents, technologies, operational and management practices, customer relations, organizational arrangements, and other structural knowledge assets. The task of management is to renew, organize, evaluate, protect, and increase the availability and marketing of these assets (Wiig 1997a).

Personal knowledge can be integral to business strategy, which emphasizes personal responsibility in acquiring knowledge-related investments. Knowledge assets are interpreted within each individual's area of responsibility. A knowledge-creation strategy emphasizes organizational learning, basic and applied R&D, and motivating employee innovation. Finally, the knowledge creation strategy focuses on the systematic transfer of knowledge, involving knowledge sharing and the adoption of best practices (Wiig 1997a).

Network Strategies

Intellectual capital can be approached with reference to a network approach to business and marketing (Håkanson and Snehota 1989; Anderson et al. 1994; Borg 1991, 2001, 2009). Networks can be essential in developing and maintaining intellectual capital, allowing companies to enhance their knowledge and search for new information by relying on competence from outside their individual boundaries. The importance of networks and networking to innovation has been emphasized by several authors (Wolfe 1994; Slappendel 1996).

In analysing company and management performance, an emphasis on innovation has replaced an earlier emphasis on efficiency and quality as sources of competitive advantage (Swan et. al 1999). Innovation can be defined as "the development and implementation of new ideas by people who over time engage in transactions with others in an institutional context" (Van de Ven 1986).

Networking can be a strategic innovation choice for management where it is essential to find the right partners and define areas of co-operation. Many innovation processes are becoming increasingly interactive, requiring co-operation across multiple communities and practices, business units, functional groups, and IT suppliers. Networking requires negotiation among various social communities that have different interests in the innovation process (Swan et al. 1999). The kind and quality of relationships can determine the ability to convert knowledge into marketable products and services. Strategic groups may be established around inter-firm networks among international companies (Dyster and Hagedorn 1995)

The Skandia model

The international financial services company Skandia very early on adopted accounting methods that consider intellectual capital (Skandia 1994, 1995); these methods are discussed in Sveiby (1997) and Stewart (1997). The Skandia accounting model, which is relevant beyond the financial sector, divides market value into financial and intellectual capital, everything that is not financial capital being treated as intellectual capital. Wiig (1997) defines the different levels of the Skandia model in the following way:

Human capital – consists of employee competence and capabilities. When an enterprise educates its employees, it increases its human capital. (In a free society the enterprise can only rent, not own, its human capital.)

Structural capital – consists of the results of intellectual activities relating to databases, knowledge bases, documents, etc. Skandia suggests that "structural capital is what is left after the employees have gone for the night".

Customer capital – consists of the value of the enterprise's relationships with its customers.

Organizational capital – consists of knowledge assets embedded in the process and innovation areas.

Process capital – consists of the enterprise's value-creating processes such as its organizational structure, management practices, systems and procedures, infrastructure, and computer systems.

Innovation capital – consists of both explicit knowledge and hard-to-identify intellectual assets such as a positive corporate culture.

Intellectual property – consists of documented and captured knowledge such as innovations, operational practices, patents, technology, educational programs, corporate knowledge bases, and the designs and specifications of products and services.

Intangible assets – consist of the value of positive corporate culture, public image, etc.

Case study: Jenoptik – mitigating the "brain drain"

Jenoptik systematically registered all its intellectual capital inside the company when restructuring around its knowledge base. After rapidly downsizing when it faced a crisis, Jenoptik found new business and rehired competent employees who were able to create an innovative company. The company was dependent on new R&D to come up with products that could be marketed internationally, so it developed a trial-and-error–oriented product development strategy. This combination of financial and intellectual capital explains Jenoptik's survival.

In co-operation with existing and potential customers, Jenoptik acted as a problem solver. After years of restructuring, the company has come to focus its research efforts in an area in which it has unique expertise, its intellectual capital strategy leading to specialization in areas in which it has a superior knowledge base. Accordingly, Jenoptik now specializes in photonics and mechatronic technologies. The network relationships the company has established have helped this former East German company survive the transition to a market economy. In a new market economy, it has been important for Jenoptik to establish strategic relationships to improve its intellectual capital.

Historical background

Jenoptik has a long corporate history, tracing its roots to the company founded by Carl Zeiss in 1846 in Jena. Jenoptik now has its main offices and largest production facilities in Jena in Thüringen (English: Thuringia). Carl Zeiss was a pioneer of the German optical industry, establishing an optical workshop in Jena that initially manufactured microscopes. Ernst Abbe joined the company in 1861; he facilitated new production and tried out new inventions, some successful, others less so. This trial-and-error method of innovation was later to become an innovation system in the company, and was applied after the reintroduction of the company into a market economy.

Ernst Abbe, the second of three founders of Carl Zeiss, also brought a broader theoretical background to the company. Abbe was a professor of physics at the University of Jena. The third founder was Otto Schott, who developed the glass manufacturing aspect of the company.

In the pre-World War II era, the Carl Zeiss company grew rapidly into a world-famous manufacturer of optical instruments for science, industry, medicine, and the military. Carl Zeiss produced cameras, lenses, and binoculars as well as astronomical and medical instruments. In April 1945, the Americans arrived in Jena. In Operation Paperclip (also called "Operation Take the Brain"), 200 key employees of Carl Zeiss, along with product blueprints and samples of drugs were taken to Baden-Württemberg to capture the intellectual capital of the company. In addition to the American capture of intellectual property, at this time the Russians also captured people, moving them eastwards: in 1945, about a thousand employees were sent from Carl Zeiss in Jena to Belarus, only being allowed to return after 1950. There were huge protests in West Germany at the brutal methods used by the Soviet regime; in East Germany, of course, no one was allowed to protest. Production equipment from Jena was also taken to Russia as part of war reparations.

Germany was divided between the British, French, Americans, and Russians at the Yalta Conference, and Jena and all of Thuringia fell under Russian control. The Americans left Jena and Thuringia in accordance with the agreement made at the Conference. The Carl Zeiss company in Jena was nationalized in 1948 and renamed VEB Carl Zeiss Jena, while in West Germany, a new Carl Zeiss company was founded in Oberkochen, Baden-Württemberg. Until unification, Germany possessed two Carl Zeiss companies, one in the west and the other in the east. In the 1970s, there were legal struggles over the use of the Carl Zeiss brand. These were resolved by giving the West German Carl Zeiss company the right to use the Carl Zeiss brand name in western markets and the brand name: Opton in eastern markets. The East German part of the company used the name Carl Zeiss in eastern markets and Jenoptik in western markets. For its East German customers, the Jena-based company produced fire-control systems for Russian tanks and multi-spectral cameras for the Russian space industry. Despite the company's advanced knowledge, it had few products that could be sold in the western market.

After German unification

By 1989 the East German company had grown to about 70,000 employees, but was highly inefficient by western standards. After German unification, the company in Jena was re-established by the German restructuring entity Treuhand, renamed Jenoptik Carl Zeiss Jena, and downsized to 30,000 employees. A contract was signed with Treuhand in 1991, providing the company with 3.6 billion Deutschmarks (DM) in fresh capital: DM 700 million from Thuringia and DM 2.9 billion directly from the German government. At this time, it was vital to identify the company's intellectual capital and to concentrate financial investments in projects where this intellectual capital could best be used.

After the contract was signed with Treuhand, further restructuring was undertaken. The company downsized again, first to 10,000 and later to 3000 employees, as some of what was considered Jenoptik's best business was moved to Carl Zeiss in western Germany. This small remaining entity became Jenoptik GmbH. After dealings with Treuhand ended in 1995, Jenoptik launched another survival strategy. Only DM 1.1 billion remained of the original DM 3.6 billion of capital provided through Treuhand. DM 600 million had been spent on a pension plan for employees who had retired during the early restructuring of the company, and Jenoptik had accumulated losses of DM 1.2 billion.

Surviving the market economy

In the first years after German unification and the introduction of a market economy, the former East Germany experienced an influx of would-be entrepreneurs from the west of Germany. Managers who had not succeeded in the west came to eastern Germany, which they saw as offering them a second chance. Jenoptik was beset by two main problems: lack of managerial skills and the shortcomings of Treuhand, the institution handling the restructuring. The company probably survived because of its independent ideas about its future.

The main survival strategy was to downsize the company rapidly and salvage the intellectual capital needed to innovate and produce new products. After German unification the company had little idea of what to produce; production almost halted at the Jena factories, as people stayed home while still drawing salaries. The last year the company fired any employees was 1995. That year, Henry Birner, a senior manager, came up with the idea of collecting descriptive data about all former employees to gain an overview of their skills, and perhaps to salvage intellectual capital that might be important to the company's future. This led to the compilation of a computerized database of skills and intellectual capital at Jena.

Another factor that helped in hiring knowledgeable people and developing intellectual capital was the recruitment of a new CEO, Lothar Späth from Baden Würtenberg in western Germany. He had good connections in the west and brought with him knowledge of how to run a western-style company. Jenoptik's existing structure was very hierarchical, with several layers of management that made it inefficient. Under his direction, the work environment was restructured and obsolete buildings were torn down. As well, the company contributed to the urban renewal of Jena: the local university campus was improved, a new city shopping mall and a new hotel were built, new streets were built, and power supplies were improved.

An additional survival strategy was simply to stay in operation. The company had to find new business areas, so a trial-and-error innovation technique was adopted, in line with the early traditions of Carl Zeiss. The company developed a laser instrument with which to measure the colour of teeth to match new fillings. This technology worked well when used on ceramics, but had major deficiencies when used on real teeth. Though this instrument turned out to be a "flop" and was never mass produced, it gave the company experience in product development and raised the aspirations of the innovators in the company.

Another product innovation attempt was the development for Saudi Arabia of a photochromatic sun umbrella that darkened when sun was shining on it. An attempt was made to sell the umbrella for use in Mecca, where people sometimes faint under the intense rays of the sun. Saudi Arabia decided not to buy the umbrella, providing the pilgrims with water bottles instead.

Jenoptik kept on trying to develop new products, markets, and business, undeterred by initial failures in innovation. The company was divided into three major business areas: laser technologies, precision technologies, and optoelectronics, the last area including military and semiconductor technology. In 1994, Jenoptic became a global player in cleanroom systems and photonics. The same year Jenoptic acquired Meissner and Wurst for DM 300 million, becoming the first former East German company to acquire a western German company. At the time, Jenoptik considered moving its headquarters to Stuttgart where Meissner and Wurst was located. This plan never materialized, and Meissner and Wurst was later sold. Another acquisition was the 1997 purchase of ESW (a Daimler subsidiary) and Krone AG, a telecommunications company, for DM

500 million. Krone was later sold to an American company.

Jenoptik inherited an impressive history and tradition from the nineteenth-century Carl Zeiss company, and it has been part of the company's task to intentionally modernize, salvaging the best of the old traditions while getting rid of what the management describes as the "ghosts of Carl Zeiss". An example of one such ghost was the granting of privileges to senior employees (e.g., window seats in the factory) regardless of their efforts or productivity.

In 1996, Jenoptik transformed itself into a joint stock corporation, and has been listed on the Frankfurt stock exchange since 1998. CEO Lothar Späth has involved himself in marketing, frequently travelling to Asia to market its semiconductor products. Späth is a formidable driving force in the company; he has considerable influence in western Germany and was able to negotiate directly with former German Chancellor Helmut Kohl. Späth has taken the company from a money-losing communist-style organization to a successful global enterprise capable of competing in the global market.

Under Späth, a well-organized management team has emerged, differing greatly from the politically organized leadership of the communist era. The company had lived in isolation in the Eastern Bloc, sheltered from market forces, and then had to face the sudden change to operating in a market environment. The new CEO had to address many challenges connected with this transition. Späth also had significant help from key personnel of the old company, while many new managers were recruited from western Germany. Key account managers have been assigned, each responsible for a major product field.

By 2006, revenue started growing and many new opportunities were visible to the company. Business-to-business marketing has been Jenoptik's main emphasis, and its main customers are large companies. Jenoptik created a new logo and changed its corporate identity. A major marketing strategy is participation in trade shows. After German unification, the company lacked experienced salespeople, so it trained its engineers to fill the gap. These salespeople were initially "too honest": they would offer a product, but explain that a new innovation was on its way and would be available next year. The customer would of course tell the salesperson to come back next year when the new product was developed. Jenoptik has since become more experienced in industrial marketing, and now spends two to three years developing a new customer. Salespeople have also been hired from western Germany.

The company's business is governed by patent seeking. Under communist rule, scientists were forced to apply for patents, regardless of whether they were relevant to production. As a result, the East German Carl Zeiss company retained more patents that did its sister company in the West. Nowadays, patent applications are closely related to identifiable market opportunities; patents are sought for marketable products and services, and not merely for the sake of seeking patents.

According to the annual report for the company, Jenoptik specializes in photonics and mechatronic technologies that put light to use as an industrial tool in the areas of lasers, optics, sensors, and mechatronics. Its vision for the future is that the twenty-first century will be the "photonics century", when light tools will change the world of technology.

Case study: Freiberger Compound Materials – attracting new investments

Freiberger Compound Materials has used every opportunity and involved every possible stakeholder in order to ensure its survival. The company has been supported by both public and private investments and has identified a small geographic area in which to become a market leader. Attracting new capital on a large scale has been a cornerstone of Freiberger's survival strategy, and both regional and central governments have offered financial support for the restructuring.

Later on, international investors invested in the company. At first, it did not matter where the risk capital Freiberger attracted came from, but for the longer term is was essential to have risk investors that knew something about the particular line of business. Moving from attracting public support to gaining private investment has been important for the company's long-term survival. Freiberger has also moved from serving customers in the public sector, such as the military, to producing for the private computer industry.

Freiberg has subjected its high-tech products to testing by certification bodies respected in the global market. Meeting the highest standards of quality has been a cornerstone to their survival in the global market. In marketing products to new international clients, it has been essential to provide solid evidence of high production standards.

The Freiberger company was founded in 1957 and represent a more than

50 year tradition of making electronic components to be installed in electronic products and equipment. The company had under the DDR time fallen behind the technological development in the West. After the unification, the company found it difficult to find buyers willing to pay for electronic components in Western currencies. The company had little experience in selling to Western markets. The company needed to develop new products and new product development took between one and two years for each new product to reach the market.

The company had 1700 employees under DDR and this number had to be reduced. All military production, which previously had been important, ended with the unification. The company sought to find new investors, but this was a difficult adventure. The production did not match western standards and the company had to go through trials to qualify as a sub-contractor to company in the West. Freiberger proved to have a high standard in its production and was able to qualify in different areas of production after showing good test results.

The company tried to defend its most essential competence and intellectual capital. Some of the less essential production is removed. The most successful product soon becomes the production of gallium arsenide, a compound of two elements gallium and arsenide. This material can be used for integrated circuits in cellular phones. With the increased markets for cell phones, this material soon becomes the main product delivered from Freiberger Compound Materials. The precision is high in the making of the microchips. To illustrate the precision of the surface of the microchips, the managers suggest that if the chips were to cover the entire surface of Germany, the level of tolerance on the surface would be a maximum height difference of 10 centimetres.

Compounds made of gallium arsenide became a strategically important product for the company. A western competitor had decided to move out of this area and Freiberger's strategy soon became to move into this segment of the market that suddenly had become vacant. The company was now strategically positioned to deliver components to the cellular phone industry. The company hired 130 persons from the western company that had given up its production of gallium arsenide components.

After unification the West German company Wacker Chemie cooperates with Freiberger in a co-option where Freiberger is capable of taking over technology and production tools. Wacker places some of it production in Freiberg and Freiberger Compound Materials can get access to some of Wacker's customers. Freiberger now employs 450 persons, down from 1700 at the time of the transition. The company also received government support during its structural change. The company stakes out a new future for the production in Freiberg. The research unit remains in Freiberg. The managing director of the company, Dr. Tilo Flade is offered several attractive positions in Western Germany, by companies that are interested in his advanced skills. Dr. Flade decides to stay in Freiberg and work for the revitalization of the Freiberger company. The company is rescued much thank to Dr. Flade and his dedicated management team that successfully privatized the company.

The company had at the time of privatization three production areas, first the Silicium products, secondly the gallium arsenide production and thirdly the solar cell production. The company tried to divide up the three areas and sell off the two first areas. The solar department is sold to Bayer Leverkusen. Bayer needs more production capacity for these products and sets up new production capacity in Freiberg. Together, Freiberger Compound Materials and Bayer Leverkusen builds an advanced material cluster in Freiberg. In 1994, Wacker Chemie AG takes over the third production area – the solar production from Freiberger. Now only the gallium arsenide production remains under the control of Freiberger Compound Materials.

A new era of the Freiberger company is started in 1995 when the company is bought by an Israeli family enterprise, the Federman enterprise with its head quarter in Tel Aviv. Federman now owns 87% of the Freiberger company. Wacker was no longer interested in the company, but took over the micro electronic division of the company. Federman, the new owners work very closely with the managers in Freiberg. The company is under the new leadership expanding its sales in the cell phone industry where their solutions for integrated circuits is the preferred solution by many cell phone manufacturers. There are four major competitors world wide in this area, and Freiberger Compound Materinals is doing well in this competition.

Of the factors that ensured the survival of the Freiberger company the two managers Dr. Flade and Dr. Weinert suggests that a functioning management team was important. The financial support for research and development that the company has received has also been instrumental to the survival. A good tradition of handling intellectual capital and using new technology has been important. A stable long-term ownership, and owners that are interested in the long-term survival of the company has been important. The employees at the company have a good work ethics and are willing to work hard for the company. People care for the company and the region in which it is situated.

5. Creating customer value

Creating customer value can help companies survive. By delivering customer value that is greater than the cost of purchasing a product, companies can ensure a future in a market economy. Customer value can be defined as the trade-off between customer perceptions of benefits received and sacrifices incurred when purchasing a product or service (de Chernatony et al. 2000). Value can be difficult to measure since it involves a subjective notion of what buyers perceive in a product or service; *customer* value, moreover, is a dynamic concept that develops over time (Jaworski and Kohli 1993). Although a company may aim to deliver value to its customers, it can experience difficulties assessing value and gaining an appropriate return for the value delivered to customers (Anderson and Narus 1999).

A market economy is characterized by competition among producers for consumers who compare different market offerings. It is difficult to measure how consumers establish and compare the values of offerings in a competitive market. Value is viewed as the benefits sought from a product minus the sacrifices incurred to obtain it. Several value-based benefits and sacrifices have been identified in association with product offerings in a market; these can be regarded as value-based drivers (Lapierre 2000). Companies can gain competitive advantage by supplying superior customer value.

Three identifiable value strategies can provide companies with competitive advantage: operational excellence, product leadership, and customer intimacy (Wiersema and Treacy 1993). Building customer intimacy offers a good way to achieve superior customer value. By building long-term relationships with customers, companies come to be viewed as value providers. These relationships may be characterized, for example, by a focus on customer service. Competitive advantage can be achieved when a company becomes the preferred supplier by building close relationships with its customers. By engaging in product and service development, a company can establish product leadership and provide value perceived by its customers to be superior.

Market value issues

Several essential issues are related to the creation of market value (Duchessi

2002), and management must keep all of them in mind when attempting to deliver superior customer value. What do the company's customers consider real value? After all, value is evaluated through the eyes of consumers. A company must communicate with its customers to understand what is valued by them as individuals. Management must also find ways of systematically planning and controlling the business to ensure it delivers value. How can value be delivered to consumers at all times and what do consumers expect of a company from which it buys specific products and services? Does business need to change and, if so, at what pace in response to customer demands?

How, for example, does a company respond to breakthroughs made by competitors? In a volatile market, competitors will constantly attempt to provide superior value to customers. Finding ways to respond to these attempts can be crucial. What changes must be made and what methodologies and frameworks are available for planning and executing these changes? What tools and techniques are required to improve customer value? Internally, one must question how employees are to be managed in order to shape the customer service encounter. Finally, the company must identify the relevant information technologies needed to implement a customer service strategy.

Some of these and several other issues are treated in the following theoretical discussion of the importance of producing customer value. When a market is changing rapidly, constantly delivering superior customer value can be a solid way to preserve company fortunes in an otherwise turbulent business environment. Relating properly to customers can allow the company to gather information about what the customers value. Together, the customer and the company can achieve a value proposition that is competitive and compares favourably with what is offered elsewhere on the market.

Stages in customer value management

Outstanding quality is related to efforts to achieve superior customer value, so discussion of how to achieve quality has been overtaken by discussion of how to achieve customer value. Quality, which can be a strategic weapon, and value are related issues. Customer value management can be divided into four stages (Gale 1994), as discussed below.

The *first* stage deals with conformance quality. To achieve value, production must conform to specifications. Quality control can be a means of achieving better quality and, as a result, superior customer value. Specifications can be formulated to ensure that the company gets it right the first time, rather than endlessly learning from its mistakes. At the same time, companies must seek every opportunity to reduce errors, and to scrap and rework faulty products and services. Products must not only have no defects, but must confirm to what the customers want to buy. While the focus on quality is intended to reduce faults, the emphasis on customer value shifts the focus to include customer preferences.

The *second* stage involves customer satisfaction. If a quality programme is to create happy customers, it must first define customer satisfaction. How can customer desires be understood and fulfilled? Several areas must be involved to achieve customer satisfaction. The company must have access to the appropriate information and be able to analyse it. Strategic planning must be in place, and human resources must be managed correctly. The company must forge close relationships with its customers. Process quality needs to be properly managed. Finally, the entire company must focus on its customers, and that involves understanding their needs and expectations.

The *third* stage in managing customer value entails comparing the company's market-perceived quality with that of its competitors by using a customer value analysis. The Malcolm Baldrige Award can be adopted as a system for measuring quality improvements made by manufacturers, services, and small business (Curkovic and Handfield 1996). The Baldrige criteria can be divided into measures of progress and goals.

The measures of progress are:
- Product/service quality
- Productivity improvement
- Waste reduction/elimination
- Supplier quality

The goals are:
- Customer satisfaction
- Customer satisfaction relative to customers
- Customer retention
- Market share gains

Companies usually attempt to gauge customer satisfaction, and measures of progress and goals are commonly used for this. Although companies conduct considerable research into their customers, they often know little about why they win or lose them. A customer satisfaction focus can help company efforts to understand what happens in customers' minds. Customer satisfaction surveys may fail to explain why certain customers turn against a product or service and take their business to a competitor. Companies may report high satisfaction on the part of existing customers and still lose customers to competitors.

According to Gale (1994), the *fourth* and final stage is customer value management proper, which includes the activities of the three previous stages. Companies can use value analysis to track competitiveness and decide what business to be in. It is essential that a company concentrate on business areas in which it is the most competitive. Capital investments can be made in business areas in which the company has a competitive advantage and acquisitions can be made in these areas. The needs of the targeted market may dictate how the business is aligned. Customer value management can be a strategic tool for companies seeking to deliver superior value to customers and create sustainable competitive advantage in a market economy.

Customer value principles

Some basic principles can be followed in achieving customer value, in addition to earlier comments about promoting customer value in the company (Naumann 1995). These principles are general and apply across several industries. They can be summed up as lessons that companies can learn about customer value and that contribute to a basic understanding of the role of value in the business literature.

Lesson one: It is essential to let the customers define what constitutes appropriate product and service quality. The customer ultimately also decides what is a reasonable price for this quality. It is thus in interaction with the customer that the needed level of quality can be determined. Managerial guesswork can lead to wrong assumptions about price and quality, ultimately leading to a failure to provide reasonable customer value. Companies can easily fail when launching a new product by failing to correctly interpret customer desires.

Lesson two: Customer expectations of specific product or service offerings are formed with reference to competitors' alternate market offerings. Interpreting what customers think of your product must be done in the context of the broader market for similar products and services. This underlines the need for competitive benchmarking. Competitors that change their perceived market value demand a response. Many companies seek to make ongoing improvements to their customer value and, to remain competitive, a company must meet or exceed its competitors' pace of improvements.

Lesson three: Customers' value expectations are dynamic and ever increasing. Investigating the value a company provides a customer yields an impression applicable at only a single moment, as customer value expectations will have changed the next moment. Having a constantly updated image of customer value expectations is a matter of ongoing interaction with customers. Expectations are influenced by technological innovations and the general competition in the market. The company is not alone in influencing customers' value expectations; competitors can be just as influential, even in the case of loyal customers. As expectations increase, customer value decreases. It is a matter of keeping up with the pace of the customers.

Lesson four: Product and service quality is the responsibility of the whole organization, not just the manufacturing department. The previous emphasis on quality often focused exclusively on improving manufacturing quality. Quality standards must be set both upstream in the production channel and downstream in the distribution channel to provide the highest value to customers. Coordination of efforts is essential in order to achieve customer value; for the company this entails a relentless search for ways of improving value to customers.

Lesson five: The search for customer value involves the whole organization. Involvement and commitment are necessary for ongoing improvement in the value offered in the market. No stone can be left unturned inside and outside any organization operating in a competitive market. There are numerous examples of companies that have been turned around by paying greater attention to customer satisfaction. Many companies have a tendency to be inward looking and to forget their customers. This is a grave mistake, as a customer focus can significantly improve profitability.

Value as pleasure

The search for maximum pleasure has been an issue in academia since Jeremy Bentham's discussion of utility. The utilitarian principle refers to providing the maximum utility to as many as possible, or, as Bentham put it, "the greatest happiness for the greatest number". The success of a utilitarian approach can be gauged by adding up the pleasure and subtracting the pain incurred by individuals. This can also guide companies in attempts to provide more value to customers. Value itself can be defined in terms of pleasure. The Canadian anthropologist Lionel Tiger (Tiger 1992) identifies four kinds of pleasures: physio-pleasure, socio-pleasure, psycho-pleasure, and ideo-pleasure (Jordan 2000).

Physio-pleasure refers to pleasure felt by the sensory organs. What we see, hear, smell, feel, or taste can be pleasurable sensations. Producers can add and improve sensory features to increase the value of products or services. For example, a pleasant scent can be provided in cars, restaurants, or offices as a service to improve value. How a product feels to hold and use or how a car door sounds when shut are essential to customer impressions of them.

Socio-pleasure derives from human interaction and the relationships between people that can be enhanced by consumption. People may buy transportation by bus, car, or bicycle to be able to move, interact, and meet others. Consumption can enhance social contact and thereby be of value to the individual. Socio-pleasure also refers to relationships between individuals and society as a whole. Consumption can enhance this, as buying status symbols can raise the social standing of the individual in society. Consumption enhances and creates identities, and one can even suggest that we largely become what we consume. Previously, we were identified with what we produced; the post-industrial era, however, means that consumption is more identifying than production.

Psycho-pleasure is related to people's cognitive and emotional reactions to consumption and to specific producers or service providers. People react psychologically to experiencing a product or service. Consumption arouses emotions, and positive psychological reactions can be viewed as a customer value. People can become angry when things do not work properly or if offended when receiving a service. Handling the service encounter well, keeping the customers' psychological reactions in mind, can be a way of creating value.

Ideo-pleasure derives from peoples' value systems. Consumers are frequently ideologically involved in consumption, and can take an ideological stand through consumption. For example, one may express environmental concerns by consuming environmentally friendly products. Not consuming certain products may also be a way of expressing ideo-pleasure. As people take stands for and against issues through consumption, offering choice or an opportunity for people to express their opinions can be a means of providing customer value.

Case study: MIFA - Surviving by rapidly increasing productivity

The two owners of the Mifa bicycle company had started a computer company after the German unification. The company was called Hurricane, and was started in 1990. They imported parts of computers from the Far East, mainly Taiwan and put the computers together in Eastern Germany. The main customers were mail order companies that bought computers from Hurricane. The managing director of Mifa, Peter Wicht, had previously been working for the East German computer industry at Robotron in Dresden. East German computer manufacturing had lagged behind Western production of computers and no essential parts of the computers made in Eastern Germany could be used for modern computers in the competitive Global market for computers.

Historical background

The Mifa biscycle company has a history that dates back to 1907. At the beginning all parts of the bicycle was made at the factory. A collection of classical bikes can be seen on display at the present factory in Sangerhausen in Thüringen, or Thuringia as it is called in English, in Eastern Germany. The bicycle technology has basically stayed the same for one hundred years, but the way of producing them has changed dramatically. Under East German state ownership, however, the old fashion way of producing all parts in-house was practiced at the production facilities in Sangerhausen. The factory was started as a public company after World War II and was taken over by the Russians that came to Thuringia. In 1950 the company became a people owned company or what was called a Volkseigener Betrieb (VEB), which was the official name for nationalized East German companies.

The Mifa bicycle company was first bought from the Treuhand by two Swiss owners for 1 German mark. The Swiss owners did not make the company profitable and where not increasing the productivity enough to be able to compete with competitors in the west and in the Far East. In 1995 the two initial owners went bankrupt. Peter Wicht and his business associate Michael Lehmann were looking for a second leg to stand on, and to alternate the computer production with the production of bicycles. They came to the conclusion that the modern production of computers is in some ways similar to the production of bicycles. Parts were bought from China or Taiwan and could be assembled in a factory in Eastern Germany. Peter Wicht had learnt how to purchase parts from China, and he had also learned English through his international business interactions. These two skills helped him when running the Mifa company.

The production of bicycles at Mifa increased rapidly over the years. In 1914 the production had been 10.000 bicycles a year, and had only increased to 20.000 by 1995 when Peter Wicht had bought the company. They paid 750.000 DM to the Swiss owners for the company that was established as a GmbH – a public limited company. They needed to increase the productivity to make the production profitable. By 1999 the production had increased to 100.000 bicycles and by 2007 the production totals 800.000.

Increasing productivity

A good measure of productivity is the number bicycles that are made per employee per year at the factory. Under the planned economy of Eastern Germany the productivity was only 200-250 bicycles per employees. These figures are not comparable to today's figures as all parts of the bike were produce in-house at the factory. During the first years of production the new owners of the Mifa factory increases the number of bicycles produced per number of employees from 1000 to 1600 bikes per employees.

The productivity increase is a good explanation of why the company has survived after unification. East German companies under a planned economy had huge problems with productivity. Ideology played a major role in the leadership of companies. There was little or no market competition and companies were viewed as a source of employment. Although efficiency was a concern for the ruling communist party and there was a shortage of labor, productivity could not keep up with the west. There was neither a real competition between different producers.

In order to survive, The Mifa company had to increase productivity to Western levels of production. The labor costs are only slightly lower in Eastern Germany compared to Western Germany. Eastern Germany is by no means a cheap region to produce in. Another source of survival was the access to capital that the company could have after unification. In 2004 the owners of Mifa took the company to the stock exchange and sold 1.5 million shares that gave the company 8-9 million Euros in investments.

Before 1995 the company had a bad reputation among creditors and bill would have to be paid in advance. The owners looked closely at the cost of production and increased productivity. The reputation of the company improved later in the 1990ies. The organizational structure of the company was kept simple. They adopted a flat management structure with a direct line of communication from the factory floor to the two managers at the top of the company. The company developed into becoming the cost leader in the business, and the production facility had the highest productivity in the business. This enabled the company to make money even in the lowest price segment in the market.

The owners of Mifa worked closely with the market and followed the marked trends as they rapidly changed. As a new trend appeared in the market, the company would make drawings and sketches of new bikes and send them to Taiwan for production. The subcontractors would come oup with final drawings that could be approved by Mifa. The company is deliberately not a market leader in new design, but a follower of regional and global trends. It is too risky to come up with a new and unproven design, and better to wait and see what the new trends will be. A new trend is bicycles made with carbon frames, and the company is watching closely to see whether the market is going in this direction.

The people working at the factory have rapidly understood the difference between a planned economy and a market economy. People have adapted to new means of production. The company has also recruited new key personnel at the factory. The managers are working 70-75 hours per week to keep the business going. They are adopting a problem-solving attitude. Gone are the days where every decision at the factory had a political aspect and party bosses where calling the shots at the factory. Immediately after the unification of Germany very few wanted to buy an East German bicycle. East German products had such a bad reputation both in the East and in the West. Mifa managed to improve its reputation and sold 80% of its production under other the retailers own labels. Only 20% of the production is sold under the Mifa label which today has a good reputation of being a reliable bicycle. The market relationships are managed by the two CEOs as well as by ales force of two people. All marketing is conducted business to business to the retailers. The close relationship to the dealers is also the main source of innovation. Mifa makes the kind of bicycles that the retailers predict they will sell in the near future.

The survival factors of the company in the market economy have been cost leadership through high productivity and high quality. The company is responding rapidly to changes in customer preferences. The market hit a slump in 1996 after a cold winter when the weather did not permit people to ride bikes. Peter Wicht underlines that bad times are good times for good people. The company was rationalized to keep up with the changes in demand. The production is more automated than any other bicycle factory in the world and robot technology is used in the productions.

When asked what reasons the company survived the transition to the market economy the CEO upholds that the managers and engagement in the production process has been a major factor. Innovations and good ideas have also been important. Furthermore, they have had good luck and fortunes in their business adventures. Finally, the good employees at the factory have helped them survive the turbulent first years of market competition. There is an informal management structure at the factory. Everyone can come directly to the managers. It is said at the factory that: "if you go through fire for me, I will go through fire for you". This has helped solidify the relationship between all that are working at the factory, which in turn has helped the factory survive. The collectivist ideology of the past has been replaced by a team spirit.

The company has found a market in the unified Germany. They have also engaged in exports to France the Benelux countries and Scandinavia. However, more that 80% of the production is sold in Western Germany. Only 5% of the bikes are sold on exports, a figure which is not increasing at the moment. The CEO suggests that the bicycle is used differently and for different purposes in different countries. In some countries like the Scandinavian countries and in Holland the bike is a means of transportation. In Great Britain it is used for fun and leisure activities. The four main branches of the markets are mountain bikes trekking bikes, city bikes and fun bikes. These are sold in different volumes in various countries.

The company is ensuring that customers are provided with a high level of service. The company has agreements with bicycle service providers throughout Germany. It is essential that customer can be helped with potential problems with their bikes. The company has a hotline where it provides answers to questions customers may have. A high level of service to customers is viewed as important to compete in the market for bicycles.

The business strategy of the company can best be describes as an action – reaction ability. The company reacts rapidly to changes in the market. The company does not adopt large market studies to find out what to produce in the future. It is through the close relationships with the retailers that the market knowledge needed for innovation is gained. The company is known for delivering on time and is working closely with the Chinese subcontractors to rapidly respond to market forces. The computer aided design (CAD) is conducted by the subcontractor undertaken from sketches made by Mifa.

Case study: Hedwig Bollhagen (HB) – "For me, rethinking wasn't necessary"

Life and survival in four German states

Hedwig Bollhagen is 83 years old when she submits her application to the Treuhand Agency for the reprivatization of her business in 1991. A year and a half later, she takes over – as she had already done in 1934 – the *HB-Werkstätten für Keramik GmbH* in Marwitz as artistic manager. The oldest young entrepreneur in Germany, as she is called with humorous respect, makes her entrance into the adventure of the market economy:

"I thought a lot about it, at my age... But if I hadn't submitted my privatization application, everybody would have been made redundant. (...) In my opinion, unemployment is one of the worst things happening in this country; it breaks people. At least the Treuhand treated us well in the end. Frau Breuel was here, and wanted to get to know the colorful old bird. I had respect for this woman in such a position. It's real madness to have to get rid of the companies in an entire country. After the formalities had been completed, all I knew was that I would hardly be able to handle the market economy alone. The most diverse people applied to me for employment. I felt like a snobbish princess, with none of the suitors pleasing me – until the right one came along. This was someone who had worked earlier at the Royal Porcelain Factory in Berlin, was well-acquainted with the profession and knew how to secure subsidies and sponsors."[73]

---

73 1 "Ich mach doch nur Kaffeetöppe." Hedwig Bollhagen – Deutschlands älteste Unternehmerin. Freitag No. 47, Berlin, November 15, 1996.

She took care of marketing herself. With humor and enthusiasm, she speaks and responds to uncountable reporters to ensure that her newly established company also becomes known in the West.[74] To this end, she also accepts invitations to appear on TV talk shows. It costs this lady, who buys her first television at the time, a large amount of willpower:

"Sometimes I look at snippets of these shows. All this fuss, with a host and the audience that constantly claps stupidly! Terrible. I have experienced it at first hand. I was once on a talk show with Juliane Bartel, who behaved like a schoolmistress, which made me wonder why she was asking questions if she already knew everything. Before the show, 'Lisel' from make-up was supposed to paint around my face with a brush, but then this 'Lisel' said that at my age, it wouldn't make any difference."[75]

Who was Hedwig Bollhagen (1907-2001)?

On the subject of her life's work, the Chancellor of the Federal Republic of Germany, in her capacity as patron of the anniversary exhibition for the 100th anniversary of Hedwig Bollhagen's birth, said the following:

"The signet HB stands apart, representing an unmistakable, independent style and functionally and esthetically sophisticated forms: timeless beauty, simple and clear, modern, but not fashionable.

"HB ceramics are, unique pieces in serial production, Afficianado pieces for daily use. /.../ Hedwig Bollhagen was one of the most significant ceramists and designers of the 20th century."[76]

Already during her "years of learning and wandering" in the Weimar Republic, the concept grew within the artistically gifted potter of producing attractive and affordable everyday ceramics with hand-painted decorations. The idea was to offer "the buyer the possibility of breaking away from the really very tasteless, false crockery that was brought to market by the china and stoneware industry."[77] The individual esthetic quality of hand-painting, giving an unmis-

---

[74] Cf. Gert Streit, Gudrun Gorka-Reimus: Annäherung an ein Phänomen. In: Hedwig Bollhagen. Ein Leben für die Keramik. Book accompanying the exhibition. Published by Gudrun Gorka-Reimus. Deutsche Stiftung Denkmalschutz, Bonn 2007, p. 12.
[75] "Ich mach doch nur Kaffeetöppe." Ibid.
[76] Introductory speech by Dr. Angela Merkel, Chancellor of the Federal Republic of Germany, at the restrospective *Hedwig Bollhagen. Ein Leben für die Keramik*. In: Book accompanying the exhibition, ibid., p. 9.
[77] Ceramicist Hedwig Bollhagen on herself. Ibid., p. 20.

takable originality to the pieces, was to be retained even in industrial manufacturing and provide a differentiation from the unattractive and lifeless mass-produced goods. This proposition was in line with the ideas of like-minded people in the *Deutscher Werkbund (German Handcrafts*organization, to bring together art, industry and handcrafts. The aim was for the creations of these free spirits to become homely in a broad sense. Not least, functional design without frills for everyone was a requirement of the Bauhaus movement, founded in Weimar in 1919, whose significance for modern architecture and interior design is undisputed today.

It was to this concept, which was entrepreneurial and artistic in equal measures, that Hedwig Bollhagen remained true for her entire life. With her humorous understatement, "I simply make coffee pots," she survived three of the German states in which she worked: the Weimar Republic, the Third Reich and the GDR. The coffee pots remained, while political systems and their leaders changed. And indeed, if you look back at her more than 70 years of artistic creation, there is an almost uninterrupted continuity. She sets out already before she is assigned to head the painting department of the stoneware factory Velten-Vordamm/Werk Velten. She proceeds with the designs and decorations of the young artist, which today "are bought by the latest Berlin middle class with the same enthusiasm as the East German intelligencia did in GDR times."[78] In 1937, she receives a gold medal at the World Fair in Paris for a small Fayence vase. After a visit to the Potsdam anniversary exhibition 70 years later (see above), the critic from the *Frankfurter Allgemeine Zeitung* summarizes the importance of Bollhagen as follows:

"Mainly developed from original geometric shapes, such as spheres and cylinders, visibly inspired by some of the Bauhaus works, the coffee pots and sugar boxes displayed characteristics already at the beginning of the 1930s that, soon after the War, contributed to the triumphal advance of Scandinavian design: distinct outlines, clear surfaces free of ornaments, smooth bodies, strong, but sparingly applied colors. Anyone looking at Bollhagen's tea service might be led to believe that there was never a war and two dictatorships in Germany. Unperturbed by all of the historical disasters and ideological shifts, she threw,

---

[78] Heinrich Wefing: Im Fadenkaro durch die Zeit. Frankfurter Allgemeine Zeitung, July 13, 2007.

painted, scarified and fired her beautiful pieces and seems never to have particularly cared for politics."[79]

This is a modified truth, which is qualified not least by the critic:

"She had to get over the emigration to New York of her best friend, Jewish woman Nora Herz; as with many of her friends, she felt persecuted as a ‚degenerate' artist; she had to produce ceramic casing for air-raid shelter boilers and food dishes for the SS; her workshop close to Berlin came under fire more than once toward the end of the War."[80]

To this can also be added that, in 1931, Bollhagen experienced the bankruptcy of the Velten-Vordamm, which was the result of the global economic crisis, and became unemployed as a result. However, the way in which politics relentlessly interferes with the realization of her concept of producing simple and attractive household crockery is not only clear from the examples of the Weimar Republic and Hitler's Third Reich. It is particularly remarkable to look at the business survival strategies that the artist developed during the 40-year existence of the GDR.

In 1945, the HB workshops in Marwitz are in a desolate state because of bomb hits and destruction by the Red Army. With 36 employees, Bollhagen begins the clear-up and restoration work of the reopened company, which she manages alone after the flight of her partner into the British occupied zone.[81] Until 1972, the workshops remain a private company against the backdrop of a system that is increasingly organized as a plan economy. There is a shortage of capital, means of production and work material – a situation that takes on permanence after the foundation of the GDR.

The products made by the private company are all the more in demand. These not only include the timeless household crockery, refined by HB particularly in the 1950s through shapes and decoration, which becomes a classic. Just like before and during the Second World War, Bollhagen and her employees increasingly accept assignments for building ceramics. In the rebuilding of destroyed German cities, there is an almost never-ending demand for listed building work, but also the artistic decoration of new buildings. The HB-Werkstätten, using

---

[79] Ibid.
[80] Ibid.
[81] Cf. Susanna Wurche: Die HB-Werkstätten für Keramik im Nationalsozialismus und in der Nachkriegszeit. In: Begleitbuch zur Ausstellung, ibid.

old handwork techniques, clean up parts of the Red City Hall, Schinkel's Friedrichswerder Church in Berlin, and historical buildings in Potsdam Sanssouci. Numerous churches and monasteries, technical and administrative buildings, residential and park facilities, particularly in Brandenburg and Mecklenburg-Vorpommern, now bear the mark of the workers from Marwitz.

Anyone acquainted with the rules of the market economy would conclude from the excellent order bookings, available human capital and the manager with her artistic and, now, financial experience, would conclude that this was a prosperous business. These were certainly also success factors in the GDR. However, the political and economic framework conditions were always permanently in the way of favorable prerequisites.

The state victimized private companies through the allocation of resources, bans and obstacles to the import of materials, constraints on the goods to be produced and demands regarding buyers. Wage levels were also prescribed by the state and these were considerably less than those for state-owned companies.

Also here, experts with a market-economy approach, would assert that the situation could not be better: the state allows the private entrepreneur to pay wages lower than the standard rate – a measure that reduces costs and increases company results.

Indeed. But in the GDR, labor was also in short supply. It was thus a distinct possibility that employees of the company could change to better-paid jobs in a state-owned company. This was the precise reason for the order from the state.

This left an increase in prices. What could get in the way of this when demand showed a tendency of being infinite?!

Once again, the state got in the way. The selling prices had to correspond to those of 1940, despite higher costs.[82] The contortions to which Hedwig Bollhagen was forced to obtain price approval for new products is demonstrated by a Price Permission Document from the Government of the German Democratic Republic, Office of the Government Commission on Prices, Central Department Glass/Ceramics, from 1961.[83] This document is a textbook example of

---

[82] Arno Röger: "Volkseigentümlichkeiten". Die HB-Werkstätten in der DDR-Zeit. In: Begleitbuch zur Ausstellung, ibid., p. 177.
[83] See Hedwig Bollhagen. Ein Leben für die Keramik. Ibid., p. 178.

German officialdom, now equipped with self-appointed legitimacy to represent the people. Bollhagen's several threats to throw in the towel become easier to understand after reading such documents.

Officialdom also interferes with the artistic interests. At the fifth German Art Exhibition in 1962, in the reopened Albertinum in Dresden, Hedwig Bollhagen exhibits a black, cylindrical mocha service, which attracts the fury of Walter Ulbricht during a tour by the state and party leadership and is described by him as "devoid of spirit."[84] This accusation helps the service to become particularly popular.

In 1972, the HB workshops are nationalized. Over a period of years, HB had successfully defended herself against government participation. But now she can no longer prevent integration with the VEB Steingutfabrik Rheinsberg. The new "Volkseigentümlichkeiten" ("people's possessions"), an ironic play on words by HB, do not have exclusively negative consequences. Suddenly, wages are the same as those in nationalized companies; there are funds for urgently needed reconstruction measures. However, the artistic profile and program risk being lost in the production company and for this reason, the state art trading company takes over in 1976. All goods must now be supplied to its galleries.[85] The rumor alone that HB ceramics are available leads to long queues of buyers in the stores. This arouses conflicting emotions in Hedwig Bollhagen. As someone who allows no cuts in the quality of her work, she asks what is in particular demand. The answer is that it does not matter as everything is sold without exception.[86] HB suppresses the intrinsic demotivation by the system by working. In 1981, at the age of 74, she relinquishes the business management of the workshops at her own request, to focus on artistic management. She remained "the good spirit, watching over everything," as one of her former employees puts it.[87]

How could a business of the nature of HB-Werkstätten survive under the

---

[84] We received the reference to this event from the curator of the Potsdam exhibition „Hedwig Bollhagen. A life for ceramics," Frau Gudrun Gorka-Reimus, whom we thank for her expert and empathetic guided tour. For the context of the formalism accusations, including those against Bollhagen, see Hein Köster: Schmerzliche Ankunft in der Moderne. In: Wunderwirtschaft. DDR-Konsumkultur in den 60er Jahren. Cologne, Weimar, Vienna 1996, pp. 96-103.
[85] Cf. Arno Röger, ibid.
[86] Author's discussion with Frau Gorka-Reimus in Potsdam, October 3, 2007.
[87] Arno Röger, ibid., p. 179.

regressive political and economic premises of the GDR that are merely hinted at here?

The existence of the workshops stood and fell with their shrewd, charismatic leader. Artistically, she went her own way relentlessly, almost stoically, and to the end remained open to experiments and innovation. In order to give herself the scope for creativity, she accepted occasionally crazy state and municipal regulations. The inevitable ideological speeches of loyalty are something she delivers in an inconspicuous small format. Every year, the company employees demonstrate on Labor Day using the simple motto, "Long live the First of May," knowing full well that this was also the date of the establishment of HB-Werkstätten.

If something did not work that was an indispensable requirement for her work, it was made possible through contacts, compromise, "bribe" goods produced in-house and once, when it was necessary, an abrupt threat of consequences. Obtaining work material alone requires the pursuit of complicated methods that were not foreseen by the plan economy:

"The red firing clay was always sourced from Westerwald until this was no longer possible because of a shortage of hard currency. A similar clay could only be sourced from Poland until they discovered the Western market with its hard currency and no longer supplied the GDR. Eventually, a solution was found. Since many listed building assignments were carried out for churches, the church received gifts of Westerwald clay from its 'sisters' in the West, which was then delivered through GENEX[88]. We then bought it from this organization, used some of it for state (!) assignments in preserving listed buildings and used the rest for freely created pottery goods."[89]

But the real explanation of the survival of the company comes only from the understanding of the characteristic HB company atmosphere. A potter and building ceramicist recalls:

"If there was not enough money, we received our wages from her private money. Many of us experienced this. We joined the company through our parents, who already worked here. My father, my mother, my sister-in-law and now my daughter works here. Some of us were given compulsory work at the

---

88 See also explanation of terms on p. 158.
89 Ibid.

Hennigsdorf steelworks, but after my military service, I didn't return to the steelworks, but came back here, although I had been earning twice as much there. It's not always a question of money."[90]

A painter says:

"Earlier, there were 80 employees here. But she spoke to each individual and knew a lot about them, such as the names of their children. The family belonged here, too. We also did a lot together. You spoke about your family and in this respect, she was always very helpful."[91]

It is HB's caring approach that binds the team to her and her company and allows offers from far better-paying nationalized companies to be spurned: "We all stayed here. We felt at home."[92] Year after year, as Father Christmas in an old military overcoat from one of her employees, she makes speeches in which she unburdens the frustrations of her soul and expresses criticism among the praise, as one potter says.[93] As a respected manager, she is for most people "the mother," and this is no contradiction. The plotting group comes to appreciate the niche that she has found in the overly ideological society of the GDR. "Father Christmas knows that you are all fed up to tears here," says HB during her appearance as Father Christmas, "and for that reason, each of you will receive three handkerchiefs."[94]

The niches open up with the Turnaround. The GDR niche society is breaking up. "Did you have to rethink things in relation to the new situation?", Hedwig Bollhagen is asked in 1996. She replies:

"Not in terms of work, because in the GDR, I had to ensure that I could produce my crockery. The State Art Trading company, to which I belonged at the time, would have preferred to keep us on a narrow path. No, I did not need to rethink, but maybe my people did. It took a while before the sales staff in our shop, from which we make sales from the workshop, became friendlier and understood that their position of power had ended. Earlier, they literally grabbed the products out of our hands..."[95]

---

[90] Günter Sens in: Ein Leben für die Keramik, ibid., p. 45.
[91] Iris Scheja, ibid., p. 47.
[92] Magdalena Glaubitz, ibid., p. 45.
[93] Helma Dalibozak, ibid., p. 48.
[94] Hilda Starun, ibid., p. 44.
[95] "Ich mach doch nur Kaffeetöppe", ibid.

During our company visit on October 4, 2007, we speak to the President of HB-Werkstätten, Herr Wolfgang Scholz, about the present and future of the business, in which 22 persons remain employed. His view of reality is unvarnished, allowing himself to be only cautiously optimistic. The HB legacy requires hand-painting. Screen printing, decals and stencils are still not used. But the hundred of mechanical steps that are required before a cup or pot is finished, have their price nowadays and this is reflected in the selling price. Customers who visit the workshop and see the artistic effort with their own eyes understand this. But others who compare with industrially mass-produced crockery allow themselves to be distracted by its low price. These customers can no longer differentiate between unique and uniform and the value of the former remains alien to them. For HB, these customers are lost.

But this does not mean that HB is lost, says Scholz. He ejects potential buyers who show an interest in the business because they smell the opportunity to make something completely different out of it. "That is not an option for me. I share HB's intentions." That is not easy in a country in which the slogan of an electronics company, "Geiz ist geil" ("Saving is Sexy"), has a hypnotic effect on customers, who then storm their branches and break all purchasing records.

The HB brand has its "ostalgically" loyal fans and new ones, who largely come from the eastern part of Germany and are a cross section of every age group. "This is where I see the opportunities of the future. Also because the tradition of our grandparents' generation is dying out, that of keeping china crockery ‚for best' and letting it merely grace a cabinet. An HB service is used and the blue and white, demanded by half of our customers, is only enhanced through use." The exhibition for HB's hundredth birthday also attracted new buyers.

We ask about exports. "Four to five percent goes to Switzerland, about the same amount to a Japanese retail chain, where we ended up almost by chance. We are hoping for a similar miracle in the US. HB is simply not sufficiently well-known abroad."

During our discussions and the subsequent tour of the company, it seems that a little of the niche from GDR times continues in Marwitz.

6. The safe anchor of Ostalgia

The Greek word *nóstos* means *return* (*to home territory*), while *álgos* means *pain*. The Brockhaus dictionary defines nostalgia as "a feeling filled with undefined longing, triggered by discomfort in the present, in which the conception of the time in question is revived through fashion, art, music or similar aspects " (*Brockhaus, Deutsches Wörterbuch*). When felt as home-sickness, nostalgia can make a person ill because it can even be a longing for what has been lost forever.

Nostalgia is a human phenomenon proving that our identities are formed in the past. We turn back to the past in times of trouble and turbulence, trying to anchor ourselves.

For this purpose, our memory activates colors, smells, objects, people, places and moments stored within us. Frequently, such as in the case of migrants, it seems as if the memory comprises an entire country.

"I lost my homeland," says East German movie director Konrad Weiß in 1992, "this gray, confined, ugly country. This beautiful country, the summers in Mecklenburg full of openness, birdsong and greenery, the winters in Vogtland with the children in the snow. And the dirty, concrete, stinking, noisy, vibrant, brave, peaceful Berlin. I grew up in this country; it was the country of my first love, the country of my dreams, the country of my wrath. It was the country of my children, and it should have been the country of my grandchildren, born and as yet unborn. Now it is being pulled away from under my feet. My hope is drying up and my dreams dying. I am becoming an immigrant in my own country."[96]

The way in which the GDR as a country became something else after its fall – also something else in the evolving memory – was felt by many of its citizens at the time. The country, in which time and money were quite separate

---

[96] Konrad Weiß in *Der Spiegel*. Quoted from Frank Thomas Grub (2003): „Wende" und „Einheit" im Spiegel der deutschsprachigen Literatur. Bd. 1: Untersuchungen. Berlin, New York: Walter de Gruyter, p. 580. Grub's dissertation records a 35-page Overview of the theme "Ostalgia" in German-language literature from 1990 to 2001. Some of his texts that are meticulously listed and commented on with captivating feeling served as working and comparative material for this study.

things, during the final years of which many felt that they were sitting in a waiting room and some had internalized – what the poet Volker Braun called "the insight into the missing outlook" – this country was suddenly gone. The peaceful uprising had brought about its fall and torn down its boundaries. It was now open: filled with unlimited expectations in terms of the new liberties and their first disappointments, but also leaving a void in a large and unexpected way: the Trabant that was cherished and cared for, for which you had to wait more than ten years, suddenly seemed to be worth less than its scrapping fee, which had to be paid in Deutschmarks. Ten thousand tons of books from the GDR, a country with a joy of reading, were shredded or, due to time shortage, discarded at the dump as they were. They had to make way for the products of the West German book chains. In the markets, there were sales of dimensions that could never have been imagined. The country's products, good and bad, those that had been subsidized and those once referred to as "luxuries," were peddled at the edge of marketplaces, often for far less than they cost to produce. Was nothing good enough anymore? In times when hundreds of thousands of jobs were being eliminated, was the biography of the country and its individual citizens only there to be cast away?

Nostalgia did not arrive overnight. A new daily life was sprung upon the people and no amount of time seemed to be enough to cope with it. Experiencing the exuberant world of Western goods, the labyrinth of the new, strange bureaucracy, the search for work and order in the chaos, apparently left no room for reflection on yesterday.

But wasn't there already a sense of nostalgia in the words of Weiß, who spoke of a country that had been and which he obviously loved?

Stigmatization of Ostalgia

At this time, 1992, looking back to the time of the East is no longer unusual. Ostalgie – a portmanteau of the German words *Ost* (east) and *Nostalgie* (nostalgia) – becomes a fact. The reaction in the west demonstrates a lack of understanding. Was it not "dangerous (that) the birdsong of a Mecklenburg summer obviously has an established, intractable link with the state of the Socialist Unity Party"?, as rhetoric Professor Ueding aptly concludes, literally shooting the bird down. Another dangerous component comprises the "myth that claimed that significant human and social values had been preserved in the East, while these had reputedly been sacrificed in the west long ago." This myth was "completely useless for orientation in a newly changed reality" (Gerd Ueding, quoted by Grub, p. 580) The investigative commission of the German Bundestag, "Overcoming the consequences of the Socialist Unity Party dictatorship in the process of German unity," addresses "the causes of the retroactive transfiguration of GDR reality." Politicians and publicists, particularly but not exclusively from the right-wing camp, form a front against the growing atmosphere.

A decade later, with Ostalgia now an alienated term adopted by media throughout Germany, the East Germans are assigned a "special awareness," that "contains a demarcation of politics and society in the West." However, it is generously permitted and there is a quietness in the west "with acquired gallantry" regarding "the bottomless barrel," according to a features editor of the daily *Süddeutsche Zeitung*, who, at the end of his philippic against the truly tragicomical aspects of the commercialized form of Ostalgia, lets the cat out of the bag: Whoever receives "transfer payments (as) a kind of hush money" deserves no "cultural victory" (Bisky 2004).

As was once the case in the GDR, an attempt is made to wage campaigns against the undesirable trend. "Through a campaign against rising Ostalgia, the CDU aims to stop the progress of the Left Party throughout the Federal Republic," report the media already three months prior to the CDU Party Congress in Stuttgart in December 2008 (*Financial Times Deutschland* 2008). Nineteen years after the fall of the Berlin Wall, Ostalgia is denounced in speeches and interviews as "dementia" and "the suppression of that which was the GDR" (Schipanski 2008). Is Ostalgia dangerous? Is it an accurate accusation that Ostalgists were demanding to have the GDR reinstated?

Jürgen Kuczynski, economy expert and historian, an authority who was both a party-conformist and critic, felt himself gravitating increasingly to the brigade of "angry old men" under Honecker. His response to the question put to him already a decade and a half ago: "Is there nostalgia for the GDR?" was: "No way! Who would wish for a return of the command system of the Politburo, under which press freedom was more restricted than under Frederick the Great, under which grassroots democracy was even more poorly developed than in the old Federal Republic? But nostalgia for a social system in which the apartments were maybe bad, but nobody needed to be homeless, in which labor productivity was perhaps far below the level of the Federal Republic, but there were no unemployed, in which pensions were low, but nobody had to starve, for a social system, in which, as is recognized by West German social scientists, the 'elbowing society was underdeveloped,' yes, this type of nostalgia exists. And not without good reason!" (Kuczynski 1994).

Early analyses

The first scientific study to my knowledge on the phenomenon of Ostalgia (Fritze 1997) arrives at similar results to the first comprehensive empirical survey (Stolz aufs eigene Leben 1995).

The research by the totalitarianism researcher Lothar Fritze finds only a few indications of a longing for a return of the GDR. "There is," according to Fritze, "among former GDR citizens, no socially relevant number of people who would wish to return to the former conditions of the GDR, including the political system." GDR nostalgia in this form is nonexistent as a "conscious, politically notable phenomenon" (Fritze 1997, p. 94).

Observers from abroad confirm this thesis. "Many former GDR citizens," writes Dominic Boyer, for example, "did experience the end of the GDR with a sense of loss and even grief. I would emphasize, however, that this was often more grief at the foreclosure of the utopian and humanitarian fantasy of socialism than grief at the end of the GDR *per se*. In hundreds of interviews with former GDR citizens, I have never once heard an East German of any age fantasize about the return of the GDR" (Boyer 2006).

According to Fritze, this in no way ruled out "that certain aspects or partial aspects of GDR reality – also and perhaps specifically in retrospect – are valued positively. (...) Whoever – instead of diffuse transfiguration – attaches a positive value to specific features of the GDR, obviously has reason to assume that the corresponding social conditions were equipped to better meet certain personal needs. If one wants to talk of 'nostalgia' in this context, the rational character of such an orientation should at least be emphasized" (Fritze 1997, p. 94).

Fritze uses the term "sighing nostalgia" (Fritze 1997, p. 105). People who expected a rapid improvement in their living standards from the new market economy conditions, but now find themselves in the midst of a society full of unpredictability that remains alien to them, make comparisons with their earlier manageable lives. Despite frequent abrupt and rigorously expressed judgments, they understand very well that this time will never return. With their expression of regret ("sighs"), they signal the fact that the past they long for cannot be repeated and give vent to their feelings. The accusation that they wish for a return of the GDR is inappropriate for them and is met with a lack of understanding: Nobody knows better than those who have only recently tried to bridge the gap between pipe-dream and realistic politics about just what has to remain a utopia.

Not least, Fritze warns of generalizations. "Whoever did not unconditionally support Germany unity, but rather urged a continuation of the GDR, need not necessarily be (...) a supporter of the Socialist Unity Party, (...) nor can they be accused of GDR nostalgia in the sense that they are interested in having the former GDR conditions" (Fritze 1997, p. 111). People, who experienced the active freedom of participation during the fall of the Berlin Wall and afterwards, had only tested grassroots democracy and codetermination for a short time and now complained of their loss in the united Germany, are in only very few cases defenders of the old GDR regime.

The opinion poll on GDR nostalgia that was conducted in 1995 by the Bielefeld *Emnid Institute* on behalf of *Spiegel* confirms an ability to differentiate and a sense of reality among the majority of the 1,000 respondents. Both prohibit a return to former conditions *per se*, which only a few would like to see. Frankly, if not causally, good and bad in the GDR are mentioned, a result that largely removes the basis for the idyllizing Ostalgia. When asked about the most negative memories of the GDR, the responses particularly refer to the effects of a society of shortages, the absence of freedom to travel, the interpretative rights of the Socialist Unity Party, spying, incapacitation, powerlessness in relation to the state bodies and the arrogance of workmen. "The worst thing was the lie that we lived with. On opening the newspaper, you could read about successes and plan-fulfillment and everyone knew that this was not true" (Stolz aufs eigene Leben 1995, p. 42). This statement is symptomatic. It tells of a "we" feeling that did not disappear and a powerlessness, still felt afterwards, of an inability to overcome the standstill in the GDR within the framework of the ruling system.

Responses to the question regarding the most positive memories of the GDR bear witness to a society in which competition largely remained an alien term, in which citizens enjoyed security, which cared for children and in which "nearly everyone" was equal, taxes and social insurance were administered unbureaucratically and social aspects – in contradiction to the teachings of Marx – held primacy over economics: "A job was created for each person, whether it was needed or not" (Stolz aufs eigene Leben, p. 42).

In the direct comparison of the living conditions in the Federal Republic and the GDR, the poll reveals no surprises. Accordingly, 89 percent of the East Germans are convinced that "the cohesion of people among each other in the GDR was stronger than it is today." Lothar Fritze, interviewed by the *Spiegel* editorial staff in this context, explains this phenomenon as "a specific kind of solidarity and sense of belonging together that is less typical in modern, Western society." Because, the all-knowing *Spiegel* editors explain assiduously, the reasons were: "a shared sense of defenselessness against the leaders" and a "one hand washes the other" attitude, which alleviated some of the shortages (Stolz aufs eigene Leben, p. 49).[97]

The loss of security is mourned by nearly all respondents: the secure job and basic provisions that were affordable for all, such as low rents, cheap food and free medical care for patients (Stolz aufs eigene Leben, p. 43). Missing from this are the facts that the state subsidies for the so-called basic provisions comprised one fifth of the GDR's state budget, disproportions in economic life opened doors and ultimately exceeded the financial resources of the country. The conscious preference for apparent security was an illusion, economically and ecologically, with the latter getting a raw deal in the survey. Not only the answers, but also the counterarguments relate to simple, almost paradoxical truths: "On the basis of the rents," according to the *Spiegel*, "the apartments could not even be maintained" (Stolz aufs eigene Leben, p. 43).

Discarded: East German experiences

However, other aspects also comprise a paradox. Positive East German experiences in individual areas were not even considered, but were in some cases already rigorously discarded prior to unification. Among East German respondents, this triggers anger and a lack of understanding – in the *Spiegel* survey in 1995 and successive empirical surveys through to the present day. One aspect

---

[97] Two causes merely mentioned generally and pragmatically here. Explanation and differentiation are provided by Michael Lukas Moeller and Hans-Joachim Maaz in: *Die Einheit beginnt zu zweit. Ein deutsch-deutsches Zwiegespräch*, Rowohlt, Berlin 1991, and further by Hans-Joachim Maaz: *Das gestürzte Volk oder Die verunglückte Einheit*, Argon, Berlin 1991, and idem: *Die Entrüstung. Deutschland, Deutschland, Stasi, Schuld und Sündenbock*. Argon, Berlin 1992.

that is constantly mentioned is the practice in the GDR of gathering physicians with varying specialisms in policlinics. This did not comply with the West German system of dispersed private practices and the policlinic system was disbanded, but is now a model that enjoys a high level of recognition. Another aspect is SERO, the system for the recovery of secondary raw materials, hailed by experts as the most efficient system of its kind worldwide, which did not survive the Turnaround and was phased out.[98] A further aspect is East German teacher training in accordance with a system that was adopted in its entirety by Finland and is today considered by experts to be a significant element of this country's PISA victories.

The experience of children's daycare centers is another of these matters. When visiting Sweden in 2009, CDU Families Minister Ursula von der Leyen found that 78 percent of children in Sweden under the age of three attend a daycare center, while only 18 percent gained a place in Germany. And "the parental home belongs with the daycare center or school in the daily routine as the moon and the sun belong with each other" ("In Schweden ist Erziehung nicht nur Frauenthema" 2009). East German readers look back: doesn't this seem familiar, both in content and the flowery, propaganda talk?

Is this why they have Ostalgia? Every bit as little as Frau von der Leyen, because in this case, they are mourning circumstances that are in no way lost forever. These are real social experiences made by them, which if you take these seriously, offer solutions for yesterday and, most of all, the existing social problems of today. In 1990, these experiences were burdened by the prejudice-infected stigma that they originated from the East, whose political system had failed. They still carry this stigma for many West German decision-makers. But times do change. In 1990, it was self-evident for numerous, mainly male, CDU and CSU politicians that mothers belonged at the stove in the home with the task of raising children. Today, this is different. Not least, gloomy demographic forecasts of the future demand a more modern approach to such matters as the combination of motherhood and career. The CDU Families Minister is

---

[98] See also Christoph Dowe: SERO – abgewickelt und vergessen? In: Wolfgang Dümcke, Fritz Vilmar (1995), *Kolonialisierung der DDR. Kritische Analysen und Alternativen des Einigungsprozesses*. Münster: agenda, pp. 195-207; and Paul Janositz: Ein Ex-Weltmeister im Wiederverwerten, Stuttgarter Zeitung December 12, 1990.

enthusiastic about the "Swedish way": "But it seems to me that the decisive factor is that Swedish fathers are just as involved as the mothers in bringing up their young children. They often take parental leave to be with their children, but also want to advance in their professions. As a result, they automatically turn the combination of career and family into a matter for the entire Swedish economy and society. Raising children in Sweden is not exclusively a subject for women" ("In Schweden ist Erziehung nicht nur Frauenthema" 2009).

This was not the case in the GDR either, where, as in Sweden, 92 percent of women had experience of the labor market. A key requirement for this was the conditions created by the state for the combination of motherhood and career. Added to this was the growing understanding among male partners for shared responsibility in raising children and doing housework, which could not be achieved through legislation. This required time and at the end of the GDR, analyses found that there was still a double burden for women, who were responsible for 60-80 percent of household duties. The monthly housekeeping day that was available to women took this imbalance into consideration. For the GDR, which was economically weak compared with the Federal Republic, this day was an economic achievement that it maintained until the end and a relief of the burden on families with children. Its abolition in 1994 created potential social conflict and contributed to a dramatic decline in births.[99] Contemporary witnesses, who have good memories of the social achievement of the "housekeeping day," are no regressive enthusiasts who glorify the GDR. They ask why the relatively prosperous Federal Republic prevented something that helped to create a component of equal rights and child-friendliness.

---

[99] The housekeeping day, which was not counted as vacation time, was introduced for married women in the GDR in 1952. From 1965, it was also available to unmarried women with children under the age of 18 and, from 1977, to women over 40 with no children who worked full time. The housekeeping day was also provided to single men with children or in the case of a wife's illness. In 1994, it was abolished in the East German Länder.
In the Federal Republic of Germany, housekeeping days were only granted in Bremen, Hamburg, Lower Saxony and North Rhine-Westphalia. In 1979, the Federal Constitutional Court declared it to be in contravention of the constitution because of "Unequal treatment of both sexes" Cf. Carola Sachse (2002): *Der Hausarbeitstag. Gerechtigkeit und Gleichberechtigung in Ost und West 1939-1994*. Göttingen: Wallstein.

Myth of the GDR?

"Is the GDR really mythified?" asks the journalist and novelist Christoph Dieckmann. He replies in the words of Immanuel Kant: "The true myth is one's own youth." The GDR is remembered in different ways. "Some celebrate what they loved, others that they managed to survive it. No matter what, Ostalgia ends dispossession. Ostalgia insists on their being a personal story, an unabridged biography. Ostalgia responds to the doctrines of history-writing with a cheerful 'but'" (Dieckmann 2003).

The "cheerful but" sometimes becomes a piece of craziness. In all seriousness, 16 years after the fall of the Berlin Wall, the Eisenhüttenstadt online shop Osthits.de offered Trabant exhaust smell in cans and immediately received orders from throughout the world. What moose droppings in jars are to smart Swedish businesspeople, the preserved Trabi fart is to the East German entrepreneur. It is explained on the company's website that the two-stroke-engine car defined the street image of socialism and it is possible to obtain the original two-stroke smell for the daring home by buying the ostalgic cans: "A smell that doesn't only provoke women." The concept of the seller and its advertising is aimed at customers with humor and a willingness to remember that is combined with a love-hate feeling. It is precisely this tone that is applied to the advertising for another East German product: so-called Hängolin tea. This drink that supposedly suppresses sex drive, served in its day by the National People's Army, was notorious for its obtrusive bland taste and smell. "For world peace in the camp bed," the mail-order firm promises, a slogan that combines the congenial ideological peace rhetoric of the brothers-in-arms with the promise of potency suppression.

At the same time, it is wrong to simply reduce the phenomenon of Ostalgia to an apolitical memory of moments carved into one's own biography. Ostalgia is also, as the former Minister-President of Saxony-Anhalt, Reinhard Höppner, calls it, a "defiant approach to justification." As a result of demonstrated West German superiority and the demolition of their own life's achievement, "many East Germans unjustly get the feeling that they have an inferior biography. Some even believe that they need to apologize because they didn't flee to the West like others did" (Höppner 2000). The current CDU Minister-President of Saxony-Anhalt, Wolfgang Böhmer, expresses it similarly: "Today, you almost need to say apologetically that not all 18 million GDR citizens were on the starting blocks waiting to flee" (Böhmer 2009).

Ostalgia contradicts such an apology. It opposes the fact "that it is constantly being explained to us how we lived," as it is put by the inventor of the term, Uwe Steimle, actor and cabaret artist from Dresden (Steimle 2006). In 1993, when the birthrate in East Germany fell to a third of the 1988 level and, at 0.77 children per woman, was by far the lowest birth rate in the world, with the exception of the Vatican City[100], the explanation given by the (West) German Families Ministry was a "shift in the function of children": "this means that fewer material values are associated with children than in the past (such as provisions for old age or in the case of illness, assistance, passing on property, and other factors), while there are stronger immaterial values (emotional, being affectionate, watching children grow and other factors). But for this, a smaller number of children is sufficient" (Federal Ministry 1994). One journalist commented sarcastically: "If necessary, teddy bears and Barbie dolls would also be fine for the emotional needs of East Germans. By now, they really should be used to being regarded by the West German leading class as inferior human material" (Köhler 1994).

The assertion in the Family Report by the Ministry is that East German families had less emotional involvement with their children in GDR times compared with today and that their numbers of children were primarily materially motivated. The fact that "passing on property" is named as one such motivation is evidence of a complete lack of understanding of East German realities. To East German mothers and fathers who read this report, it was an insult, based on conceit, lack of knowledge and political calculation. They did not recognize themselves in this report, which was one of many and definitely no exception, although they did understand who it related to. They saw themselves as being devalued to the role of puppets, who had fulfilled state procreation assignments for reasons of bourgeois self-interest. It was such disparagements that contributed to the emergence of an "East" identity that had never existed in the time of the GDR. In turn, the compromising of this identity – or rather: what this identity was considered to be – by the West German-dominated media industry, simply fuelled the fire.[101] Christoph Dieckmann hits the nail on the head: "Anyone who catalogued the GDR under P for penitentiary simply provided ammunition for its defenders" (Dieckmann 1997).

---

[100] Tagesschau, March 16, 2006.
[101] Typical examples of the "domineering West German discourse about the East" are presented by Thomas Ahbe in: *Der Osten aus der Sicht des Westens. Die Bilder von den Ostdeutschen und ihre Konstrukteure* (Ahbe 2005).

Ostalgia throughout Eastern Europe

Prominent representatives of the now international and cross-discipline Ostalgia research, see in this one of, if not the main reason for the existence of this phenomenon. "The greater trauma," Dominic Boyer, for example, writes about the East Germans, "was not the collapse of the GDR and its lifeworld but rather the discovery that postunification public narratives reduced the GDR to the prison camp of a criminal regime and reduces them to this camp's abject inmates" (Boyer 2006). The writer and mathematics professor Helga Königsdorf, popular in the GDR because of her socially critical texts, says: "Reducing the history of the East to a story of crime and inaptitude is possibly a way of creating room for maneuver. But it is an abuse of history. The country was not primarily a land of victims and perpetrators. Above all, it was a country of completely normal people faced with conditions with which they had to live and also could live, despite all of the burdens mentioned" (Königsdorf 1992).

Königsdorf speaks about the history of the East, meaning by this East Germany. However, the phenomenon of Ostalgia exists under other names and with other characteristics in all of the former Eastern Bloc countries. An interdisciplinary colloquium entitled "Nostalgic View of the Communist Era. Is a new collective memory emerging in Eastern Europe?" organized in Berlin in 2005 by the Franco-German Centre Marc Bloch für Sozialwissenschaften, looked at the reasons and consequences of this. The Italian Germanic expert Eva Banchelli, drawing a balance, speaks of the "recognition of Ostalgia as a form of broad and multifaceted remembrance culture." It articulates the uneasiness of rapid, forced adaptation to the alien, global and mobile present at the time of the millennium. At the same time, it is "a kind of resistance against the dominant discreditation of the real socialist past as an era of compact totalitarianism." Ostalgia looks behind the facade of the former dictatorship. It uncovers there an astonishing capacity for creativity, innovation and distancing oneself through ironic humor "under the strict conditions of political control and economic neediness." On the basis of these capacities, also under the new circumstances, it reinforces the current need for identity and defends personal biographies (Banchelli 2008, p. 59).

Let's test these theses on the example of East Germany!

In the early 1990s, *Ostalgia* was foremost an expression of the longing for social security and order in a turbulent and chaotic reality. It was so it began. Ostalgia mirrored the East Germans' loss of identity and many people's belief that their own biography had suddenly lost its value. West German laws and regulations were imposed, thousands of companies went bankrupt due to the lack of profitability, the now demanded earlier debts to the East German state, the collapse of the (export-) market or uncertainties regarding ownership.[102] Under these circumstances, Ostalgia meant more than a passive and misconceived memory of the 'good' old days. To remember the real or imagined values of their former life became for many East Germans an active choice, strengthening their self-confidence in a situation in which nothing from the Eastern part of Germany seemed worth keeping besides the green arrow traffic signal.

Against the background of this active choice, the rigorous and immediate rejection by East German consumers seemed unfitting and was met with expressions of surprise by observers. It only becomes understandable if one considers the special characteristics of the GDR's plan economy and some of its complicated consequences.

Socialist plan economy à la GDR – an excursus

This plan economy was anything but an economy that ran according to plan. The sheer boundless popularity of the Danish *Olsen Gang* movies in the GDR was attributable, among other things, to the constantly repeated plot: Gang leader Egon Olsen has an ingenious plan that promises the earth, but never works out. East German viewers drew comparisons with their own economic system.

A cornerstone of this system was the so-called basic provision. Parts of this system from the 1950s still existed at the time of transition. No one should have to starve, freeze or become homeless. For this reason, basic foods, housing, children's clothing, health care and public transport, to mention some examples, were heavily subsidized. While the aims of subsidization may have been praiseworthy especially after the suffering during and after the War, the consequences became more and more devastating for Eastern Germany's public finances. The maintenance of a policy of low prices at any cost took the country to the brink.

To be able to boast at Socialist Unity Party and Bloc parties' congresses in the 1980s that consumer prices were still the same as in the 1950s, fixed prices

---

[102] See chapter 3, p 49.

were maintained that pathologically strengthened the already existing disproportions throughout the economic system.

For example, the price of 5 Pfennig for a bread roll that had been maintained for nearly 40 years exceeded the cost of ingredients and labor long before 1989. Bakers were forced to comply with the prices prescribed by the state. It was an open secret that there were farmers and breeders who fed their animals bread. It was cheaper than producing one's own animal feed or buying feed when it was available.

Since bakers could make no profit on bread rolls, only losses, they produced only the amount prescribed by the state. In turn, this needs calculation took no account of diversified wholesale purchases – they did not fit into the idyllic image. The ideology was not permitted to be sullied by facts, as it is put sarcastically by the author mentioned above, Helga Königdorf, in her writing.[103]

The result was a consumer run on the bread rolls constantly produced in the same amount, which was evident from the frequent lines of people queuing in front of the bakers' shops.

The lack of bread rolls that was blamed on politics was only one – certainly extreme – example of hundreds that bear witness to the consequences of ideologically based dogmas, when these are applied to the rules of the market.

The permanently damaged, but unavoidable market rules had their revenge. They forced the state to constantly come up with new stop-gaps in the framework of the party-based command economy. This was quite rightly accused of being rigid and inflexible. However, the daily practice of its protagonists was anything but rigid and inflexible. They had to find solutions and, if necessary, complete the miracle of squaring the circle. To them, the economy equaled "a colorful fairground magic booth, complete with tightrope dancers, jugglers, escape artists and magicians of all kinds," as historian Stefan Wolle writes. "There was a plan, but improvisation ruled nonetheless" (Wolle 1998, p. 189).

For example, improvisation had to be applied in skimming off the growing amount of money held by the population without the associated infringement on the principle of unchanged fixed consumer prices becoming too obvious. With the sale of high-value products, also known as luxury goods, at higher prices, the money mass was restricted, while at the same time the growing

---

[103] Helga Königsdorf (1982), Der Lauf der Dinge. Geschichten. Berlin and Weimar: Aufbau.

national fury dispelled that involved claiming that there was nothing to buy for one's money. Luxury goods were not only cars or Meissen china, but also the 100g bar of East German chocolate, which quality-wise could be compared to a low-quality Western type. The standard price for this of 3.85 GDR Marks corresponded to a total of 77 subsidized bread rolls – just one of many plastic examples of disproportions that distorted the market.

To foreign or West German visitors, the extremely low standard prices for some goods and extremely high prices for others were a complete puzzle. If visitors had freely convertible currency, such as DEM and made an albeit illegal but ubiquitous exchange for GDR Marks, a bread roll cost just one Pfennig at an exchange rate of 1:5. The GDR's prescribed "Minimum exchange for visitors from nonsocialist countries and West Berlin" at a rate of 1:1 had little effect on this.[104] The stable standard prices for basic goods, celebrated to the end as a social achievement by the GDR's state and Party leadership, were in reality a waste of the national wealth, a fact known by every economist, but which none dared to mention. This was because such a judgment brought consequences as it was regarded as an attack on the apparent "unity of economic and social policy." The effort required to maintain this waste doubled in real terms from 1971 to 1980 due to increased world market prices (Hertle, Wolle 2006, p. 266) and doubled once again from 1980 to 1989 because of the halved proceeds in convertible currency.[105]

Without many people seeing through it, the citizens' enthusiasm for this policy was held within boundaries. It is a general human experience that anything obtained almost for free tends not to be valued greatly. The attitudes of the generous fathers of the nation that were displayed with propaganda-style pomp were not appreciated by most citizens. Instead the power of being accustomed reigned. East Germans, with the exception of pensioners, were normally only allowed to travel within the Eastern Block where they encountered a similar system of subsidies. At the end, many people regarded it as normal and simply

---

[104] Introduced in 1964 at a rate of DEM 5; for visitors from West Berlin, the rate was DEM 3. 1973: Increase to DEM 20; DEM 10 for visit to East Berlin. 1974: Reduction to DEM 13 and DEM 6.50 (East Berlin). Exemption from minimum exchange for persons under the age of 16 and for pensioners. 1980: Increase to standard DEM 25, also for pensioners. Children from 7 to15 years, DEM 7.50. 1983: Abolition of the compulsory minimum exchange for children. 1984: Reduction of the exchange rate for pensioners to DEM 15. December 24, 1989: Abolition of the minimum exchange.

[105] See Chapter 3, p. 62.

part of everyday life. They had not been confronted with any system but this one. Experiences with the market system were only made after the unification when things like free dental care were no longer available.

The state management of shortages that came to nothing became increasingly apparent. A well-known joke that emerged at the beginning of the 1980s tells of a customer in a department store who inquires on the ground floor about kitchen furniture. The assistant tells him he is in the television department, where there are no television sets. "No kitchen furniture can be found on the third floor."

East Germans often bought reserve supplies and were always armed with a net shopping bag for this purpose. This was a strategic safety measure shared with the citizens of other Eastern European countries. They did not buy what they needed, but what was available. There were seldom spare parts for the Trabant that often needed repairing, but because nearly every Trabant owner bought reserves, they were even scarcer. The book from the Transpress publishing house, *Ich fahre einen Trabant* (English: "I drive a Trabant"), with "maintenance and repair tips," was the most-sold book in the country.

The East Germans constantly compared their modest standard of living with that of their relatives in the Federal Republic. The expanding gap was all too obvious and led the party propaganda to absurd levels. Every East German could receive Western radio and 70 percent could receive West German television. The product advertising shown there seemed artificial and out of reach. It reflected an alien world. But the inability to obtain these products that seemed so tangible made them all the more desirable and lent them an aura of exclusivity.

From 1959 until 1976, the East German state countered with its own television advertising because it could not be tolerated, as the Party daily *Neues Deutschland* stated, that "the capitalists in West Germany" had used television advertising to create an "illusion of the economic miracle," "while we voluntarily hid our light under a bushel" (quoted from Tippach-Schneider 2004, p. 53). "The separation from the West German market," which Tippach-Schneider presents as the main reason for the PR offensive, did more harm than good. Wherever an economy of scarcity dominates, advertising rapidly becomes superfluous, if not a sheer anachronism. What could be done when the advertised product was once again unavailable? In this context, the assignment was to propagate "socialist lifestyle and provide good examples of such," which ultimately resulted in advertising that resembled product-oriented Western advertising, featuring, for example, beautiful women reclining in foam baths. Reacting to the subsequent criticism, the makers brought in "unpolished cleaners," who "presented the spirit of order and cleanliness" (Werbung in der DDR 2004). However, this did not really encourage the purchase of the cleaning products presented. Not uncommonly the East German TV ads could have quite the opposite effect. People stopped buying the advertised product. They were skeptical about the political propaganda, why should they believe in the ads, ordered by the same bigwigs? "Something must be wrong with the product if they want to get rid of it," they thought. And in actual fact, the party ideologists relentlessly misused the "Tausend Tele-Tips" broadcast for campaigns. If there was not enough meat, the cholesterol-promoting slogan was "Take an extra egg"; if shelf-warmers had accumulated, they were touted – but obviously without success. In 1976, the Council of Ministers decided to end television advertising in the GDR once and for all.

Reality told a different story that not even the most stubborn ideologist could ignore. The relationship between buyer and seller in the GDR was one of dependency that could not even be concealed by the best advertising. It was well-known that the seller was king, using the regionally colored "We don't have it" as his sales pitch, but who could also pull the desired product "out of a hat" if he actually had it.[106] In the GDR, "a need was met," goods were "made available," there was the term "to buy up": the customers had bought up all supplies of something, which now, in grim reality, the people's economy had to once again begin producing laboriously. "The announcements regarding the supply of goods, in their choice of words and structure, were reminiscent of reports from the front" (Wolle 1998, p. 193).

Reports on GDR economic policy, particularly in the 1970s and 1980s, actually tell of a never-ending fight with numerous unknowns, officials' fights in the wings behind the scenes, real shooting or at least artificial thunder from the superpower, the Soviet Union, West German humanitarian requirements in return for assistance and, not least, the tragicomical erroneous decisions made by the embattled leaders.

A cardinal mistake that was made in 1972 was the nationalization of 11,800

---

[106] Nowhere is this relationship of tolerance more authentically described than in Christoph Hein's novel, "Der Tangospieler" (1989), Berlin und Weimar: Aufbau, p. 96.

private and semi-state-owned companies. The victims of this were not only world-renowned export companies, including the furrier and fashion industries, musical instruments manufacturing and the toy industry. Even worse was the resulting sudden absence of the consumer industry's "1,000 small things," whose production was later forced upon the combine groups of companies. These were obliged to contradict their own profile and often had to design and manufacture consumer goods that were unrelated to their own industry, with huge effort and a lack of experience. The way in which these problems hit back at their instigators was demonstrated by no other than SED General Secretary Honecker himself in an interview that became known as the "Knickers Report." Honecker: "For example, for a long time, there were no women's knickers for sale, not in Berlin, nowhere in the Republic. I heard about this and brought it up with the Politburo. Then Inge Lange said: 'Didn't you know? The Women's Association is now issuing instructions on how to sew knickers.' This is scandalous! A country with a huge textile industry and enormous exports can't produce enough women's knickers!" (quoted from Engler 1995, p. 21) Naturally, the self-made political scandals that caused this "scandal" in the first place were never mentioned.

Honecker's consumer socialism that was announced in 1971 is based on the erroneous assumption that it would be possible to pay back Western loans in the second half of the 1970s through aggressive exports. However, the goods that now carried the ideologically sound "Made in GDR" and no longer the world-renowned and popular "Made in Germany," attracted only moderate interest in the global economy. The plan fails and increases the GDR's debt to the West, which grows further in the 1980s and prevents urgently needed investments in companies. Thanks to the intervention of Bavarian Minister-President Franz Josef Strauß that secured the guarantees from the Federal Government for two loans totaling DEM 1,950 billion provided by West German national and private banks in 1983 and 1984, the GDR succeeds in regaining its international credit worthiness.

From the time of its foundation, the existence of the GDR was dependent on the supply of raw materials from the Soviet Union, which used this as a means of political leverage. The decision in 1981 by the General Secretary of the Communist Party of the Soviet Union, Brezhnev, to reduce the contractually agreed supplies of crude oil by two million tons per year is a nail in the coffin. The GDR survives only as a result of the laborious and expensive nationwide conversion of power stations to lignite, which enables the export of processed fossil oil products, but also has catastrophic ecological consequences. In the second half of the 1980s, billions in investment money that is desperately needed elsewhere are tied up in the attempt to become the "Japan of Comecon" in the area of microelectronics. The lag of six to eight years behind the West proves impossible to bridge, even if an unprecedented media propaganda of lies suggests otherwise. The one-megabit chip presented to Honecker in 1988 is made by hand and is not suitable for serial production; the successor 64-Kbit chip costs 93 Marks to produce, but is already available on the world market for a dollar. The 256-Kbit chip is available for two dollars, while the GDR version costs 534 Marks.[107]

In a confidential report to the politburo on May 16, 1989, the Chairman of the State Planning Commission makes it absolutely clear that GDR will be at risk of bankruptcy not later than 1991.[108] Already since the end of the 1970s, all means had been justified to meet the steadily rising interest on the loans raised from the West: the sale of political prisoners, and, later, weapons export, the sale of illegally confiscated antiques that had been privately owned, and even paving stones torn up from East German streets.

What are the country's own products worth?

Let us return from this digression to the matter of the East Germans' rejection of their own domestically produced goods.

Without generalizing, the observations, evidence and contexts presented above show a tendency. This can be described as the insecurity of consumers and, to a large extent, the producers, regarding the value of the consumed and produced goods. An entire network of factors contributed to this insecurity. These factors were connected invisibly and strengthened each others' effects.

The usual conversion of the product value into East German currency functioned at most until the introduction of the DEM with the start of the Economic, Monetary and Social Union on July 1, 1990. Value was reflected in equivalent GDR Marks through subsidies of, in some cases, highly discounted goods, just

---

[107] Quoted from Hertle/Wolle, p. 293.
[108] Quoted from Hertle/Wolle, p. 296.

as some goods were made very expensive and were designated as luxury articles. This value was purely artificial and applied only on the domestic market of an isolated GDR, which diminished rapidly with the opening of the border to the West.

The maintenance of this artificial system that could not be abolished overnight was something that was exploited by a huge number of speculators. In markets in the West, often close to the former border, they offered consumer products that were still subsidized for DEM and hereby accelerated the sell-off of the GDR.

The mere use of a separate, non-convertible currency in the GDR domestic market had been thwarted for more than twenty years by the DEM, which increasingly assumed the position of a second currency in the GDR during the 1980s. The factors that determined the private, black market rate at any given time were the availability of illegal exchange sources and the desirability of the products that could be purchased with DEM.

Decades of disproportions caused by financial policy, with a system of arbitrary pricing and the fact that they were accustomed to scarcity of goods and services had led to a value framework based on these conditions becoming established in the heads of the consumers by which they acted. This value framework had evolved over a long period of time. Repeated experiences in practice had proved its validity.

The Western realm of consumer goods literally broke into the value framework overnight and made it collapse like a house of cards. What still applied? What were the new rules? The once so inaccessible products of the alien, far-off TV world made their entry into lives and lent them an air of unreality.

One could not even rely on the usual shortages any more: now everything was available!

Thirty models of percussion drills in the West German Baumarkt DIY store near the border replaced at a single stroke the complicated barter transaction to get hold of one of these tools that, in the GDR, was mainly reserved for export and without which you could not even hang a single painting in a prefabricated reinforced concrete apartment.

In the local specialty chocolate shop, only five months after the fall of the Berlin Wall and for three times the Western price converted into GDR Marks, 40 kinds of chocolate enticed shoppers. They sold like hot cakes.

Now only a few went out of their way to get the once so popular and nearly always sold-out "Bückware" ("bowing goods")[109] that were produced in the GDR. By habit, these people bought only what they knew. The hysteria and rush for Western products made them nauseous. Statistically, they formed a minority, as evidenced by surveys into the consumption of food and luxury food items. In January 1991, only 21 percent of the East Germans had said that they preferred East German to West German food products. Sinn and Sinn attribute the preference for Western products, alongside general quality, to "curiosity or simply a ravenous appetite for goods (...) that had been virtually unavailable to date" and talk of a "subjective concept of the value of Western product." As food for thought, they state that West German suppliers in the second half of 1990 spent a further DEM 475 M on advertising in East Germany (Sinn and Sinn 1993, p. 97). East German producers had no money for such activities. As shown in consumer surveys conducted by the *Süddeutsche Zeitung* and weekly *Die Zeit*, West German products drove many East German goods almost completely off the shelves – and this happened while the GDR still existed in September 1990, a month before German unification.[110]

After this, GDR products turn quiet. With the excessive offering of Western products, their sales fall rapidly, if the firms survive at all. Even earlier frontrunners like Rotkäppchen sparkling wine, chocolate from Halloren and Delitzscher or Wernesgrüner beer are under threat of bankruptcy.

East German brand products in retrospect

Nonetheless, the figure of only 21 percent of East Germans who expressed "a clear quality preference for East German goods" had suddenly grown to 56 percent only a year later, in January 1992, with this number giving East German products precedence over West German products.[111] What is the explanation for this sudden and astonishing change of heart?

The tendency referred to above of insecurity regarding the value of domesti-

---

[109] The term "Bückware" or "bowing goods" was used by consumers in the shortage society of the GDR, by which the buyer had to „bow down" to the salesperson, that is, ask politely for the goods, which the salesperson, similarly bowing down, would then bring out from underneath the counter.
[110] See Sinn and Sinn 1993, p. 97.
[111] Süddeutsche Zeitung No. 15 from January 18, 1992. Quoted from Sinn and Sinn 1993, p. 98.

cally manufactured goods, as well as the lack of clarity regarding the new living conditions, required an antidote that gave promise. "Almost all nostalgic thoughts and feelings of the East Germans could be traced back to a single word," was what was stated in the Emnid survey commissioned by *Spiegel* that is mentioned in the introduction. "That key word is security" (Stolz aufs eigene Leben 2005, p. 43). Compared with easygoing, predictable, "comfortable dictatorship" GDR (Grass) the new situation offered civil liberties, an open world and adventure. The accustomed security of East German sympathy was not on offer.

In existential decision-making and upheavals, it can be helpful to hold on to what is familiar, reflection on one's own roots. Would reflection on the society that had only just been eliminated be of help? Whose politicized and ideologized structures seemed unfitting as a possible shield with which to overcome the present. But there were emotional ties to aspects of the earlier life that were unrelated to politics and whose disappearance was perceived as a loss.

This context includes the rediscovery by consumers of consumer products made in East Germany, the ones with which they grew up, with which memories were connected and they did not want to forego taking this piece of familiarity into their new circumstances.

Initially, the demand now expressed for East German products was only seldom politically motivated, although it angered many consumers how quickly the process was of eliminating products that had not been in demand for a short time and that when they visited the West or went there to their new workplaces, they virtually never found East German products on the shelves of West German supermarkets.

Moreover, only a few consumers chose East German products as a type of solidarity action. Certainly, awareness had grown in the months since the fall of the Berlin Wall regarding the relationship between job losses, company closures and purchase decisions. However, Products that proved to be of inferior quality to their competitors did little to help the situation. The number of company bankruptcies increased further in 1993 and 1994.[112]

Quality was the deciding factor in the purchasing pattern of East German

---

[112] Cf. Hans-Werner Sinn (2005), *Ist Deutschland noch zu retten?* Berlin: Ullstein, p. 48.

consumers. Their decision for or against an East German product – insofar as it was still available or available once again – was made in competition with the West German product, which had often been tried by them. Numerous multi-industry and industry-specific consumer surveys bear witness to the fact that the preference for various East German products in eastern Germany was not a short-lived fashion, but a sustained, stable, statistically proven trend. In the Emnid survey cited above, 53 percent of the East German respondents answered the question "What is your approach to buying food and household articles?": "I only buy according to quality and price," 2% "I buy Western products where possible" and 45% "I buy Eastern products where possible" (Stolz aufs eigene Leben 1995, p. 43). The importance of quality is quickly recognized by East German food producers: "By April 1991, 150 East German firms had already been allowed to use the seal of approval of the German Central Agricultural Marketing Association (CMA) on their products" (Sinn and Sinn 1993, p. 97).

A look at branded products from the East in retrospect shows that these went hand-in-hand with the self-confidence of the East Germans. These were interdependent and supported each other. While in June 1990 66 percent of East Germans felt themselves primarily to be Germans and only 28 percent as GDR citizens, the trend turned around in 1992. "The percentage of those who primarily identify themselves as East Germans has fluctuated since then until the present time between 60 and 80 percent" (Ahbe 2005, p. 281).

Use of home advantage

The product advertising that reflects this self-confidence would be worthy of a separate survey. The "Hurra, I'm still alive" on the advertising posters for East German Club-Cola in 1992 hit a nerve with the consumers in the East. Did the "I" refer to the product or the consumer himself? The ideal goal of a marketing specialist had been achieved, commented an observer, "product history and personal biography could no longer be kept apart." Memories of the post-war period were aroused, with banners at demonstrations bearing the words "Hurra, we're still alive." Later, this also became the title of a novel by best-selling author Johannes Mario Simmel (Lay 1997).

The advertising for Club Cola, as well as for Burger crispbread ("Ein knackiges Stück Heimat" – "A crunchy piece of home") or Kathi baking mixes ("The East has chosen: Kathi"), proves that people had learned to use the „home advantage," that is, the familiarity and earlier fondness for the brands. It even applied to products whose origins were not apparent. "What are the reasons for filling up with gas at MINOL?" ran the advertiser's copy in a newspaper ad for the East German chain of gas stations, with the answer: "Several. You can find us almost everywhere, we are the East German champions of modernization and we speak the language of our customers. We come from here" (Minol Advertising 1993).

Since 1996, North Rhine-Westphalia spirits company, in cooperation with an East German bottler, has achieved an unexpectedly high turnover by selling sometimes up to 1.2 million bottles monthly liqueur "Erichs Rache" (Erich's Revenge) in the new Federal Länder. The bottles, which all carry the portrait of Honecker, are available in such flavors as "DDR" ("Der Deutsche Rachenputzer" – "The German Stomach Cleanser"), "SED" ("Spirituosen-Einheitsdrink" – "Spirit of Unity Drink"), "FDJ" ("Fruchtiger denn je" – "Fruitier than Ever") and "LPG"[113] ("Leckeres Proletarier-Gesöff" – "Tasty Proletarian Slush") (Anderer 1997).

Under the heading "Typically East German," the German magazine *Wirtschaftswoche* addressed the issue of "How companies from the West with traditional East German brands profit from GDR nostalgia." There are numerous examples of companies clearly indicating their East German origins and referring to these in their advertising. "In the East, the brand is strong and strengths must be strengthened," says one manager. Overcoming the low level of awareness in the west from case to case would be too expensive, so strengthen the focus on PR specifically aimed at the East (Wie Konzerne ... 2003). The US tobacco group Philip Morris, which took over the Vereinigte Zigarettenfabriken Dresden, with the GDR brands of F6, Karo and Juwel, directly after the Turnaround, also adopts one of its own advertising slogans for Marlboro "Test the West" in this context, one of the first advertising posters in East Germany that reflected the prevailing atmosphere of the time. Now the slogan has become "I smoke Juwel because I already tested the West. Juwel. One for us." In the West, such advertising would be an obstacle to sales. This is particularly fitting in the case

---

[113] Really the official acronyms for *Deutsche Demokratische Republik (German Democratic Republic)*, *Sozialistische Einheitspartei Deutschlands (Socialist Unity Party of Germany)*, *Freie Deutsche Jugend (Free German Youth)* and *Landwirtschaftliche Produktionsgenossenschaft (Agricultural Cooperative)*.

of the rebellious slogans for the other brands, as social scientist Thomas Ahbe finds: "In the GDR, *Karo* was regarded as the cigarette of the maladjusted, the intellectuals and artists. They prolonged their image using the slogan 'Attack on the taste of unity!' The East German cigarette *Cabinet* presented itself as 'unadulterated and unperfumed,' thereby addressing the East German stereotype of the false, highly polished and perfumed West Germans" (Ahbe 2005, p. 278).

Typical Western lifestyle exaggerations and status symbols hardly work in the East, while rational purchase arguments work all the better. "When I see the housewives in West German ads with their polished fingernails, it makes me shudder," says the East German marketing expert who created the commercial for Club Cola together with a colleague. Whoever is familiar with East German sensitivities and does not confuse the slogan of the East German Monday demonstrations, "We are one people" with "We are all Westerners" has a genuine chance of selling in the East (Dolmetscher der Träume 1999).

For Ahbe, Ostalgia is self-empowerment, contributing to the productive stabilization of East German identity (Ahbe 1997, p. 614). This often occurs with humor and satire. Particularly in the first few years after the Turnaround, Ostalgia helped East German consumers in their return to products, which producers sometimes believed had been lost or had already given up for lost. The unexpected push in demand was, from an economic perspective, a saving anchor for tens of thousands of jobs. In the time of the introduction of a market economy without a market, as Treuhand President Breuel called it[114], this signal of encouragement was of particular value. Most East Germans could unite around this. Accusing them of wanting a resurrection of the GDR seemed singularly tragicomical and misplaced. Foaming, perverse reactions to Ostalgia only reinforced this. As political zealots were still fine-tuning their treatises and weaving their counter-campaigns against Ostalgia, the market had long recognized and used their potential.

---

114 See Chapter 3, p. 63.

Thematization of the East

Two movies contribute to an all-German curiosity regarding the phenomenon of Ostalgia, without detracting from it. Both of them are bold enough to permit a generally more relaxed view of life in the GDR that nonetheless does not deny the ever-present themes of the Berlin Wall and Stasi. The creation of a "cheerful, self-ironic communication between East and West" is how East German theater director Leander Haußmann explains his "Sonnenallee" project that was begun in 1997. In the industry, it initially met with "bitter shaking of heads": "They said that nobody wants to see films about the East." "The East stinks," is what he is told. But after the amazing success of *Sonnenallee* (1999)[115], including in the west "the Ossi theme suddenly seemed to be of commercial interest" (Haußmann 2003).

The amount of interest is demonstrated in 2003 by more than six million German cinemagoers who see the, also internationally, highly successful movie *Good Bye, Lenin!* by West German director Wolfgang Becker, with the screenplay by Bergisch-Gladbacher Bernd Lichtenberg. It is basically a family story surrounding life lies, love and differing perceptions of reality, only this takes place in a 79-square-meter prefabricated GDR apartment. The protagonist tries to protect his Party-faithful mother, who has had a heart attack and has recently come out of a coma, from the shock of the news of the fall of the Berlin Wall which she has "slept through" by bringing real existing socialism back to life. The story is told with a fine sense of the various methods of comic acting and is full of factors that can be recognized and identified by both East and West Germans – and by foreigners observing German unification. This explains its success. It is highly unfair to continually connect the film in retrospect only with one of its episodes, namely the hunt by the film's hero in June 1990 for an East German product that is simply no longer to be found: Spreewald gherkins.

This is partly related to a deliberate phenomenon in literature of meticulously including East German product and brand names in fictitious and documentary texts about the GDR and to present them almost exclusively in a positive light.[116] For whatever reasons this happens, the tendency that has been

---

[115] Screenplay: Thomas Brussig and Leander Haußmann. In the same year, Brussig published his novel "Am kürzeren Ende der Sonnenallee," Berlin: Volk und Welt.

[116] Cf. Grub, ‚Ostalgie' und Ostprodukte, pp. 563-573. Quite justifiably, Grub indicates that this tendency is unusual. His critique of one novel is: "The composition of dishes is designed to its own ends, especially considering that, in literary texts, brand names are not usually specified when candy or puddings are being eaten" (Grub 2003, p. 564).

sustained from 1990 to the present day emphasizes the importance of those East German products that represent identity. Sometimes they seem almost to be invoked with magic. "The past becomes an enormous supermarket and consumer museum, in which the collective memory seems at least to be better cared for than in any official memorial" (Banchelli 2008, p. 67). It banishes the weighty feeling that German unification was essentially driven by others and not themselves. Even such an author as Uwe Tellkamp, who denounces Ostalgia as the "sweet sickness of yesterday" in his novel "Der Turm" (2008), indulges in accurately presented product descriptions.

Secondly, the featured Spreewald gherkins make it clear that the effect of *Good Bye, Lenin!* reinforced or initiated independent and sudden trends, which the filmmakers had never guessed or intended. Accordingly, immediately after the premiere, the business of daily Trabi safaris in Berlin exceeded "the wildest expectations" of its Dresden-based owner, who said that he really should transfer money for the marketing effort to the makers of "Good Bye, Lenin!" (Neue Ostalgie-Welle rollt 2003). The prefabricated apartment in the film, a construction in the movie factory at Berlin-Adlershof, became "Germany's best-known living room" and could subsequently be rented for EUR 250 per night. "Perfect for an Ostalgia party," wrote *Bild*. A week in a people's police uniform was available for EUR 55 (Sylvester 2003).

Commercialized Ostalgia

There was no more doubt: Ostalgia itself had mutated into a brand item. As such, it suddenly gained a market value that was no longer concealed even from the television media. In autumn 2003, public service television and private television competed to have the best GDR show.[117] Before and after, the German supplements competed to have the most credible and witty interpretation of this unexpected phenomenon.

With the advent of these GDR shows, the time was over at last, when dogs

---

[117] *Die DDR Show* (RTL), *Meyer und Schulz – Die ultimative Ost-Show* (SAT 1), *Die Ostalgie-Show* (ZDF), *Ein Kessel DDR* (MDR).

appeared more frequently on television than East Germans, as one of the numerous media analyses found.[118] Had sufficient justice been done?

Doubt may be cast on this. The Stern reporter Holger Witzel from Leipzig wrote: "Anyone watching television nowadays acquires a tinted view of the GDR in a manner in which, plain and simply, not even GDR television would have dared (...). The 'real life' in the East was of no interest to anyone before and the situation is no different today. (...). The evil GDR is boring. Other aspects are now coming to the fore, 'the nice memories,' (...). The real cheek is the approach with which 'the real life over there' is discovered. Suddenly, after 13 years, it is admitted that the Ossis did not spend every day spying on each other, but did in fact laugh, love and somehow managed to survive in a humane manner. This is the height of arrogance. If possible, they should also be thankful for this. (...) It is like in the theater: After tragedy comes comedy, and ultimately, farce."

Sarcastically, Witzel describes the potential effect of the GDR shows on viewers in the West: "Take a look here at the people in the Zone: Did they actually have something like an everyday life, sometimes even something to laugh about? Listened to the radio and spun dry their washing (both electrical), bravely ate their own chocolate (...), enjoyed naturism and the Young Pioneers, doing voluntary work and in their collectives. To this day, they still feed themselves on pickled gherkins and sweet sparkling wine, but nonetheless they had a happy childhood. Who would have thought it? (...) Hats off to them!" (Witzel 2003).

A similar view was expressed in "Das Magazin," which stated: "The mummy has now been released" (Ach, wie niedlich 2003). Leander Haußmann regarded it as "monotonous," "the way in which the East German zombies led themselves by the nose ring through the TV arena and were applauded for it" (Haußmann 2003).

The reactions in the west were in a similar vein: "The Ostalgia surrounding 'Good Bye, Lenin!' doesn't please everyone. It is mainly 'young bankers, Web designers and advertising people from the West,' who go to the cinema in blue FDJ shirts, the 'Frankfurter Rundschau' writes. 'The Zone is cool. The West

---

[118] Cf. Thüringen Study by the Hamburg Bredow Institute and the University of Leipzig, Leipzig 1999. Quoted from Mühlberg 2001.

snuggles up to the dictatorship of the proletariat'" (Neue Ostalgie-Welle rollt, 2003). Even the "ugly training jackets of the National People's Army" sold in the west like hot cakes, while they remained hanging "like lead in the East." "Nobody who had ever been forced to wear this jacket would put it on again voluntarily (...), only a Westerner like Oliver Geissen of RTL could manage it" (Witzel 2003).

The Ostalgia that was alienated in the artificial media spotlight united Germany, East and West, in their rejection, at least in the supplements. In the service of commerce, Ostalgia was trivialized and turned into something banal. In this form, it was and is easier to stigmatize it.

But it would be biased only to see its negative and occasionally even repulsive side; the media spotlights also highlighted problems, one of which was the virtually nonexistent offering of East German products in the West. The media attention created demand, at least for some periods of time. Numerous West German companies established in the East used the forum of the GDR shows to advertise their products.

Unified but not united

A genuinely liberating aspect was the approach of young people in East and West to the devotional items of the wild East that were now growing in popularity. The ideological burden weighing on them from both sides, the back-and-forth of the offensiveness of one side against the insulting of the other on the golden scales of political correctness seemed to have been banished at last. However, this kind of lax adoption of the symbols of the past was also not fine enough for the magazine. But on at least two occasions, it gained attention: "Whatever the young people of today do in colorful FDJ Group jackets or Präsent-20 suits, whatever makes them put on little Mielke hats on hip-hopper heads or Boxer jeans on their behinds, is free of all deep ideological meaning. In their perception, the GDR state mutated long ago into a general artwork. (...) Their approach to the GDR follows the old principle of negation of negation. Freely from Hegel to Marx, things are happily pulled out of the VEB hat that can guarantee coolness here and now on MTV and VIVA" (Ach, wie niedlich 2003).

But it is only true for those born later. Ten years after German unification, scientific cultural research finds distinct differences in essentially all areas of life between East and West Germans and these exceed the findings of psychologists and sociologists immediately after the Turnaround. The differences comprise eating habits, sexual behavior, money management, daily routines and the rhythm of these routines, the relationship with one's own body, the type of self-expression, garden arrangement and apartment interior design, party preferences and election behavior (cf. Mühlberg 2001). Also added to this list could be East-West differences in matters of equality, working mothers and the approach to work in the home, the role of confession and preferences in choice and use of media that deviated from each other.

Today, 20 years after the fall of the Berlin Wall, these differences remain. With those born in 1990, there is a generation coming up that has no authentic experience of GDR character. Ostalgia with ideological traits is not a subject that affected them, nor will it ever be. An estimated minimum of one third of these young adults have turned their backs on their homeland and seek perspectives in West Germany or abroad. However, they are also impacted by the socioeconomic conditions, particularly those remaining in Eastern Germany. Also here, in the East German provinces and the few urban centers, what belongs together has grown together. Leading Social Democratic politician and cultural academic Wolfgang Thierse states: "After the rapid adaptation of the East to the West proved to be an illusion, the following can be said: Whoever remains will not do it without one or the other form of identification with East Germany. If migration, resignation or muted reaction are not to become the characteristic signs of Eastern Germany, if a lack of perspective and fear of the future are not to continue alternating and social instability in many regions is not to remain a basis for right-wing radicalism, politics must do more to promote a feeling of self-confidence, belonging and identity" (Thierse 2001).

This applies today more than ever. From the demonization of East German identity through the politics and tolerance of East German culture, only in museum form if at all, the politically motivated assignment has become that of promoting an East German identity – a late insight, which opens up a broad perspective through one-sided West German conditions.

Case Study: Halloren - Taking Ostalgia to the stock market

Germany's oldest chocolate factory uses tradition and region as its platform for the world market

At the time of its foundation in 1804, the *Halloren Schokoladenfabrik AG* in Halle an der Saale was a honey cake bakery with cocoa products. The *Mignon* filled chocolates created in 1880 eventually made the firm - *David & Söhne* at the time - famous throughout Germany and this was later reflected in the name *Mignon Schokoladenwerke*. The latter is the name given to the business after 1933 under the Nazi regime, which removes the Jewish-sounding family name. Chocolate production ends four years after the start of the war. From 1943, the company serves as a subsidiary department of an aircraft works. It produces parts for aircraft wings.

The maker of one of the best-loved filled chocolates in Germany becomes a supplier of aircraft parts – it could not be worse. In the GDR's economy of scarcity, the company, which was nationalized in 1950, organized under the *Kombinat Süßwaren (confectionary combine of companies)* and assigned the name *Halloren* from 1952. It produces "Bückwaren," literally "bending goods." This was what they called the products that were in demand and always in short supply, and which the sales assistants kept under the table for good customers, for which they and quite often the customers had to "bend down" to get.[119]

After the fall of the Berlin Wall, hardly any customers bothered about Halloren products any more. Interests lay in what sort of chocolate the West could offer, now that it could be tested personally. Chocolate was one of the most popular products in packages sent by relatives in the West and in the *Intershop*.[120]

---

[119] In popular parlance, these products were known as "FDGB": *Für die guten Bekannten ("for good acquaintances")*. FDGB was actually the acronym for GDR's united trade union confederation, *Freier Deutscher Gewerkschaftsbund*.

[120] State trading organization founded in the GDR in 1962 with the aim of generating freely convertible currency. Most of the products only available against payment in hard currency were manufactured in the GDR for Western companies. The ban on GDR citizens owning Western money was removed by the Council of Ministers in 1974. However, from 1979, GDR citizens were not permitted to pay in the Intershop using Western money, but had to convert the money to Forum checks in the State Bank of the GDR. The Intershops and the Geschenkdienst- und Kleinexporte GmbH (*Genex*) created a two-class society in the GDR and enabled price-quality comparisons with the usual offering in the GDR retail sector.

"Just imagine," says Marketing Manager Tino Müller, "for almost 40 years, these quality products enjoy a special status as goods in scarce supply and from virtually one day to the next, they have to compete with a gigantic confectionary market, in which the East Germans want to try something new and the West Germans don't know us." About the period between 1990 and 1992, mind-boggling stories circulate. Among the more than 800 employees, euphoria quickly gives way to concerns about their jobs and the production process never comes to a standstill. The Treuhand Agency offered this traditional business to several companies. However, interest in *Halloren* was extremely low and nobody recognized the brand potential. The initial years after unification were characterized by extensive actionism, aimed at not allowing the products from the GDR times to be assigned to history. Employees loaded our wares onto trucks and sold them in the new markets, straight from the truck.[121]

In 1992, Chartered Accountant Paul Morzynski from Hanover acquired the company from the Treuhand Agency and made a contractual commitment to retain 120 employees for at least four years and to invest DEM 13.5 M in the factory.[122] The agreed amounts are exceeded.

At the time of privatization, the social atmosphere in eastern Germany is quite different compared with the time of the Turnaround. Now, in 1992, most consumers know the consequences of turning their backs on their own quality products: company closures and lost jobs. At the same time there is a longing for products that belonged to the GDR period and provide a sense of custom, confidence and identity. In GDR times, gaining access to these products was often difficult; it was as if the effort associated with getting them also increased their value. Now, in times of forced adaptation to unaccustomed power and market structures, the absence of these products is felt as one of the numerous losses.

The logical decision by the Halloren company management is: The original production shall be maintained and the range shall be extended in a marketable manner.

It is a decision for which there is no time to be lost in implementation and the risk associated with the company's outmoded and fault-prone production

---

[121] Author's discussions with Tino Müller in Halle/Saale on April 20, 2007.
[122] Westdeutschland ist für Halloren noch ein unbekanntes Land. *Frankfurter Allgemeine Zeitung*, October 22, 2004.

facilities has to be taken into the bargain. The decision is based on the assumed return of East German consumers to the quality and brand products that they know.

At the core of these measures is the *Original Halloren Kugel (Original Halloren Kugel globes)*. These were created in 1952 and were the company's best-loved product during GDR times. They are as well-known in East Germany as Haribo in the West. The name is established regionally. Halloren are a brotherhood comprising the descendents of the medieval and early modern-age salters, to whom Halle an der Saale owed its wealth at the time. The globes are supposedly a reminder of the buttons on the clothes that are still worn today on festive occasions by the 50 Halloren.

In the Halloren Kugel globes, initially only sold in the East, the company's most important product from the GDR time survived, and together with it, the entire company. In 1995, the *Halloren Schokoladenfabrik GmbH* puts into operation the most modern production line in Europe, in terms of chocolate products, for the "Original Halloren Kugeln." "The globes," as connoisseurs and company employees call them, gain the same cult status in Eastern Germany as the Spreewald gherkins, F6 cigarettes, Bautzner mustard and Rotkäppchen sparkling wine. In conjunction with the company's 200th anniversary in 2004, four confectioners devoted six months of free time to working on the largest and, at 200 kg, heaviest Halloren Kugel in the world in accordance with the original recipe.[123] As part of the *Schokoladenwelten* ("chocolate worlds") exhibition, it is displayed in 35 selected cities in eastern and western Germany between 2004 and 2008. In 2009, the company has an offering of 14 different kinds of Halloren Kugeln, comprising the classic made of the same high-quality ingredients as in GDR times and innovative types.

In 1998, the Halle company expands its range, including the reintroduction of another once successful Eastern brand. Success is secured through the adaptation shortly afterwards to three-shift operation, which was normal under GDR conditions.

During our visit to the company in April 2007, the first thing that catches our eye is the bright red and blue Trabant in front of the company building. In the factory shop, we acquire 10 cm, silver foil-wrapped GDR Marks made of milk

---

[123] Sie ist nicht zu übersehen: Die größte Hallorenkugel der Welt. *Volksstimme* Magdeburg, May 24, 2007.

chocolate, with a reverse that carries the GDR national emblem. On the company website, there is a link to the useful mail order service for East German products, offering not only condoms with the motto of the GDR Pioneers, "Be prepared, always prepared," but also Halloren Kugeln globes and other products from the Halloren Schokoladenfabrik. "Does Ostalgia promote sales?" is the question we put to Tino Müller.

"Definitely. There have been two waves of Ostalgia. Naturally, the first emerged in the chaos after the Turnaround, when everything from GDR times seemed to be no longer of any value and people wondered if this could be true. The second wave, an artificial one, was created in West German TV studios when there was a desire to hear something other than Stasi and wall-building in relation to the GDR. We have made use of both waves, like most other former East German companies. In a time when we had neither money for PR or other investments, we were in the pleasant position that people missed products that we were able to offer. Suddenly we were once again loyal to each other, but it was only possible because it was a matter of quality products. If they had been anything else, we would have been hopelessly lost. The second wave confirmed and accelerated all of this once again, with West Germans becoming aware of East German products. In 2004, we also decided to produce a new version of the collapsible boxes from the 50s, 70s and 90s, which were well-received by consumers because they served as a reminder of old times."

However, *Halloren's* market strategy is by no means aimed exclusively at the market in eastern Germany. Müller specifies the sales figures to the East as 70 percent and those in the West as 25 percent. Today, in 2009, the latter has grown to more than 30 percent.[124] This is a success, considering the Western proportion was only 4 percent in the year 2000. Five percent, with a rising trend, is exported to the US, Scandinavia, France, Spain, Italy, the Czech Republic, Slovakia, Austria, Hungary, Japan and Israel.

Halloren's East German image is not always helpful in the West. Even nearly two decades after German unity, old prejudices are an obstacle. "The brand's blessing of having its roots here is also its curse," says Halloren President Klaus Lellé, who originally comes from the Palatinate.[125]

---

[124] Halloren setzt auf Mövenpick. Schokoladenfabrik strebt ins Premiumgeschäft. *Frankfurter Allgemeine Zeitung*, April 4, 2008.
[125] Starke Marke. *Frankfurter Allgemeine Zeitung*, October 13, 2006.

The strategy of at last becoming known in the West has to be achieved without company-financed, cost-intensive media advertising. "Ferrero or Storck spend EUR 20-30 M for a new product," says Lellé. "That corresponds to our sales for a year."[126] Instead, smaller firms known in their respective regions of West Germany were sought, whose products suited Halloren. In 2001, the *Confiserie Dreher GmbH* in Bad Reichenhall (Bavaria) was acquired and production was relocated to Halle. The takeover was primarily related to the best-known Dreher product, the Mozart Kugel globe, a product related to the Hallorenkugel globe. "This was a door-opener to the shelves in the West," says Lellé.[127] Through the recognition of the Mozart Kugeln in the West, the Halloren Chocolate Factory succeeds in making the long-awaited introduction of its entire product range to such major food chains as Edeka, Rewe and Kaufland. Two years later, the integration of small West German producers is continued with the acquisition of *Confiserie Chocolaterie Weibler GmbH* in Cremlingen, near Braunschweig. In 2004, in order to generate capital for further purchases and investments, Halloren issues 10,000 bearer bonds with a nominal price of EUR 1,000 Euro for private investors, with an interest rate of 7 percent and a duration of five years.[128]

With its entry on the Frankfurt Securities Exchange on May 11, 2007, the medium-size company secures additional capital of approximately EUR 12 M, while old shareholders receive a good EUR 5 M. Through this issue, it is intended that awareness in West Germany should grow, to increase sales there and pave the way for further acquisitions.[129] In 2008, the sales of the company, now transformed from a limited liability company to the *Halloren Schokoladenfabrik AG* (public limited company) and employing 460 people, rose to EUR 38 M from EUR 30.5 M in the preceding year. The main product, the Halloren Kugel globes, contributed to this success, but so did the focus on high-class pastry products. The takeover of the Saxonian Delitzsch production facility also made a positive contribution to business. This company was acquired in insolvency in the autumn of 2008.[130]

---

[126] Ibid.
[127] Westdeutschland ist für Halloren noch ein unbekanntes Land. Ibid.
[128] Ibid.
[129] Halloren-Aktien kosten zum Börsenstart 7 Euro. *Frankfurter Allgemeine Zeitung*, May 11, 2007.
[130] Halloren 2008 mit Rekordumsatz, *Volksstimme* Magdeburg, February 2, 2009.

A particular success factor is the license acquired from Swiss fine food producer Mövenpick, allowing pastry products to be produced in its name, a cooperative practice already established earlier with the Munich fine food producer Käfer. This means that, in addition to offerings in the lower and middle price segments, there are also products in the upper range, corresponding to the trend in the confectionary industry. The pastry goods achieve higher margins, which is why the business wants to grow particularly strongly in this area, according to Lellé.[131]

Furthermore, Halloren also produces for other retail brands in the West and takes this route to the major discount stores. "Halloren is also included, where it is not stated on the packaging," is the jokey factory version of a Nutella slogan.[132]

Despite price increases in the raw materials market, Halloren anticipates double-digit growth in 2009. Sales of EUR 54 M are planned. In terms of profits, the aim is to maintain pre-tax earnings of EUR 2,3 M.[133]

What is the secret behind the success of the *Halloren Chocolate Factory* after the fall of the Berlin Wall? In his reply, Tino Müller continuously returns to regional establishment. The company knows its local customers and ensures in all possible ways that the customers get to know the company. For this purpose, there is the Chocolate Museum, founded in 2002 and lovingly created and extended at the time. It is housed in the company's own traditional building, which has been the domicile since 1896. But also part of this is the local press in the building opposite, who "always want to know if we have any news and we are only too happy to keep them informed."

The company is interwoven with the history and culture of the region through many visible and invisible threads. A large portion of its innovation is taken from regional tradition: The *Mignon Mozart Kugel* globes were the basis for a complete product range, which the company's own traditional brand *Mignon* was once again brought to life. Two exclusive Halloren Cafés in the center of the city of Halle carry on the coffee-house tradition of the David family owners from the 1920s. Individual products and product series emerge through coop-

---

[131] Halloren setzt auf Mövenpick, ibid.
[132] Starke Marke, ibid.
[133] Halloren hat große Pläne. *Tagesspiegel*, Berlin, June 25, 2009.

eration with regional winegrowers associations and beer breweries. These are only three examples that are evidence of a proven concept.

Even the currently trendy event culture, which almost no company in the industry can avoid, is a tradition-related activity for the Halloren. This is not necessarily the case with the largest chocolate cuckoo clock in the world, but it is so with the largest Cat's Tongue in the world, made for the company's 200th anniversary and included in the Guinness Book of World Records. In the same year, the "Chocolate Room" was created in the museum, an artistic Biedermeier drawing room, consisting mainly of chocolate and marzipan, creating a link with the period of the company's foundation.

Its regional involvement makes the business distinctive and lends it established roots. One result of this is customer loyalty and a fabulous degree of recognition in the East of 98 percent[134], but also "an almost zero turnover" in its own business, as Müller explains. "There are employees who have been loyal to us for 40 years." In this regard, he also mentions continuity, as demonstrated by Klaus Lellé, who has been President since 1997. The chaotic Turnaround and post-Turnaround periods are now history.

From Halloren it can be learned how a chocolate producer disseminates product-related identification and communications messages that are now also accepted outside its home region. The name of the travelling exhibition mentioned earlier, *Schokoladenwelten* ("chocolate worlds") is thus also fitting.

---

[134] Starke Marke, ibid.

7. Attractive product design: Opportunities and obstacles

This text discusses the various challenges and opportunities faced by small and large design companies in global competition. The challenges imply that the design company's ability to understand and sense different cultures, both outwards in the marketplace and inwards in the organization, is crucial to success. A designer's education should be both broad and interdisciplinary, in preparation for leading and strategic positions in the company. The second best choice for this task is a broadly trained manager, skilled in both design matters and technical engineering in addition to business administration.

Is design management necessary?

Design has become a management concern, giving rise to the field of design management, in which design refers to visual design, aesthetic concept, and lifestyle and event design as described in Pine and Gilmore (1999). Roughly speaking, design management concerns the use of design as a competitive tool when developing new products. Researchers regard design as a strategic resource for company success, a resource that should be consciously integrated by management when researching and developing new products (Svengren 1995; Bruce and Cooper 2000; von Stamm 2004). Design management also highlights marketing-related factors, for example, how the production and marketing of aesthetic design are successfully harmonized and synchronized from the very start of the production process (Borja de Mozota, 2003). Design-related questions, raised by the company's designer staff, are nowadays often taken seriously, though why this is so is a matter of discussion. Traditional design management discourse suggests that design adds value that is crucial to company leadership in an established marketplace. This is especially important when the company cannot beat its competitors using price as a tool. Therefore, to succeed in adding value specifically by design, design management is necessary.

The design value of products is becoming increasingly important in the global market (Bruce and Cooper 1997; Bruce and Bessant 2002), making design management the centre of attention. One obvious conclusion is that globalization challenges both the practical and theoretical aspects of design management, especially concerning "obvious" cultural differences.

Bruce, Daly, and Kahn (2007) suggest that preparing for and managing the global product launch process offers unique challenges, as each targeted country can display unique differences among design categories, for example, different country mores, languages and colloquialisms, and technology infrastructure. A healthy balance between a customized and standardized approach must be found when globally launching a designed product. The authors conclude that the greater the differences between the above-mentioned four design categories, the more customization is needed for each global region, which means that companies active in the global market must rethink and adapt their design management. Bruce, Daly, and Kahn (2007) further argue that managers responsible for global product launches should co-operate with the owners, distributors, and retailers of currently popular brands to gain competitive advantages in local markets. Thus the availability and capability of local trade partners within each global region must be considered. Distribution channel owners should have a role in determining the launch time, in certain design matters (e.g., colour and form), logistics, and Internet presence. Furthermore, these authors believe that successful product launching in a particular global region depends on a company's ability to understand the key issues in local cultures and how to respond to them.

Recent research has discussed productive ways executives can manage design when launching a product in a market in another culture. However, when it comes to identifying, understanding, and handling a local market's particular characteristics, a designer's role should be developed in order to frame the conditions for design management.

The designer's role when competing globally

According to Simon (1981), a design-centred product has a particular character as an intentional human artefact. This intentional factor is closely connected to what Weick (2001) describes as "sense-making". Latour's translation model (Latour 1998) considers sense spreading as lying in the hands of human beings, every one of whom can behave differently. According to his actor–network theory (ANT), human intention and "sense-making" are crucial to determining whether or not a product is saleable in the market. The market and its local culture can be seen as a "nonhuman actor" and the designer as a "human actor". Consequently, the local adaptation of a designed product is optimal when the designer is included in the local actor network, and, in some senses, lets the artefacts develop when people meet and interact, people being the "nodes" in the network. At the same time, it seems that certain elements of a global product launch can be standardized for efficiency purposes. That is why it is often inefficient for a globally active company to let the designer be part of one specific region's actor network.

It is more efficient is to identify, understand, and handle the distinguishing characteristics of various local markets. The company must create a local meaning in a given region using a visual, aesthetic language: The intentional factor is appreciated by the local market if it is regarded as meaningful in the local context. As the designer is most familiar with the company's genuine form language, a conclusion is that a market launch is considered more likely to be productive when it is customized by the designer. Nevertheless, as designed products are intentional artefacts, a customized product launch cannot build a bridge over cultural obstacles, but only act as a well-functioning local complement.

As discussed above, intentionally creating a human product takes competence and skill, which are often possessed by professional designers. This means that design management should give professional designers adequate influence throughout the process of developing a new product. Furthermore, the importance of a designer's influence is heavily emphasized by global competition in many culturally distinct markets. However, a hierarchical management structure, especially in larger firms, often complicates the efforts of design staff. Inherent creative capacity is therefore never used as a resource, and never becomes a tool for a competitive advantage. On the contrary, the creative strength that comes with design is often regarded as a risk that is better avoided (von Stamm 2004). Thus, design management has organizational implications in the sense of how and whether management decides to integrate design into the overall company culture (Svengren 1995; Hakatie and Ryynänen 2007). According to Svengren (1995), management and the board of directors have the main responsibility for design matters and must guarantee that they are prioritized. Ways of guaranteeing this are to include a company designer in the board, or to train designers for management positions.

Even if the company does not give its designers strategic responsibility, the company still needs designers who, besides their design skills, have expertise in brand management and strategy formulation, as emphasized by Borja de Mozota (2003). She argues that a lack of financial resources to hire staff designers with a wide range of professional skills, or high transaction costs in the company, has prompted the outsourcing of design at a conceptual or idea-management level. In that case, the consulted design firm creates the entire concept.

Even if design work is outsourced, the company's executive group must be more than theoretically committed to every design project. Furthermore, it is a mistake to think that the quality of industrial design services will necessarily be improved simply by switching agencies (Hakatie and Ryynänen 2007). It does not matter whether design is an internal function or outsourced, because companies that do not succeed in "breathing design" (Dumas and Mintzberg 1991) do not earn a healthy return on their investments. Such firms risk their long-term survival, according to Bruce and Cooper (1997) and Bruce and Bessant (2002). This is why the designer's role in global market competition is both intuitional (i.e., identifying and interpreting channel parameters, country mores, language and colloquialisms, and technology infrastructure) and strategic in nature. One conclusion follows from all this: Companies should understand the designer's crucial role. This implies that they ought to reconsider and improve their design management philosophy, to compete in the global market.

Designing services: Culture and business-size factors

In the service context, intangible goods such as experience are often in demand. Pine and Gilmore (1999) relate this to what they call the "experience economy". They identify the importance of designing the experience itself, and ensuring that it is presented properly. Experiences are consumed repeatedly whenever the consumer decides to remember something, for example, a day in a Walt Disney theme park. This implies that the experience as such should be perfect, because any failure cannot be erased from the consumers mind.

Consumer experience design is a research subject in the design management field. For example, one research question is how to guarantee positive aesthetic memories. Thus, experience design concerns connecting feelings to the product offered or the service bought. Pine and Gilmore (1999) argue that information technology provides but one way of "~ ing a thing", i.e., adding experience to a product.

Cultural factors are not the only challenges facing a company designing a product or service and competing in the global market. Rapidly changing environments, such as Internet-based services, are also major questions to be handled in theory and practice, according to Verganti and Buganza (2005). They consider it a shortcoming that existing literature focuses only on innovation processes in the development stage. It is not enough to be able to design a good service; they instead argue that a high degree of *service life-cycle flexibility* should be established and maintained. They define service life-cycle flexibility as:

… the capability of introducing incremental and radical innovations during the service life cycle (i.e., to adapt a service to contextual changes and opportunities after it has been first released onto the market) at low costs and in the shortest possible time. (Verganti and Buganza 2005)

According to these authors, service life-cycle flexibility is particularly important when it comes to environments where technology and market needs change rapidly. The authors identify five "inertia factors" determining the maturity stage of a product: (1) technological inertia, (2) internal organizational inertia, (3) external organizational inertia, (4) customer inertia (towards changes in the service package), and (5) customer inertia (towards changes in the service interaction design). Verganti and Buganza propose design practices that reduce these five inertias. Two conclusions can be drawn from the demand for service life-cycle flexibility. The first one calls for reconsideration and improvement of a company's design management philosophy. The second conclusion: as rapidly changing environments (e.g., Internet-based services) partly depend on cultural factors, the designer's role should not be underestimated when it comes to establishing and maintaining the company's service life-cycle flexibility.

The role of new product development (NPD) models in design management

Borja de Mozota (2003) claims that design management involves managing the product, the process, and the organization. In the context of global competition, product design is often complemented by service design. In the new product development (NPD) process, systematic design methods have come to be widely used. The stage-gate process has become a popular model for developing and introducing new products in the market.

As suggested above by Verganti and Buganza (2005), the effects of the inertia factors are reduced when it comes to mature services. In any case, service life-cycle flexibility largely depends on how a product-supporting service was designed in the first place. Thus, NPD as a stage-gate process is still useful in the context of global competition, where there is a demand for increased service life-cycle flexibility. Even so, recent research claims that the stage-gate process approach has its weaknesses. The cause for this is discussed below.

Questioning the stage-gate process

A stage-gate process is referred to as both a conceptual and an operational framework for taking new product projects from idea to launch and beyond. Its purpose is to manage the new product development (NPD), increasing its effectiveness and efficiency. The stage-gate process has been developed as a method for avoiding weak organizational action and management in creative teams, and offers a solution for projects lacking clear goals and planned structure. The stage-gate process was initially the result of research that modelled winning behaviour (Cooper 2004). Nowadays, Cooper (2008) claims that a traditional stage-gate process approach is far from sufficient for a design firm, as it applies only to part of the products and processes in NPD. Its most serious weakness is that it often leads to the over-bureaucratizing of the process, which in turn blocks creativity, despite its being neither a linear process nor a rigid system; that is why the stage-gate process approach has been reinvented by progressive firms. Traditionally closed approaches have therefore been abandoned, in favour of the open innovation model. Instead of just taking stock of their core competence and of business intelligence, progressive companies find that customer experience offers a rewarding appraisal of their business efforts. This relates to all three aspects of the innovation process (i.e., ideation, development, and commercialization). The stage-gate process has also been modified to accommodate open innovation.

Cooper (2008) stresses that this approach has reinvented NPD practice and created more value throughout the process. Obviously, the weakness of the stage-gate process is especially relevant to the creative flow. As discussed earlier, global competition and service life-cycle flexibility lead to increased creativity in the firm. Overcoming the shortcomings of the stage-gate process approach is crucial to design firms competing in a global market.

Leenders, van Engelen, and Kratzer (2007) suggest a modified approach for better communication when developing new products. According to them, improved communication leads to better efficiency and creative performance. One of their concerns is whether organizations can exert control and provide structure for NPD activities while encouraging and managing creative performance. They agree that any NPD project requires some level of creative effort and that genuine creativity is paramount, stressing the need for an approach that is planned, optimized, and verified. They argue that the effect of a systematic design methodology on NPD team creativity is mediated by its communication patterns. They propose that four principles be incorporated into modern design methodology: hierarchical decomposition, systematic variation, satisfaction, and discursiveness. These principles affect NPD communication by determining the establishment of subgroups, the frequency of communication, the level of agreement or disagreement within the team, and the level of communication centralization. Each of these four principles individually shapes NPD team creativity; nevertheless, all design principles work together and must be considered as an integrated whole, to manage creativity effectively.

Recent research, as referred to above, highlights essential factors in managing the organization in order to improve creativity. Still, global competition and shorter life cycles challenge management to improve the organization's approach to creativity in the sense of *who* ought to manage *what* in order to guarantee flexibility. Referring to earlier discussion, designers who have expertise in brand management, strategy formulation, and people management in addition to their professional ability should manage the organization. It is obvious that the shortcomings of systematic design methods used in NPD often originate from the fact that non-designer company management manages the design perspective.

Design-related problems for small and medium-sized enterprises

Few companies have sufficient resources to retain in-house designers, especially small and medium-sized enterprises. At the same time, they are forced to act in a competitive global market, with its demand for service life-cycle flexibility. This is obvious concerning big-sited companies. When it comes to SMEs, the problem remains, despite the fact that they often only can afford to outsource design.

Moultrie, Clarkson, and Probert (2007) agree on the importance of good design for company success. However, they believe it is apparent that despite strong evidence, design skills are often marginalized in small and medium-size enterprises (SMEs). They suggest that small companies use an audit tool, based on process maturity principles, which targets design-related activities in NPD. This tool encourages managers to pay greater attention to the design-related elements of NPD. The tool consists of action plans for improving future performance, and explicitly distinguishes between management- and design-related activities in NPD. Management awareness of the design-related elements within NPD is essential to the survival of small and medium-sized enterprises, even if the company has outsourced its design function, as is often the case.

The independent designer

When small or medium-sized business firms choose to outsource the design function, this brings in a partner, i.e., the independent designer. Small and medium-sized enterprises should carefully consider such outsourcing, due to their financial constraints. Looking at the situation the other way around, what is the situation of the independent designer? Jevnaker (2005) notes that specialist designers have emerged, offering a range of services to companies and other organizations still largely ignorant of design approaches and expertise and often unfamiliar with their qualifications. Her main concern is how dynamic capabilities in designing might be *enabled* in connection with companies when organized agents are working, often temporarily, with non-designers. She zooms in on *living–working relationships* between designers and organizational people to understand their interacting abilities and "lifeworlds" when trying to co-operate. She understands that, when creating new products for a company, designers and manufacturers operate in what she calls a "messy" world. Although this world is a highly creative environment, it often needs more structure, because every creative "mess" benefits from a stable basis. She concludes that if the division of responsibility between designer and manufacturer is clearer from the start of a process, and if there is mutual understanding of and respect for each party's core competence, new innovative products will reach the market more easily. This view has significance, not least for small or medium-size companies.

The important role of silent designers

Besides professional designers, there are *silent designers* who undertake many design activities, without being aware that their work is a part of a design process. They do not even look on themselves as designers. A technician helping develop the latest bicycle helmet, an operator in a service company, or a customer sales rep in the company's call centre are all good examples. It should be obvious that silent designers play a bigger role in a smaller company than in a worldwide enterprise. Gorb and Dumas (1987) claim that one cannot rely on professional and silent designers to spontaneously co-operate, without management, to achieve a common goal if the goal is to win in market competition. One condition for a successful design process is that different categories of "actors" with different rationales, including silent designers, be integrated in the NPD process (von Stamm 2004; Veryzer and Borja de Mozota 2005). One conclusion is that in global competition, with its need for service life-cycle flexibility and increased creativity, both NPD and design managers must rethink how best to integrate the various disciplines involved throughout the NPD process. Furthermore, they must facilitate communication across disciplinary boundaries. This includes not only explicit disciplines such as research and development (R&D), industrial design, engineering, marketing, and marketing research, but the implicit and fuzzy professional area of silent designers. The relationship between design and management is relevant to all areas of design (Sebastian 2005).

A different structure for design management: Methodology and application

According to Sebastian (2005), the structure shared by design and management has its shortcomings, and a new structure ought to be devised. Furthermore, these shortcomings concern inadequate approaches to design management. The main approach (discussed earlier in this text, i.e., managing the product, the process, and the organization) has several weaknesses. When managing a product, design is treated as a static entity, the value and execution of which are predefined – which is almost impossible in reality. When managing the process, there is no guarantee of good results, even though all work may be performed according to the directives. Furthermore, Sebastian stresses that it is a flaw in company management that design management is not involved in design activities as such.

Besides the above-noted weaknesses, Sebastian (2005) claims there are three obstacles to the successful study and practice of design management: (1) design management as a concept is new, (2) a firm scientific basis is lacking, and (3) existing approaches cannot perceive the core tasks of a designer. He points out that nearly all popular concepts of design management have been developed by people who do not design anything, for example, company executives, engineers, and scientists. This, he says, is perhaps why many designers are reluctant to accept design management as a field. It explains why he has sought common ground between design and management, and why he argues it is located between the actor, the action, and the setting. He concludes that the common ground arises from the fact that both management and designers choose methods for improving situations and human-made artefacts. An interface between those parties consists of a common vocabulary and a scientific paradigm. From there, he pleads for a new perspective, based on cognitive science, which is central to the science of design management. Sebastian considers that a socio–psychological approach to design management has great potential, since it increases designers' awareness of society's complex reality during and after the design process.

As the above discussion has shown, designers and non-designers in a firm must communicate, as do independent designers and their clients, or the creative process will be hampered or paralyzed. These conditions are valid, regardless of whether the company is small, medium, or large: in all cases, management must communicate with the in-house design team or the external design firm to foster creativity. The lack of a common language, arising from the actors' different rationalities, is often regarded as the core problem (e.g., von Stamm 2004). According to Sebastian (2005), on the other hand, the core problem lies in the inappropriately structured methodology and application of design management. One conclusion is that all these weaknesses together contribute to inefficiencies when developing a new product. Misunderstandings appear when partners with different professional backgrounds execute design projects together and there is a lack of appropriate methodology and of understanding of inertia factors. Furthermore, our discussion has highlighted how the design company's ability to recognize and understand different cultures, both externally in the marketplace and internally in the organization, is crucial to the success of small and large enterprises in the face of global competition. It also highlights that the main approach, like that of Borja de Mozota (2005), has been challenged by global competition and shorter product life cycles.

To overcome global competition and satisfy different market demands for service life-cycle flexibility, another serious matter must be targeted: the motivation of individual workers, i.e., personal commitment. If communication is difficult, if there is no guarantee of success – even though the production map has been strictly followed – there will be no motivation for the participants. The engagement will result in the participants performing a barely adequate job, according to given instructions: there will be no individual commitment to overcoming misunderstandings arising from different professional identities.

These insights highlight the necessity of seeking a new framework for design management. Design is not sufficient in itself: the *organization* of it also matters. An organization's structure and culture are crucial to its performance. It is not only the design process and the nature of the design problem that make a design unique, but the people who implement the process. Once design questions are taken seriously, *who* does the management matters, in addition to *how* the design is managed. As these matters determine creativity, they are crucial to any firm active in a global market and in markets that demand service life-cycle flexibility.

Seeking solutions beyond the existing power structure

Gorb and Dumas (1987), von Stamm (2004), Jevnaker (2005), Veryzer and Borja de Mozota (2005), and Sebastian (2005) have all identified a profound problem in traditional design management. When the discipline was developing, interdisciplinary matters were not emphasized; due to global competition and shorter product life cycles, however, the importance of interdisciplinary questions has grown. Though recent research often stresses the need for a paradigm shift in design management, authors such as those noted above have all sought solutions in the organization's *existing* power structure, even when discussing new approaches. Is that approach sufficient, or must a solution be sought beyond existing organizational power structures? One radical but unlikely change to the existing paradigm would be to appoint designers as managers, giving them full responsibility for the product, process, and organization. One appropriate step in that direction would be to broaden the education of designers, inculcating interdisciplinary awareness in them, making them capable of occupying leading and strategic positions in companies. Simultaneously, there is also a need for broadly trained managers who are skilled in design matters and technical engineering in addition to business administration. If, for example, a designer with technological/engineering and economic skills developed a marketable product, would not this offer the best chances of business success? Instead, under current conditions, work tends to proceed the other way round. Perhaps smaller companies, where the distance between management and the design team is shorter, could lead the way. That would almost certainly challenge the existing power structure in organizations.

Case study: Meissen - Survival by design management

Several design-related companies in the former East Germany have survived despite their past under a different market system. Meissener Porzellanmanufaktur has survived by building aesthetically attractive design into their tangible products, making their "East German" porcelain products marketable in western Germany. Their style of design is considered classic and enduring, and consumers who prefer Meissen's products do so because of their design.

By means of *Fingerspitzengefuehl* – intuitive flair – the company's designers have succeeded, and are still succeeding, in creating aesthetically pleasing and classic design. This allows consumers to respond both physically and psychologically (Houze 2002). Classic, enduring design attracts people, independently of a given zeitgeist, much as fine art does. The Meissen case proves that if design is well executed, it is marketable; moreover, if design is both well done and classic, it is marketable for many years. The company's core competence is its ability to create superior and timeless, aesthetically pleasing designed products, which guarantees long-term competitiveness.

Meissen was established in 1710. Its marketing manager is proud that Meissen design has survived several different market systems. German unification represents only one of many transformations in the company's business environment:

"Meissen started three hundred years ago[135]. Unification is one of the historical moments that the company has survived. It has resisted many other societal changes: the European Seven Years' War (1756–1763), the First World War, the Weimar Republic, the Monarchy, capitalism. After the Third Reich, at first there was a phase of finding oneself. Meissen was not threatened, because it was not a company to be deconstructed by the Russians." (W. Kolitsch, Oct. 01, 2007)

By means of its production, Meissen helps preserve a living artistic tradition. It has enormous experience in porcelain and in selecting materials. The Meissen style has spread from its origins in Meissen to worldwide fame. Compared with other companies, generation after generation of Meissen's workers have understood how to balance the preservation of aesthetic tradition with the development and innovation of aesthetic understanding. Meissen's position in both German and European culture has given it an overview of the unfolding of history, and helped it understand its place in it. The product range has grown over three hundred years. The Blue Onion from 1739 (Zwiebelmuster) is a classic and still available pattern, and the product range has developed especially in recent years. The "new" Wave pattern has only existed for ten years, but it has already become a classic part of the product range. Typical motifs have been kept, when decorating and forming the products:

"Artists have always played an essential role. In different periods, they have been more or less innovative. The artistic influence was less from the end of the eighteenth century to the start of the nineteenth century. At the end of the nineteenth century, there was a boom, when the bourgeoisie imitated and copied the aristocracy. Then demand decreased, when many other companies were founded, and others disappeared. At the beginning of the twentieth century, many important things happened: For instance, Jugendstil and Bauhaus arose. When looking back at the first half of the eighteenth century, names like Kaendler showed artistic potential. Such potential was then challenged and supported by Pfeiffer, Meissen's director from 1918 until 1933: He employed well-known artists, such as Scheurich and Esser." (W. Kolitsch, Oct. 01, 2007)

Good and timeless aesthetic values were and still are to some extent influ-

---

[135] Johann Friedrich Böttger experimented with gold making in the beginning of the 18th century, but instead he found the "white gold" i.e. porcelain. As a result the cradle of European porcelain is found in Meissen.

enced by an admiration of upper-class tastes, as described by Tollhagen-Åkerhielm (2003). Company management is completely conscious of the image of Meissen products, of their value as status symbols, and of the competitive advantage this gives them in the market. Management is also aware of changes in consumer tastes; for example, young couples now prefer to buy their own modern dishes, rather than regarding Meissen crockery as a valuable, high-status inheritance.

Marketing Director Wolfgang Kolitsch has been working at Meissen since 1995. Earlier, he was employed in another company in Saxony, where he observed the negative consequences of German unification. Those negative experiences differ greatly from what he has since experienced at Meissen:

"Unification as such was full of uncertainties. There was no consensus when looking at how things should be in East Germany. Today, we notice that many things have changed since the East Germany existed. So it's not too late to discuss how Meissen survived, the survival strategy, and how time has been managed." (071001)

As the economy was forced to adjust to new market conditions, former East German companies had to offer their goods in line with new and real market conditions. There were no artificial measures to cushion the adjustment. One result was a considerable rise in prices. As far as Meissen was concerned, the market could deal with that relatively well. Immediately after unification, it was apparent that Meissen products were being sold too cheap. The western market bought Meissen's entire high-quality production for effectively bargain prices during the GDR-era and immediately after the unification. If there had been market transparency in East German times, Meissen could easily have adjusted its prices to market levels. According to Kolitsch, being fenced off from the free market was Meissen's biggest problem.

Meissen had often been regarded as an exception among East German companies. It was one of a few companies with special permission to export 100% of their production to the non-socialist world. The company's exports had been administered by East Germany's foreign trade organization and not by Meissen itself. Before the unification, many customers from West Germany used to visit the company.

East German citizens were barred from contact with non-socialist foreign countries. Despite this, contacts of all kinds were established at industry exhibitions, at which the company's top artists and management represented the company. Therefore, Meissen's former export market, for example, mainly West

Germany, still existed immediately after unification, though the marketing attitude had to change. In contrast, another porcelain manufacturer, Freiburger Porzellanfabrik, lost its market in Eastern Europe overnight.

Before and up to unification, West Germany was Meissen's main customer purchasing 90% of its production, while other countries collectively bought only 10%. Many areas classified as foreign non-socialist countries (such as the Scandinavian countries) were never part of the Meissen market due to the price level. Immediately after unification, Meissen decided to handle sales itself, to exploit the possibility of making independent decisions. The sales field was completely new to the company and had to be organized because of prior neglect. This was carried out successfully and responsibly, and many market opportunities were identified and secured. In the former East Germany, Meissen's products had never actually been offered to the market, which raised the question of how to organize the market in the new Bundesländer. Meissen's goods could be offered at reasonable prices but should not be cheap. There had been a general sales contract with West Germany, which quite coincidentally expired in 1990. This meant that there was no obligation to continue producing and delivering at fixed and unrealistically low prices, simply to fulfil a prior contract.

Operations after unification

One sign of success and stability is that there have been few changes in management. In other former East German companies, there was chaos as management was renewed twice a year. Today, Meissen still retains the same management team it had at the time of privatization.

Management has had to deal with various difficulties since unification, for example, advisory meetings with management consultants, demanded by the single shareholder. However, Meissen management was quite sure of its competence. When confronting situations in which, so to speak, the question marks were larger than the exclamation marks, management was able to find the right direction quite fast. Important people have stayed on with the company, although there have been exceptions. Meissen had two managers in 1979. One of them had been appointed director general before German unification, the other one, the managing director, left Meissen to join the Frankfurt Ambiente in 1980. The Ambiente is an annual fair in Frankfurt that showcases the latest products and trends for the table, kitchen, housewares, gifts, and home decor. The sales director then officially became the managing director and led the company throughout the unification period; he was appointed full CEO after unification.

It is interesting to note how frequently design management has been implemented in the company's decision processes, in terms of explicit marketing strategies and organizational efforts. Most of Meissen's artists have been employed since the 1960s, developing their craftsmanship in house. As apprentices, they acquired basic professional competence, to which they added an education in industrial design and fine art painting. Because of this extensive in-house training, they developed an artistic vision and identity that is characteristic of Meissen[136].

Several new workers were recruited by the Meissen workshop when the general sales contract with the former West Germany expired. The sales and marketing unit engaged an Austrian who had earlier been connected to Meissen for over ten years. Overall, the hiring of western German workers has been so small as to be negligible. There has been great continuity among Meissen's staff, whose average age is 42 years, who have worked with Meissen for an average of 20 years, and who closely identify themselves with the company. All that is an asset to Meissen in terms of continuity of identity, but can hamper adaptation and innovation.

It is not easy to manoeuvre a ship loaded with heavy cargo. All Meissen's workers have long highly specialized, so their flexibility had to be improved. When there is less demand in one product area, Meissen tries to develop and expand its capacity in another. For example, if there is less demand for the "Tableware" line, Meissen can develop its capacity in the "Interior" or "Modern Art" ranges. If the demand for figurines declines, production capacity in the "Accessories" or "Editions" ranges can be expanded. Once an innovation has become established, it is usually good for company business.

The need for innovation has also meant production facilities have had to be updated several times. As mentioned earlier, the Meissen factory was first established at the end of the seventeen hundreds. It was substantially expanded

---

[136] Meissen is the only porcelain-manufacturer in the world, which has the staff and ability to recreate all the 180,000 items that have ever been produced by the company.

and modernized in the eighteen hundreds. This kept the factory innovative, and technical innovations were constantly assimilated and integrated. After unification, improvements were again made to the general technical infrastructure and condition of the factory building. The entire system of kilns for firing the porcelain was updated. The modernization of the heating system alone meant that only half the former workforce was now needed.

"As a former East German firm, we had to downsize when Germany was reunified in order to be efficient. We lost employees, primarily artists." (W. Kolitsch, Oct. 01, 2007)

German unification was just one of a long series of external changes that have influenced Meissen's production capacity over the years. Once difference this made, for example, was that workers now had the freedom to give notice and seek employment elsewhere. Some took advantage of the opportunity, and started working with Hoechst in Berlin, to raise their salary by a few Deutsche Marks. Some even started businesses of their own.[137]

However, it is not easy to succeed as an *independent* porcelain artist. It is the artist's performance in combination with Meissen's "crossed swords" logo that is fundamental and synergistic: The value of an artist's work sinks the day she/he decides to leave the company and produce independently. The symbiotic value of individual artists combined with the Meissen brand is considerable, and the company has seen many conflicts arising from the inherent strains of that relationship.

It was crucial to Meissen that re-privatization occurred quickly after German unification. The Treuhand agency quickly decided to return the company to the Freistaat ("free state", comparable to a federal state) of Sachsen. They saw that the person responsible at the Freistaat, Professor Biedenkopf (occupying a position comparable to that of governor), had a feeling for what Meissen porcelain represented: he understood there would always be a market demand for such goods. Other politicians also realized that Meissen designs were timeless and classic. Private investors from the West were interested in acquiring the

---

[137] The tradition of Meissen was so strong that after the unification authorities in the former capital Bonn re-introduced the profession »Manufakturporzellanmaler« (manufacturer porcelain painter). This was also important for trainees to get a proper diploma in the profession they had learned. Without a disploma, a professional license is not approved in Germany.

company, but they probably would have been unable to preserve Meissen as a cultural institution.

The re-privatization of Meissen in 1991 meant complete freedom to act and plan, which was important for knowing on what basis to establish the "new" company, the "Staatliche Porzellan-Manufaktur Meissen GmbH". To avoid governance interference, it was thought more suitable to organize Meissen as a limited liability company. In addition, ownership by shareholders allows management a relative high degree of independence. With the government as the only shareholder, profit was not emphasized; private shareholders, however, want to earn money, and in 17 years since privatization, the company's gross earnings were EUR 45–50 million.

Conclusions

This book examines the strategies East German companies have used to survive. What strategies helped them survive when their institutional context changed overnight? How did Meissen succeed in surviving the uncertainty and paralysis Treuhand created for most companies while political agendas shaped and delayed the privatization? What strategies helped Meissen survive when Germany was reunited and a market economy replaced the planned economy? The above discussion identifies ten factors that helped Meissen survive German unification: 1) its existing market, 2) immediate management action, 3) the expiry of the contract with the West in 1990, 4) clear-sighted management, 5) core competence, 6) workforce stability, 7) downsizing and rationalizing, 8) fast privatization, 9) management stability, and 10) flexibility. Flexibility particularly explains how Meissen survived German unification. Meissen had an advantage over many other companies because its privatization was allowed to occur quickly, due to sympathy for the cultural heritage it represented and to the realization that its designs were timeless and marketable classics. There was insight into the continued viability of the company's unique core competence, on which it could build its continued existence.

Notably, the company's culture, inherited from the East German period, was in many ways free of traditional hierarchy. Meissen has the same management today as before the Berlin Wall fell, and that this continuity has helped keep its spirit alive. It has fostered Meissen's creativity and facilitated communication between designers and management. Even in the East German period, management understood its limitations regarding the company's core competence, so designers naturally accompanied management to trade fairs and joined in meetings with customers. Meissen has a long organizational tradition of giving professional designers adequate influence throughout the product development and production processes. Meissen has evolved a management solution and power structure far superior to those commonly found in design-centred organizations. Meissen is a textbook case illustrating the perspective on design enterprises introduced earlier in the chapter.

The Meissen way of design management for global competition

The German market was very important to Meissen when the Berlin Wall fell. Since then, however, Meissen's market structure has changed, and now Germany and the global market each purchase 50% of Meissen's production. As well, German consumer behaviour has changed, illustrating another side of the market challenge, namely, radical changes in the distribution structure. The retail sector in Germany has changed dramatically, as the mid- and high-price market segments have shrunk drastically. Shopping malls, "gross markets", and soft discounters have replaced traditional shopping districts and small businesses. Due to weaker demand in its traditional market, Meissen has been forced to find alternatives. Since German consumers no longer spend as much money on expensive, luxury goods, Meissen has turned to the Asian market where such purchases have risen.

Today Japan is an important market. Because design is the company's strategic resource, and because Japanese culture differs from European culture, Meissen has adapted its strategies to Japanese market conditions. Experience and discussions with foreign retailers, agents, and sub-licensees have led to products being specially developed for and launched in Japan. The artistic core competence has been crucial to this, as customization is demanded for every design, though not for the raw materials. It is essential that the Meissen artists themselves find out what works and what does not through discussions with customers in specific local markets:

"Especially on the Asian market, it is important not to offer goods haphazardly. As tradition is important in Asia, one must learn about the market conditions before producing for it [i.e., the Asian market]." (W. Kolitsch, Oct. 01, 2007)

Meissen's design management is well aware of the company's design strengths and of the challenges of a global market. New customers are recruited at fairs and through personal contacts made by the designers. No matter what market or partner the company is producing for, Meissen's designs display a consistent and timeless style crucial to the company's design value and brand in the global market.

Design as a strategic resource has been consciously integrated into the R&D of new products, as described by von Stamm (2004). On one hand, we have Meissen's technology strategy, for example, embodied in modernizing and updating the production facilities, which has determined the innovation focus of Meissen's design. Furthermore, since the 1960s, Meissen has maintained its own in-house department for developing new artistic skills, forms, and decorative motifs. On the other hand, the firm has successfully marketed its classic designs through public relations efforts such as event marketing (as described by Borja de Mozota 2003). Meissen has carefully mined its wealth of history and experience, to guarantee that its current products match what is unique and characteristic in that rich experience.

One example of Meissen's stewardship of its historical heritage is the museum it owns and runs, which attracts some 350,000 visitors a year. Busses, crowded with cultural tourists from far and near, park outside the museum every day. Meissen's first museum was founded in 1915; nowadays, however, it is more of a theme park than a traditional museum. It has expanded to include behind-the-scenes aspects of production, and includes guided tours through the working porcelain workshop to see the production process first hand. Visitors can experience all the steps in producing every Meissen product, directly observing the artists themselves. The tour starts with an explanation of the raw materials used, and ends with the finished product.

Understanding the various steps in the process is important, Kolitsch argues, in grasping the handcrafted value of Meissen's goods, compared with massproduced porcelain. By facilitating such understanding, the tour helps visitors accept that Meissen porcelain wares warrant their high prices:

"Who believes today that Meissen porcelain is made by human hands? Our artisans, during the guided tours through the porcelain workshop, demonstrate that our products are genuinely handcrafted. This is, in a very positive sense, pure event marketing, and by extension it leads to an understanding of our price structure. People are shown that we are selling genuine artistic performance." (W. Kolitsch, Oct. 01, 2007)

Another experience offered the visitors of the museum is to taste food, coffee, and fine chocolates served on Meissen porcelain. As well, an open house is held at the museum twice a year, in fulfilment of the company's commitment to the state to preserve national cultural assets, as well as being a vital, producing firm. Management has consciously turned this requirement into an investment in event marketing.

The company is always seeking new opportunities and is innovative in finding new uses for porcelain. That is why Meissen has entered markets porcelain has not traditionally penetrated, though if possible, it tries to produce only in response to incoming orders from these new markets. In this way, Meissen is being innovative, while limiting its risks by interacting and communicating with its market partners. For example, it co-operates with Glashuette Original, specially fabricating porcelain watch faces decorated with fine-art painting. Watch construction demands high precision and the porcelain used also needs distinctive tolerances; the technology required for this has been developed, and it works.

For five years, Meissen has created pens in co-operation with Mont Blanc. This innovative arrangement is good public relations, so essential to brand care, as it spreads awareness of porcelain to new markets. In co-operation with Lagerfeldt, Meissen has helped create two haute-couture dresses with paillettes made of porcelain. The media exposure, for example in the French newspaper *Le Figaro*, is important and confirms Meissen as a premium brand. This publicity is also vital in reminding the public that Meissen, while a classic and timeless brand, is still up-to-date:

"We are often confronted with the question of whether our customers are dying out. There are reports of earlier answers to the same question, actually one from as early as 1884. One important task today is re-entering, in a natural way, areas where we worked at the end of the thirties and the beginning of the forties." (W. Kolitsch, Oct. 01, 2007)

The market for antique Meissen porcelain is regarded as a parallel market; it can both strengthen and weaken the market for fine modern porcelain, and some old original designs have been put into production again. On one hand, the market for antique porcelain confirms the Meissen brand and mystique, and emphasizes that its products have stable value; in this, it supports company renewal. On the other hand, it distracts attention from newly made Meissen porcelain pieces, devaluing them in favour of antique pieces.

"Responding to the challenges of the "vintage" market is a balancing act,

requiring careful consideration from the company and making this area a very exciting field of endeavour." (W. Kolitsch, Oct. 01, 2007).

Meissen has tried several other marketing communication avenues, besides their standardized, global efforts, to raise awareness of the company brand. Regional awareness is raised by the existence of the museum, for example, making it an investment in the future.

Meissen's operations have an organic structure, where management truly supports the designers' activities. In this respect, the designers are the ones who lead the process, which stimulates their individual motivation and their commitment to the company. If communication is halting and poor, if there is no guarantee of success, even though production plans have been strictly followed, workers will not be motivated to excel. Involvement will end with the participants merely performing adequately, acting according to instructions. This is obviously not the case at Meissen: here we see individuals with different kinds of expertise committing themselves to overcoming any misunderstandings arising from their different professional identities.

8. Developing competitive brands in a global economy

In theory, brand management is about communicating messages, which are received in line with the brand owner's intention (Kapferer 2004). In this sense, branding communicates how a product differs from competing products. In the 1970s the brand itself was often regarded as an indicator of quality. Brand-name products were expected to be of high quality. In that context, conducting a brand strategy was a way to position a product's functional superiority relative to competitors' products (as Timberland, a company that produces shoes with a price guarantee and tops rated customer service. Timberland also manufactures outdoor clothing and products for active sports). In connection with that, in the 1970s people began to discuss the importance of services, and perspectives on what is actually being produced, changed. The expression "output" was redefined. It came to be understood as a value, that is, an aggregation of a product and service. We thus became aware of the symbiosis between product and service, and our view of what goes into the production chain (input) had to be revised.

In classical business economics input consisted of raw materials, capital, and labour. Since tangible values, such as intellectual property and services, often determine the "output's" value, it is obvious that the quality of the tangible values matters! In such a context the importance of symbolic values is obvious. Absolut Vodka hereby serves as an extreme example. The product doesn't differ from competitors' offerings, but the symbols create an Absolut cult value and an identification factor, which are crucial for the brand's position on the market. Symbolic value related to exclusivity and a "first class" appeal helps to create a "premium brand," which in turn justifies a higher price than the average within the producer's business range or their own niche. Advertising for "premium brands" can also validate the purchase for those in the absolute top layer - and thus reinforce the admiration of the "envied" in society (as Lamborghini and Ferrari, both Italian sports car manufacturers, providing luxury highline autos). With visibility of intangible items relevant to the value produced, a discussion of the "corporate brand" followed. The importance of harmony between the value offered and the company's trademark is discussed in Aaker and Keller (1990). The company's brand, in turn, is ensured when personality, identity, and image are synchronized. But even personal brands are being discussed more frequently. The subject is not only of interest to managers and tied to the company's brand, but also to representatives of political parties, public organizations, and associations. Positive personal brands obtained by key people in organizations provide important public relations and can be vital, not least in crisis situations. Finally, even private individuals are interested in good personal brands as these brands carry good reputations.

Since the generated value, the company brand, and key persons' personal brands together create immaterial input, they cannot really be considered individually; instead, they must be considered as interdependent parts of a whole. Researchers who believe that (1) the company's different brands (different products or values), (2) the company's brand, and (3) the company's key persons' personal brands interact argue that it is a matter of different degrees of synergy (Keller 1998; Varadarajan et al. 2006). The manifold relations are represented along a spectrum from the "branded house" to "the house of brands," including "endorsed brands" and "sub-brands" (Aaker and Joachimsthaler 2000). In order to clarify the role and function of corporate branding, Muzellec and Lambkin (2009) propose three types of corporate branding strategies within the brand architecture framework (i.e., trade name, business brand, and the holistic corporate brand). They introduce the concept of ascending and descending brand extension.

The possibility of building new brands by using established brands can increase a company's competitive advantage when it comes to wooing consumers. Christodoulides (2009), however, describes the traditional brand manager as a self-absorbed narcissist. Using one-way multimedia modes of communication, such managers want to disseminate the message that they are offering an exceptional brand. This traditional and hierarchical approach assumes that the consumer is passive and adaptive and that the brand manager is something of a control freak. The same approach faces serious problems in a media world dominated by Internet and many-to-many marketing. Suddenly the balance of power changed, and the consumer began to co-create brand meaning. This increased the importance of cultural factors with respect to branding. The brand culture concept occupies the theoretical space between managerial intent and market response; in other words between strategic goals and consumer perceptions (Schroeder and Salzer-Mörling 2006). Realizing that consumer culture is not a single, static phenomenon or something that might be standardized, companies must review their thinking when developing competitive brands in a global economy comprising many different consumer cultures.

In international marketing as a whole, perspectives have changed as a result of globalization. Approaches that focus on product, price wars, and the dominance of the market via acquisitions or alliances (Thompson 1967) are not sufficient for winning the market war. International marketing requires knowledge of how soft values, adapted to a local market's requirements, are created. These locally adapted values affect the quality of customer experience. This is why the local market response is crucial to brand managers.

One of the key issues in international marketing has long been the question of standardization versus adaptation (Herrmann and Heitmann 2006). This issue has been the subject of interest among both academics and practitioners at least since the early 1900s as a result of increasing internationalization and globalization (Ryans et al. 2003; Agarwal 1995). Despite this, there is no theoretically integrated approach in marketing strategies that specifically problematize and focus on the issue of standardization versus adaptation (Ryans et al. 2003; Herrmann and Heitmann 2006). Similarly, there is no applied comprehensive marketing strategy that takes into account the specificities of individual markets. Some researchers (Szymański et al. 1993; Levitt 1983) argue that markets are homogeneous and that similar strategies are applicable regardless of country. In Europe, the same view is often based on a notion of simplifying the EU and harmonizing the conditions in EU countries, which in turn is expected to lead to an increasing homogenization of consumer attitudes. Increasing homogenization offers scale advantages. From a business perspective, scale advantages mean that if you want to achieve scale advantages, you have to standardize (Ryans et al. 2003).

As late as in 1998, however, a comparative study of the English and French markets showed that marketers still perceived a need for local adaptation as a result of the strongly rooted cultural factors (Whitelock and Rey 1998). Given that Britain and France are among the earliest members of the European Community, the result is significant (Britain joined the European Economic Union in 1973, while France was a founding member in 1957). Other studies, such as the one conducted by Belk et al. (2003), point in the same direction. Ryans et al. (2003) argue that there is much empirical evidence that contradicts the notion that markets are homogeneous, which in turn makes it doubtful whether the standardization of marketing in the international context is meaningful.

Some researchers have even included a mixture of different strategies on the agenda Comparative studies have been carried out to examine the mixture of effectiveness and impact. Multidomestic strategies have been compared to adaptive strategies, with an overall marketing mix as a base, as well as to wholly locally and individually tailored marketing mixes (Solberg 2000; Szymański et al., 1993; Zou and Tamer 2002). Many studies have specifically focused on advertising (Onkvist and Shaw 1999; Sirisagul 2000) But, with respect to brand strategies, it also seems that researchers now understand the importance of taking cultural differences into account.

Aaker et al. (2001) argue that different cultures perceive brands differently. Kanwar (1993) and Yavas et al. (1992) discuss different perceptions of risk and brand loyalty in different cultures. In a survey conducted by de Mooj (2005), enterprise patterns are revealed, which in turn point to six different commercial strategies that companies can use when marketing their products globally. These strategies range from full standardization to adapting marketing efforts to each local market. A review of the literature indicates that most researchers agree that cultural differences lead to a diverse host. This means that in an era of mass, mega markets, mega-trends, and hyper-Taylorism (Klein, 2002), it is not clear how best to design international marketing (including branding) efforts to be effective. This creates problems for producers and marketers.

There is a lack of a comprehensive marketing strategy in the field and there is no theoretical discourse in the field. A review of frontline research shows that the problem persists, whether it concerns tangible or intangible values (Aaker et al., 2001; Kanwar 1993; Yavas et al. 1992). Tangible values are physical, hard values (respectively), and intangible values are soft, imaginary, or aesthetic values as described in Grönroos (2002), Normann (2001). The need for a comprehensive marketing strategy that meets the needs of individual market trends is obvious. To what extent is it possible to categorize the different countries' cultures in order to lay the foundation for a theoretical, comprehensive marketing strategy? Herrmann and Heitmann (2006) argue that questions connected to "standardization or adaptation" are closely associated with whether a society can be regarded as collectivistic rather than individual. The dimension individualism-collectivism (Green, Deschamps and Paéz 2005) has often been used to describe, explain, and predict differences in attitudes, values, learning, communication, self-creation, socialization, and self-concepts. In organizational research, the same dimension has frequently been used since Hofstede's intercultural studies in the 1970s. They were conducted at IBM in fifty different countries and in an organizational context. Regarding a marketer's choice between standardization and adaptation, Herrmann and Heitmann's (2006) research shows that it is important to know whether the local culture is characterized by consumers that follow the same patterns as others or if it is characterized by individualism. They further argue that their research indicates that people in individualistic societies value the choice between different products within the same product category to a greater extent than those in collective/mutually dependent cultures. This means that, instead of fully personalized marketing in a customized world (Gilmore and Pine 1997), Herrmann and Heitmann (2006) speak of adaptation to society-individual, socio-cultural trends in a simultaneously geographically distinct market. Other researchers discuss cultural differences on the basis of the same culture's appetite for risk. The perceived risk is then considered not as a personal factor relating to individuals (i.e., individual consumers), but as a characteristic of the country's culture (Kanwar 1993). Belk et al. (2003) speak in terms of a culture depending on moral values. Those are crucial to the local consumption patterns and the culture's approach to advertising and brands. Risk and morality also represent dimensions which, since Hofstede, have often been seen as related to organizational research.

A prerequisite when categorizing different countries' cultures - in order to lay the foundation for a theoretical, comprehensive marketing strategy - seems to be understanding the extent to which research can convincingly highlight dimensions that can be described. Also crucial for a theoretical, comprehensive marketing strategy is how successfully research offers explanations and predictions of cultural differences in attitudes, values, learning, communication, self-creation, socialization, and self-concept. The lack of understanding and explanation, due to specific cultural trends relating to marketing factors such as identification and personality, often leads to shoddy, superficial, and unclear descriptions of cultures. Therefore, the concept of the brand culture (Schroeder 2009) is welcomed not only for the purpose of tailored branding on the Internet, as in Christodoulides (2009), but also for the purpose of responding to local markets, once it has been decided how best to balance standardization and adaption. A key conclusion is, thus, that companies must consider cultural differences when developing branding strategies. The firm mentioned below has been able to sustain competitive brand value in the former GDR after unification; it has also succeeded in building a competitive brand on the global market, probably because it has successfully found a balance between standardization and adaptation.

Case study: Kathi does it step-by-step

Reading the website www.kathi.dk one is struck by impressive data for a company that, with no West German partner and as a private business, started anew in 1991 after the Big Bang. The question is what factors are behind the incredible success story of Kathi. From the interview with Director Rainer Thiele, it is clear that without *"the belief in ourselves"* (R. Thiele, 070420), none of this would have been possible. This belief is not only a matter of self-confidence in securing new markets in a free market economy, but also a consistent belief in a genuine family enterprise and the company's own products, regardless of the prescribed market order. In the case of Kathi, this „belief in oneself" is connected with the creativity, innovativeness, entrepreneurial ability, flexibility and capacity to adapt that had already been demonstrated by the family earlier. From his parents, Thiele had quietly learnt how a family business is built and managed, but also how it can be adapted to external conditions.

The tradition

The company was founded in 1951 in Halle (Saale) by Käthe and Kurt Thiele. Both founders came from established pastry shops and bakeries. This made self-employment a possibility for them. When the Marshall Plan set the standard in West Germany after the Second World War and the "Robber's Plan" was applied in the East, there were shortages on all levels in the GDR. In principle, the leading economic bodies expected the producers to come up with ideas, despite the latent shortages, to produce double amounts.

"Where understanding grows, there is a need for inventiveness." R. Thiele, *April 20, 2007.*[138]

The entrepreneurial couple adapted to the situation: in 1949-50, Käthe and Kurt Thiele thought about how a simple cake could be baked despite the huge shortages of many ingredients in the GDR. The minimum of ingredients were flour, sugar, starch and extracts. Based on this reasoning, Käthe Thiele had the idea of developing a quick bread based on the most important ingredients. The

---

138   All quotes in italics in the following text are taken from the discussion between the author and Herr Rainer Thiele on April 20, 2007.

advent of cake mixes in Germany came officially in 1970 through the company KRAFT. Dr. Oetker arrived in 1972. But Kathi had this idea already in 1951, which makes it the oldest producer of baking mixes in Germany.

"Necessity is the mother of invention – and it demands creativity. Mother never studied, but she had a definite autodidactic ability. Father was a born manager."

Frau Käthe Thiele also seized focused initiatives in advertising and sales. For example, the customer could receive a free recipe book by cutting out and sending in a painted Kathi house from 20 cake-mix packages. In another example, in 1950, she had the company logo painted on the delivery truck. All of this took place a t a time when advertising in the East had more of a political-economic character, with advertising being used as a tool to adapt demand to supply.

Until 1957, preparedness for innovation was fostered in the small and medium-size companies in the GDR. Kathi brought to market easily handled products in flat packages and SOS bags. Furthermore, the innovator Kaethe Thiele also thought about making dried meat with a shelf life of five years, so that it would form a good base for soup mixes. The first Kathi soup mixes had been available for only two years in the shops, when it was decided that the entire production was to be delivered exclusively to the National People's Army (NVA).

"Power before the law and the market. Cardboard drums, each containing 20-25 kg, were now being produced exclusively for the army."

The advantages of soup mixes for the army are obvious. Firstly, the soups have a high level of convenience; secondly, a long shelf life; and thirdly, a high level of hunger satisfaction. Pulses cooked in the soups are ready in ten minutes. Kathi originally held the patent that was subsequently taken over by the former "VEB Suppina Auerbach" in Vogtland after Unification, and then by the Knorr company.

Initially in the GDR, only heavy industries, banks and insurance companies were nationalized. Small and medium-size companies were actually encouraged, but later they were gradually nationalized. At first, Kaethe and Kurt Thiele had to accept 67-percent state ownership.

"Ultimately, state ownership was 82 percent. They were permitted to retain all of 18 percent."

Before Kathi became a 100-percent „people's own" enterprise, baking mixes, refined potato products, ready-to-eat soups and sauces were being produced. The business evolved, with its expansion breaking the socialist framework that had been set. For this reason, the company restricted itself to one line of goods. The decision fell in favor of retaining baking mixes. For Kathi, the fact that it was deprivatized in 1972, like other businesses, was the final step in nationalization:

"Power before rights: The machines used for the production of the two other principal ranges and their recipes could not simply be sold, but had to be conveyed free of charge to another people's own company. We had no influence on this process because the nationalized companies were free of ownership."

Following the signature required by the state for the transformation of "Kathi-Nährmittelfabrik Kurt Thiele KG" into a nationalized company (VEB Backmehlwerk Halle), Kurt Thiele suffered acute loss of hearing and was granted invalidity.

"In the process of privatization, many people went mad and there were also some suicides among entrepreneurs. My father was more of an introvert. Sometimes, I think it would have been better if he had quoted Goetz von Berlichingen. My mother also suffered a mental breakdown. She couldn't understand that all of this was possible."

The promise

It was partly because of this memory that, 17 years later, when the Berlin Wall fell, a vision emerges: Rainer Thiele thinks that he might possibly win back the Kathi business. The vision is morally set, in that Rainer Thiele makes a promise to his mother on her deathbed in 1989. He explains:

"My mother believed that the socialist system had brought ruin. But we would have nobody to take over the company. Rainer, she said, you should get the company back, if things are ever 'different.' I replied, 'yes, mother, I will do all I can to get Kathi back through reprivatisation.'"

The promise had been made and he thought about how he could manage the whole matter. After the Turnaround, he first of all became authorized signatory at Kathi.

"After the Turnaround, I first had to prove that I was 'mature enough' for the challenges of the market economy, since I had nothing but baking mixes."

But what he actually had in addition to the baking mixes were the promise as described above, a belief in himself, a good portion of luck and/or coincidence, a degree in marketing and the protected Kathi trademark. The latter had an importance for future success that cannot be underestimated:

Trademark protection

As already mentioned, through deprivatization in 1972, nearly everything in the GDR became nationalized. After this, the state wanted to get rid of the name "Kathi" from both east and west packaging, as it was a "capitalist-bourgeois" name and as such, unsuitable for a GDR product. But another problem emerged from this, since in December 1949, two months after its foundation, the GDR had recognized the international Trademark and Patent law. In 1952, the name "Kathi" was granted trademark protection following an application by the Thiele family. As a result, not even the state was entitled to remove the name "Kathi" from the packaging. However, the form of the logo could be changed and this was also done. From 1972, Rainer Thiele paid the taxes and fees for the protection of the name "Kathi" out of his own pocket, although the family business had been nationalized. Its "own belief in itself" had resulted in the family's consistent management of its trademark, as well as the fact that they were convinced that the GDR would not survive forever as a state:

"We conducted production using the Kathi trademark from 1952 because we were already 100-percent convinced that by 2000 at the latest, the GDR would only exist in history books."

It can be assumed that the continuity of the trademark management was a contributory factor to the high level of recognition in the new federal Länder. When a market survey on brand awareness was conducted shortly after the Turnaround, the result for Kathi was sensational: Kathi's awareness level was more than 90 percent, without prompting. Kathi was an established brand, an established concept.

Belief in oneself

His optimism and "the belief in himself" told him that his wife, although she had a background in medicine, was a possible qualified business partner. In the GDR, she was the manager or senior sister in charge of 42 nurses. If she was able to be in charge of 42 nurses – he told himself – then she would also be in the position to handle new challenges. He could no longer count on his eldest daughter, who had fled to Bavaria with her husband and children in the trunk of a Mercedes four weeks before the fall of the Berlin Wall. She did not want to return to East Germany.

"The first I knew of her escape was when she called from Bavaria. The call was also repeatedly cut off – four weeks before the Wall fell."

Otherwise, the family comprised 13-year old daughter Ulrike and sons Marco (18) and Thomas (23). Together with his wife, Rainer Thiele first of all took on the task of "buying back" the company. Before he could finally do so, Herr Rainer Thiele had to provide the Treuhand Agency with evidence of the legal status of the company prior to deprivatization and his entitlement to buy back the company. Thiele succeeded in this in the truest sense of "one minute to twelve." A dubious Dutch property group had presented a false concept to the Treuhand Agency. This concept contradicted all reality in terms of a concept that could promise success. They also wanted to make Kathi an exception. Rainer Thiele believes that, in his life, he owes a lot of gratitude to luck and coincidence. He says:

"For a criminologist to succeed, he must encounter such figures as 'Inspector Luck' or 'Inspector Coincidence' and I met 'Inspector Luck.'"

Inspector Luck and/or Coincidence

In February 1990, he applied for reprivatization. In May 1990, he had his first appointment with the Treuhand Agency. When he arrived for the meeting, he encountered a former high-ranking member of the Socialist Unity Party, who had played pranks on him. He wondered why this person, with such a past, could be working for the Treuhand Agency. When he opened the door to the meeting room, he saw a second comrade, of whom he had even worse memories. He had a bad feeling and it came as no surprise when he discovered that the documentation that he had so carefully compiled repeatedly disappeared at the Treuhand or were found to be incomplete. For more than a year, he canvassed all of the retail chains in Germany regarding inclusion as a supplier, at the same time as the application for reprivatisation was being processed. After more than a year, he received a strange letter from a renowned retail chain: this year, he had not succeeded in demonstrating the future legal structure of the company and its owners. However, the chain was convinced of the concept and the products, but needed to know specifically what legal structure the company would have in the future. If evidence of this could not be provided within three months, the Kathi products would have to be removed from the supplier list.

"That was the first sleepless night I had. I spoke to an old West Berliner business acquaintance and he was my 'Inspector Luck.' He said that, first of all, I should not take it personally. He knew many entrepreneurs in the new federal

Länder and my case was no exception. I needed to get a lawyer quickly, but not an East German – it should be a West German because East German law no longer applied and we came under the Civil Code of the Federal Republic. In GDR times, lawyers were affordable, but a West German lawyer cost many times more. Then Inspector Luck said to me that I shouldn't worry about it. He would pay the necessary amount and I could pay back later."

Thiele hired a lawyer from Erkrath, near Düsseldorf. When he received an appointment three months later with the County Administrative Office for the Settlement of Public Wealth Issues in Halle/Saale, he had to bring his lawyer along. The County Administrative Office for the Settlement of Public Wealth Issues was located in a multi-story building in Halle-Neustadt. The Treuhand office was on the sixth floor. However, the head of the office announced immediately that the documentation could unfortunately not be presented this day because they had mysteriously "disappeared." This case was no exception. But the gentleman from the office believed that he knew where to look and that the documentation would "turn up" again in two to three weeks.

"I said: Your words will be heard by God!" But after three weeks, he did have all of the documentation! It was with immense joy that he showed his wife the reprivatization papers, which they toasted with a glass of sparkling wine. "However, the entire 'back transfer procedure' had caused so much stress that with the easing of the tension, I suffered a heart attack."

Since one first had to know how to gain access to earlier documents, it was naturally necessary to "serve" some "eternal hangers-on" at the Treuhand. Many of them simply could not handle the fact that the GDR no longer existed. But one thing they did understand immediately after the Turnaround: take your jacket off and turn it inside out. They could not turn back the wheels of history, but by throwing sand and stones into the "wheels" they could and did more than slow down some matters in their development.

Trade fair

As one of the few East German entrepreneurs in his industry, Thiele visited some of the most important trade and consumer fairs immediately after the fall of the Berlin, including Anuga in Cologne, the largest fairs in the world for food and goods for immediate consumption, the ISM international confectionary fair in Cologne, SIAl in Paris, Fancy Food (NY) and Gail Food in Dubai.

"Fairs cost a lot of money, but they had first priority. For many East German competitors, it was more important to buy a swanky new car or a new house first of all."

In 1993, he attended a fair in Saudi Arabia for the first time. He had heard from a business partner that there was good business to be done there. In the area of baking mixes, the offering in Saudi Arabia is two to three times larger than in Germany. The high demand is attributable to the fact that, due to kosher requirements, less meat and fat is eaten. Cakes, cakes and more cakes is the rule. At the fair, contact was made with a future partner of many years, an important sheikh, with whom there is unfortunately no contact nowadays. Unfortunately, political relations have a negative impact on many things. Thiele does not know whether the sheikh is still alive.

"In such things, one is powerless."

Deliberate branding and marketing strategies

Thiele describes himself as a brand fetishist. The importance he assigns to branding and marketing strategies is partly explained by the fact that he studied marketing. He did this in the spring of 1983. As a marketing student, it was also important for Thiele to understand the theory behind market and demand research. He knew that in a free market it was not a question of managing latent shortages, but using, for example, modern marketing strategies and methods for the optimal sale of products. Thiele also says that many East German entrepreneurs misjudged the importance of using marketing to present a professional approach in the commercial field. As one of the first East German entrepreneurs in the industry, he understood the importance of professionalism in this respect and was early in having displays and folders made for the professional presentation of the Kathi brand. This professionalism also included giving Kathi a new, modern logo, because the spirit of the times had changed considerably since the fall of the Berlin Wall.

"As a result of my studies in marketing and demand research, I had a solid prior knowledge and quickly immersed myself in the market economy. It was also clear to me that entry into the market, in a market economy, also required such activities as a market survey – only, at that time, I couldn't pay for this myself. I had to take a loan to pay for it. My family declared me mad."

He believes that, if a brand is like a personality, then a strong brand is also a strong personality. It was important to build up sustainable confidence among the customers. There must never be concessions, not even concealed, in the quality in favor of attractive prices. Hard discounts are not even considered by Thiele. He produces top quality exclusively under the Kathi brand name. Departures from this strategy might increase sales in the short term, but are counterproductive in the long term.

To Thiele, sales are vanity– cash flow is health. All activities in the company have to conform to this performance principle. Yes, Kathi should grow – but not at any price.

From the beginning, Thiele subjected himself voluntarily to the product monitoring checks of the Central Marketing Authority of German Agricultural Industries in the Federal Republic (CMA). The advantage of the checks is that they are conducted by an internationally active, fully independent food-monitoring institute. Kathi produced eight products prior to the Turnaround. The competitors in the old federal Länder generally had much larger product ranges. Thiele had all of the products of all his competitors gathered and their ingredients and preparation methods analyzed. All worked more or less with chemistry or were filled into large packages, where small ones would have sufficed. The average package contents comprised 55 percent. Through the controls, a list was compiled by a neutral agency of the ways in which Kathi's products differed from those of the competition. This meant the USP (unique selling point) of Kathi was determined independently.

"From the outset, I made a grand entrance! I received the gold medal from the CMA and now I work with the CMA."

There is a conversion factor and a points score. If more than 4.25 is achieved, it is permitted to print the CMA value on the packaging. Thiele has Kathi tested three to four times a year. The checks conducted are random choice. For three consecutive years, he achieved 5.0 and thereby the golden commendation, summa cum laude. Thiele is the only entrepreneur in this industry to achieve this highly unusual result to date. Eleven out of about 80 products have this mark of quality.

PR

Thiele participates regularly in the Green Week in Berlin. It is also regionally active. In cooperation with the Händel House, it supports the Halle Festival in honor of the great son of the city, George Frideric Handel. Among other activities, Kathi has a stand in the Händel House during the opening. Thiele plans to be involved in the Hundertwasserhaus building in Magdeburg, but these plans will only be realized if the participation can be finances from cash flow. Thiele holds the position of Deputy President of the Halle-Dessau Chamber of Industry and Commerce. His company is a member of the central German Food Industry Clusterboard. On the initiative of Thiele, the company has been awarding the "Golden Kathi" since 2001, an award that includes EUR 1,500 and is presented to the best apprentice in the area of trade and commerce in the Chamber of Commerce district. Securing well-educated, committed successors is a matter close to Thiele's heart.

All machines in the plant bear the Kathi livery of yellow, red and white, since it is Thiele's conviction that color is the element that is maintained as a multiplier in seconds from inside to outside.

Halloren and Kathi have some joint business, for example, at the railway station, leading to a win-win situation for both East German companies.

Potential determined by capitalizing on changed conditions. Adaptation and gut feeling – Gut beats head

Abroad, Thiele sells Kathi products exclusively under his brand. Always quality before quantity. The amounts may be smaller, but they are no less successful for this.

Potential 1: The diabetic mix
A diabetic baking mix was produced by Kathi already at the time of the GDR. Kathi had the 100-percent market share associated with a socialist paradise, although the product was no hit.
The diabetic baking mix of the time tasted of chemicals, was hardly digestible and had an unpleasant taste. In GDR times, the diabetic mix was a disaster. After the Turnaround, Kathi developed a new diabetic mix with the addition of Hoechst artificial sugar. After a year of development, it was launched, with blind tests conducted beforehand. The test group members could not differentiate between the diabetic mix and the normal mix. Today, the range includes eight diabetic products. These are mainly exported to such countries as Iceland

and the US, where the buyers are homes for the elderly and hospitals. They are packaged in amounts of 5kg and 7kg and are Kathi's main export successes. Schizophrenically, the diabetic mix also sells well in the US, but it cannot be sold under the "diabetic" label for "reasons of discrimination":

"The 'slim' Americans would become sick!"

In the US, however, another approach to the market was proven:

Potential 2: Family tradition in the US

At some point, there came the idea of selling Cash Big Bags in the US. The so-called packs contain 65 percent flour and a relatively high share of starch. The rest of the US mix is a Kathi secret recipe. The only question at the time was how to produce it. Thiele would not consider licenses, or a joint venture. But for Thiele, cooperation on production was lucrative, realistic and viable. The cooperative partners mix the principal ingredients in the Big Bags (Packs). But they cannot find out what the small constituent parts from Kathi consist of. Accordingly, there is a win-win situation for both parties. Kathi was also quick to recognize that a producer of baking goods, who wants to export to the United States, not only has to incorporate umpteen percent more sugar, but also coarser sugar. In Germany, the finest-grain sugar is preferred.

At the Fancy Food Fair in New York it is explicitly emphasized that Kathi is a family company. A logo was also developed specially for the US market, clearly conveying the family tradition. After Kathi launches its new logo in the US, sales triple.

Asia with a question mark

In general, baking mixes are uncommon in Asia. Japan has some imports. Baking mix products for the Asian market are different. Thiele believes that it is possible that the eggs may have to be included in semi-processed form. The Japanese have a lot of high-tech equipment in their homes, but live in tiny apartments. They often have only 13 square meters for a family and have virtually no kitchen and that is why at least 70 percent of the Japanese eat outside the home. In China, this is even more extreme, for example, in Beijing or Shanghai. If baking is still done at all here, out of tradition, then it takes place in a wok.

Ad-hoc tactical solutions – The ability for immediate adaptation, flexibility and traceability

While awaiting reprivatisation, Thiele, as entrepreneur, had a vision and idea. He knew that, with the fall of the Berlin Wall in the East, there would be a push for Western products, food and non-food. But he was also sure that all GDR products would experience a renaissance, Kathi baking mixes and other commodities in short supply. The question was when this renaissance would set in. However, he was also sure that, except for baking mixes, the company would be basically unable to produce anything else. When the 20-percent sales crash of 1990-91 occurred, Thiele came up with the idea of "co-production." This was a way to bring sales back to a normal level. It was important to bridge the time to reprivatization. For the transition period, he sought a similar enterprise with new technology. He sought and he found. The requirement was to commence production and distribution without delay. Thiele found this in order, but he put his cards on the table and made the condition that the agreement must end immediately following reprivatization. In turn, the partner required notice from Thiele, not only eight days, but two to three months in advance. Through these ideas, the following was possible:

1. operation of the machines in two shifts
2. well-trained labor could be secured and they could become familiar with the new technology
3. all employees could remain in employment
4. red figures could be avoided.

Sales were DEM 4 M instead of the budgeted DEM 3 M. From the outset, the company had no red figures. The banks found this a favorable concept; the balance was extremely satisfactory and it possibly had an indirect impact on the work of the Treuhand Agency.

"For many it was inconceivable that an East German company could be in the black after only two years in the market economy. The business rose like the phoenix from the ashes. It was only possible because I always told myself: Don't put the cart before the horse – serving comes before being served!"

Self-confidence in the face of uncertainty

Rainer Thiele is of the opinion that many East German companies were inexperienced and introverted. He himself was an extrovert, which also contributed to success. At the first consumer trade fair (Green Week, Berlin) after the Turnaround, there was a hall for East German companies offered on special terms. He told himself no, I won't do this – *"I didn't want to create my profile through the tears of the East."* He needed to act in an optimal manner. Intense competition was the order of the day, regardless of whether it was in Cologne, Halle/Saale, Hamburg, Dresden or anywhere else. His inkling was that the special terms for East German companies would only be available for a brief initial period. He was the only one not to enter Hall 21 (for East German companies), going instead to Hall 23, surrounded by exhibitors from Bavaria and Baden-Württemberg.

"Was I arrogant? It was not a question of that."

Already in the GDR, Kathi had advertising slogans on expressway flyovers. In the free market economy, advertising on flyovers is prohibited because it distracts drivers. The problem was "resolved" by placing the posters ten meters to the right, in a field, because apparently there, they would not attract drivers' attention away from the road. A view that is not only incomprehensible to Thiele.

Solid foundation. Healthy, not overhasty, growth. Veracity and honesty. No setting false priorities

After the Turnaround, many Westerners came, who "heartily" embraced those from the East. In turn, Many East Germans saw the solution in large companies after the Turnaround. Thiele was also "heartily" embraced by many, but he wanted to retain his independence. He did not want to fall into the arms of a partner, which is something related to the history of his family company. As an independent entrepreneur, it was important for him to get his priorities right. Firstly, investments had to be made in production, which he carried out when it was financially possible. He prepared well for this by becoming acquainted with the most modern technology worldwide. The internal production facility is fully computer-controlled. The technology that Thiele had installed is of the highest class and quality – he compares it with that of Mercedes and BMW:

"I am not rich enough to make cheap purchases."

When a businessman from the region bought himself a big BMW, new machines and horses rather soon after the fall of the Berlin Wall, one of Thiele's sons said he thought they were doing something wrong at Kathi. Thiele reflected quietly that, unfortunately, many were making the serious mistake of getting their priorities confused.

"Wait a few years."

Relative to its size, there were some new East German companies in Halle after the Turnaround, specifically 15 food companies at the time. Today, only two remain, namely Halloren and Kathi, both companies that existed in former times, but Kathi remains an exclusively East German company.

"At Halloren, the constellation is entirely different compared with Kathi."

He is keen for the company to remain in family ownership and would be pleased if his sons would take over. But only if they are genuinely prepared to be passionate about the task. They need to be prepared to be first in the office in the morning and, as a rule, last to leave the office in the evenings. Initially, they need to make do with a small car and a small salary and always act according to the principle that you should treat everyone as though they might be your boss tomorrow.

"And if you think you can do it by yourselves, I told them, then you are free to try."

Thiele says that, in addition, he expected two things of his successors: they should have practical ability and come with a completed university education. The solid base is important and one that he also wanted to pass on to his children.

Respect for employees. Care and treatment of the "Human capital"

There is no trade union at Kathi. According to Thiele, the unions ruined their own chances at the company. Loyalty and commitment are too strong. Thiele's explanation for this is that the following motto defines the business culture: Everyone should be treated as though he or she will be your boss tomorrow. Discriminatory terms, such as "Putzfussel" (cleaning rag), are not tolerated. Each person is needed in the production and nobody shall be treated condescendingly. Bullying and discrimination are strictly prohibited. There is distinct social commitment at Kathi. This means there is, for example, wedding money, maternity benefit, vacation pay, Christmas pay and, within Halle, removal pay. Every apprentice receives a bonus of EUR 320 on successful completion of the final examination. Employees receive an old age pension of 80 percent and have done since 1994. Thiele got the inspiration for this company-sponsored pension scheme when he visited the US for the first time in 1993. There he found a social coldness that he had never before experienced. An old age pension from the state or a company is almost a foreign term. However, the employees could not immediately appreciate the value and usefulness of this pension. Some even said they would prefer a cash payment. But explanations are no longer necessary.

"I'm not saying that one system is superior to the other. Many things were better in the GDR than they were after the Turnaround. I lived there. For example, the quality criteria of agricultural association AGRA were stricter than they are today. But if a comparison is made of the good and bad factors of the 'Russianization' of the GDR on the one hand and the Americanization of West Germany on the other, the good factors of Americanization prevail."

Summary

A combination of many factors contributed to Kathi's survival and present success. The step-by-step approach, characterized by veracity and a solid base, was the prerequisite for survival, not only in the period immediately after the Turnaround, but also in the long term. Kathi's ability to make the jump to the changed external conditions – the market economy – so quickly and successfully is attributable to the will to survival and tacit knowledge inherent in the family tradition, which Thiele grew up with. The fact that Thiele had accumulated a mass of intellectual capital through his marketing studies made a particular contribution to the speed of adjustment. The following is a list of the five most important success factors of the East German "survivor" Kathi.

1) The Vision, qualified by the promise
2) The belief in oneself as a result of tacit knowledge
3) Veracity and a solid base
4) Traceability

5) Humble management style
6) Targeted and consistent marketing as a result of intellectual capital

Especially by the latter factor, Kathi serves as an example of a company, which has successfully developed a competitive brand in a global economy. This is as Thiele considered cultural differences when developing branding strategies. He successfully found a balance between standardization and adaptation when building a competitive brand on the global market.

9. Crisis management

The aim of this chapter is to examine the way a survivor managed the crisis that was triggered by German unification. This will be done with reference to a prominent example. Does the approach differ from the ones discussed in the theory, in particular the proactive and reactive approaches? Or does the survivor confirm that organizations should act as theory suggests? Is there something unique in the approach that this prominent survivor chose, and if so, does it contribute to the theoretical literature? Can we learn something from it that has not been previously highlighted in theory? The company that serves as an example of survival by successful crisis management is the pharmaceutical company Jenapharm.

In general, management tries to prepare for crises in various ways. Preparations vary depending on what particular crises imply for the organization, and what crises an organization might anticipate. Certain extreme situations are more imaginable – and manageable – than others. For example, an organization may be able to confront a hostile takeover bid, a production plant breakdown that contaminates water, and a kidnapping of a key person on a business trip in a foreign country. It may be more difficult, however, to deal with the level of crisis an event such as an earthquake can trigger.

There is therefore a distinction between crises that occur within an organization operating in a stable environment and crises that arise when the outside world loses its stability. In the first case it is easier to be proactive than in the second case. Lalonde (2007) identifies two major trends in the crisis management field: (1) planning that emphasizes the development of techniques for overcoming hazards (an internal organizational crisis in a stable environment) and (2) the sociological analysis of organizational contingencies that focus on disasters as social events (the world loses its stability). One common proactive approach is to have a well-prepared PR agenda; in the event of a crisis within the organization, that agenda will be an important tool with which to diminish possible brand damage.

When conditions in the world change overnight, organizations are affected and are often forced into reactive mode. Training and preparation may be done to some extent before any crisis arises; however, many events cannot be simulated for training purposes and others cannot even be predicted. Mitroff (2004), however, discusses how post-crisis management efforts are more socially, culturally and locally oriented. In the case of crises due to major natural or other types of disasters, this perspective is significant.

One example of a pre-emptive action focusing on disasters as social events is the internal training of individuals in the organization. Such training aims at coaching personnel to take efficient action in the event of fire, earthquake, or terrorist attack, for example; the ultimate purpose is to reduce the incidence of casualties in the form of physical injuries or mental crises. Such action may not be altogether effective, however, as there is no guarantee that individuals will act according to their training and in the collective interest when disaster occurs in reality. King (2007), for instance, argues that, when a real-life catastrophe arises, the narcissistic personality type may even act in a counterproductive manner and in his own interest rather than in the interest of the organization. One conclusion from his study of narcissistic personalities is that it is questionable whether investments made in education and training pays off in the event of a real emergency.

There is also a theoretical discussion concerning the balance between risk-taking and crisis prevention actions and the costs of the latter. The cost of training personnel to deal with crises and costs for other crisis preparation measures must be seen in relation to the risk that a crisis may occur. In this sense crisis management and risk management relate to each other. It implies that a cost-minimizing manager would perform a risk assessment before preparatory resources are deployed. It explains why the cost argument could lead a company to avoid all crisis management preparations.

In the absence of substantial crisis preparation, in cases where an internal organizational crisis is damaging to the brand, a frequent way out is to blame an individual or fire company management (Lalonde 2004). As well, the executive group could take the opportunity to use a crisis as an excuse to make major changes (Lalonde 2007). Under normal circumstances, such changes would have been regarded as illegitimate or inappropriate within the company, but during a crisis, these changes can be justified – or rationalized. These types of measures are often less productive for the actual management of the organization as they draw attention away from the problems the crisis actually generated. The real crisis-related problems are never addressed.

Whether management practices proactive or reactive measures – or has no plan at all but chooses instead to improvise in the event of a crisis – it is a problem when the organization's own experience of crisis handling is not used. Earlier crisis experience should inspire active learning, which would lead to better crisis management in the future (Lalonde 2007; Catino 2008).

Other researchers discuss how the management's perspective on the company and its surroundings influences how crises are handled. According to Ouedraogo (2007), there are three possible perspectives when managing crises: the transactional cost perspective, the resource-based perspective, and the institutional perspective. The first implies that a company in a crisis always seeks to minimize transaction costs, the second assumes that the company has unlimited access to resources, and the third takes an institutional approach. According to Scott (2001), the concept of institution consists of various semantic meanings, including behavioural patterns and perspectives, cognitive models, and the corpus of ideas, beliefs, and rules.

An institutional approach relies on shared knowledge with respect to power, requirements, and reproduction. Shared knowledge makes collective action possible; it relies on proven routines in the local culture. As a consequence, an organization, influenced by an institutional approach is externally legitimized by the state, regulation authorities, and/or professional bodies. This organization takes into account the institutional framework in which it operates and adapts to it, but is also reluctant to see things in its environment in a different way. Within such an organization, inability to see things in a different way and to adapt in a changing environment often leads to stiffness and inertia. This kind of organization tends to be slowfooted. In turn, this creates passivity, and problems are often marginalized. The significance of an external crisis may even be nullified by the organization (Pettigrew et al. 1992). In the longer run, that leads to a non-acknowledgement of failure, which in turn may lead to the release of negative energy, as described in Senge (1990). Admitting problems and facing failure can help prevent the onset of a vicious circle. In an organization, influenced by an institutional approach, action should be at the core of the crisis management strategy dynamics (Ouedraogo 2007; Martinet 1996; Hafsi 1997; Mintzberg, Ahlstrand, and Lampel 1999).

The conclusion of the theory discussed above is that *action and ad hoc flexibility* as the core for crisis management is of particular importance whatever perspective management takes.

Case study: Jenapharm - A Partisan-Strategy for confronting an external disaster and an internal crisis at a time

Jenapharm is in the business of hormone compounds, oral contraceptives and hormone replacement compounds and is market leader for oral contraceptives in Germany. The company works in accordance with international standards: the quality and environmental management is DQS-certified in accordance with DIN ISO 9001:2000 and DIN ISO 14001 (Reg. No. 233484, www.Jenapharm.de). In the acquisition of Schering AG by Bayer in December 2006, the Schering subsidiary Jenapharm, with the market cash-cow Valette, was attractive. Considering that the East German company Jenapharm might just have well disappeared in conjunction with the Turnaround in 1989, the question must be asked what the secret is behind the impressive figures and data above. To what strategies before and after the Turnaround can the successful survival of Jenapharm be attributed?

1989: Turnaround and the time immediately after the Turnaround (Privatization of Jenapharm)

In GDR times, most businesses were state-owned. After the Turnaround, a law was passed by which all "people's own" companies were to be restructured as capital entities (Law Gazette of the GDR, read more about it in chapter above: "*In safe hands. Institutional Experience on the Road to a Market Economy*"). Accordingly, Jenapharm became a limited liability company in June 1990[139].

---

[139] The origin of Jenapharm is as follows: Dr. Hans Knoll was assigned by Schott to develop glass filters for sterile purposes for Jenaer Glas. Knoll was permitted to conduct "hobby research" within his work duties. As part of this hobby research, he patented his own process for the artificial production of penicillin. After the Second World War, there was high demand for penicillin. Initially, Thüringia was occupied by troops from the US. The evacuation of Knoll's laboratory was prepared, but was prevented by the employees. Knoll, who firstly went to the American zone, but returned and remained in Jena. When the Russians heard about this, they very quickly started up penicillin production in the premises of the Zeiss eye-glass plant. In 1946, penicillin products were presented for the first time at a trade fair. Penicillin could now be produced on a large scale for the first time. Shortly after the foundation of the GDR (1949), the production site of Jenapharm became one of the first people's own companies (1950).
1991 GEHE (Jenapharm is dressed as the bride and a groom is sought)/1996 Schering (Jenapharm is acquired as a threatening competitor, when the opportunity arises) /2006 Bayer-Schering (the Jenapharm trademark as the subsidiary of a subsidiary, more to follow…)

Jenapharm was also a large company, with 3,000 employees, which meant that the company attracted the attention of the Treuhand Agency, with the management called upon to present a restructuring plan to find a suitable investor. This made it clear to the Jenapharm management that privatization was unavoidable. Nobody could know what privatization would lead to. It was a matter of "fumbling in the dark," only the uncertain was certain, major changes were initiated. Active leadership was decisive for the future success of Jenapharm. The following sections show the manner in which the company was active, instead of passively harboring hope of assistance.

Time gained through drive and an ability to act

Without waiting for the Treuhand, work on preparing a restructuring concept was soon begun, which meant that the restructuring plan could be presented as early as September 1990.

"I prepared a restructuring plan very early on – together with my team. We asked the question: How can we best build up our marketing, distribution and sales?" Dr. Taubert[140], April 21, 2007.

Having a scientific model was important for the Treuhand. The scientific model of the applicant company needed to have "arms and legs" for consideration as an investor. Dr. Taubert achieved this through contact he himself established with a Swiss advisory company He explains further:

"Initially, the Treuhand was not particularly well organized. I personally had a different view of the situation than the Treuhand and tried to find an investor by myself. If I had waited for the Treuhand, the entire process would have been delayed by a year. This often led to an "extended workbench" for the result of privatization. Interested West German parties mainly wanted Jenap-

---

[140] *Information on our contact, Dr. Dieter Taubert: graduate engineer, Dr.rer.nat., Jenapharm employee since 1979; Trainee in production and the area of research and development, team leader in the chemistry department, head of the Establishment Staff for the preparation of the steroid plant, company director of the VEB Jenapharm since 1987, President of Jenapharm GmbH since 1990. From March 1, 2004 through April 1, 2007, President of Schering Deutschland GmbH. From April 1, employed with Bayer Vital (sales organization) as Head of Women's Healthcare. In summer 2007, he moved from Berlin to Leverkusen, to assume his position with Bayer Vital.*

harm without its research, with less production, but at least they wanted a local business partner." Dr. Taubert, April 17, 2007.

Independently of the Treuhand, an investor was sought, who could endorse the restructuring plan that had been prepared. To this end, Dr. Taubert came into contact with Schering, but also with the companies Ratiopharm and Stada. A special situation then arose with the company GEHE. The Stuttgart-based company had just made a comeback in the industry. At the time, GEHE was a pharmaceuticals wholesaler. It came to the attention of Dr. Taubert because it had just acquired another pharmaceuticals company. A company like Jenapharm, which could offer other products and, in addition, had its own research and development, could provide a favorable complement, thought Taubert. Accordingly, he presented the restructuring concept to GEHE and discussed with the company ways in which joint development might be achieved. They drove the privatization project independently and submitted an almost ready-made project to the Treuhand. The Treuhand accepted the proposal, but nonetheless wanted to take other interested parties into consideration as one was not sufficient. Following establishment of a supervisory board, the management of Jenapharm was asked to evaluate other offers of privatization. Ultimately, there were three competing offers that could be negotiated. In March 1991, the game of poker for Jenapharm commenced, albeit with the exclusion of the local management as far as possible.

"Once only two companies were in the running, I made myself the partisan between GEHE and Jenapharm, without knowing how the contest would end. Happily for me, GEHE won, since I was always able to tell them what would be particularly decisive in the privatization process, such as securing jobs and binding agreements to investments at the company's location." Dr. Taubert April 17, 2007.

On July 2, 1991, GEHE took over all of the business shares in Jenapharm from the Treuhand. The restructuring plan was then implemented. This included reorganization and the closure of production units that were no longer required. In this manner, the breadth of production was reduced. Chemical production was restricted to the manufacture of sexual medications and in the area of medical finished goods, the remaining facilities were modernized, while a pharmaceuticals production facility was built on a greenfield site in Weimar. As can clearly be seen, thanks to the management's drive and ability to act, Jenapharm was able to look for new ways and adapt to the new circumstances in a focused manner without losing much time.

The importance of caring for human capital

The atmosphere immediately after the Turnaround in the GDR was characterized by a mix of pioneering spirit and new starts. However, pessimism reigned and threatened to become overpowering. This pessimism applied to West German investors. Dr. Taubert believes that people are important. It is important to have a team that can be relied upon. He believes that Jenapharm survived partly because of the focused establishment of good relations and confidence in management. The East German management's preparedness to resist the "not-invented-here" syndrome was also decisive. This syndrome refers to the skepticism of West German customers toward East German products, a skepticism that was able to destabilize and paralyze some East German companies after the Turnaround.

"But when they have nothing else and see an opportunity, the human will is so great that it can move mountains." Dr. Taubert, April 17, 2007.

He also believes that the right style of leadership needs to be at the fore in this special situation. Management must be in the position to correctly motivate the employees, who are important for the future of the company in their role as key performers. In this respect, confidence in flawlessly functioning leadership is particularly important. The success deriving from this is the best accompaniment. It works as it does in football: the most difficult thing is to score 1:0; 2:0 is easier, and 3:0 occurs almost automatically. However, a prerequisite in a big bang, as brought about by the Turnaround, is that the products "are in order," and that there is a minimum level of financial possibility. This means that a specific core competence is required that has development potential and can find markets. More on this in the following section.

Recognition and capitalization of the core area

Following the Turnaround, it was also important to define the core business of the firm in order to determine the fields of research. There had to be consideration of the area in which research was to be conducted to bring innovative products to the market as quickly as possible. The core area in terms of the company's own traditions was sexual hormones, in particular oral contraception, and hormone-replacement therapy. In the area of sexual hormones, the competition in favor of Jenapharm was not as strong as in other indication areas. There were comparable products in East and West, but the advantage of

Jenapharm was that, globally, there were comparatively few companies in this area. Focus on the core area of hormones proved to be correct: for Jenapharm, sexual hormone products comprise two-thirds of its business in the 1990s. In the GEHE period (1991-1996), Jenapharm developed so successfully in the area of sexual hormones in Germany that one of GEHE's largest competitors (Schering AG[141]) ultimately acquired a majority of Jenapharm shares in 1996, thus becoming market leader in Germany in the area of sexual hormones.

Despite competitive advantages through its targeted and successful capitalization of the core area after the Turnaround, Jenapharm did experience a time of hardship. The company had too many employees overall, while at the same time, there was a need to expand in selected areas. At this time, sales at home and abroad were regressive because the former export markets in Central Eastern Europe were no longer receptive. In other words, the dramatically changed market situation after the Turnaround was a cause for concern. In indication areas other than sexual hormones, the company suffered loss of sales, albeit not as seriously as East German firms in other industries such as food.

"In the brewing sector, for example, producers could compete using such slogans as 'Beer is the feeling of home'. At that time, TV commercials had succeeded as a means of securing the loyalty of local consumers. In the food industry, expensive television advertising is often required to become established as a concept in the consciousness of the consumer and to remain there. But TV advertising requires a large turnover volume." Dr. Taubert, April 17, 2007.

With such OTC (over the counter) products as vitamins, for which television advertising was conducted, there was an initial requirement of a turnover volume of DEM 60 M for a product to be able to finance any TV advertising at all.

---

[141] As already described, GEHE re-entered the pharmaceuticals industry in 1990. In 1996, GEHE again withdrew; it wanted to become a pharmaceuticals wholesaler once again as it was prior to 1990. The reason was that GEHE wanted stronger internationalization of its core business. For the same reason, it had recently established a joint pharmaceuticals project with a company in the UK. In 1996, 51 percent of GEHE belonged to Haniel, meaning that the majority of shares in the company were family-owned, with 49 percent in diverse ownership on the stock exchange. At this time, GEHE itself had acquired various companies and offered Jenapharm as the trump card. There were three interested parties: Schering, Organon and Wyeth. Schering was the winner, although a higher purchase consideration was offered by Wyeth. Wyeth had made a mistake regarding the US: as a bidder, Wyeth wanted guarantees from GEHE that GEHE did not want to give. Nonetheless, six years after the Turnaround, Jenapharm was so attractive that three parties immediately took an interest in the company.

Today, a producer requires a minimum of EUR 40 M! The enormous amounts required for TV advertising were simply not viable in the survival process at Jenapharm. But nonetheless, the company's products were in order and it had a financing partner. In terms of sales, it was primarily a matter of securing new markets using reasonable means. What did Jenapharm do after the Turnaround to bring to market its products for which neither expensive advertising nor expensively gained permits were possibilities?

Affordable access to the market

Immediately after the Turnaround, two factors applied: East German customers should not be captured by West German companies and Western markets had to be secured anew.

The first challenge, to take care of and retain the market in the East, was not too difficult in the pharmaceutical industry according to Dr. Taubert. This is attributable to the fact that there were established favorable and reliable relations with the physicians there. In many industries, the sudden loss of the Eastern market for East German companies was an unavoidable and bitter result of the Turnaround. Time was also required to recapture the lost 25 percent of the market in the East and to replace it. The management of Jenapharm looked reality in the eye and acted accordingly. It was aware that:

"Every day, I am losing shares of the East German market. That is why I must be active throughout Germany and gain West Germany as a market." Dr. Taubert, April 17, 2007.

The factor that partly protected the company's sales in the East German market was the same factor that created obstacles in the West German market. Customers in the pharmaceuticals industry are rather slow and do not readily adapt to a new market or a new product: a physician is acquainted with a pharmaceutical after many years of use and is thus convinced of the product quality. He does not shift his patients on to a different product from one day to the next. Regardless of this problem that was basically specific to the industry, the pharmaceutical industry was able to cope with the general problem with which East German companies struggled:

"The building of marketing and sales organizations caused difficulties for the East German companies, who were trying to hold their own in a competitive

situation. I wanted to become involved in sales myself and it was clear to me that, particularly in our area, a professional sales force was required in order to be in any way competitive." Dr. Taubert, April 17, 2007.

Since access to the market had been identified as the absolute survival factor, the company needed to recruit employees internally for its sales team or find them externally. A potential sales person in the industry should either have qualifications in natural science or be an experienced pharmaceuticals consultant. A pharmaceuticals consultant requires six months' training and also has to pass a Chamber of Commerce examination. Where possible, applicants should also live in the areas in which they will work. This means that applicants from among the company's own ranks would need to be prepared to relocate.

"In terms of new employees, the key factor was to find people who wanted to work in the old federal Länder in behalf of an East German company, meaning that it was sufficiently attractive for them to be employed by an East German company." Dr. Taubert, April 17, 2007.

From the very beginning, it was important for Jenapharm to establish its own representation in West Germany and not, as discussed in GEHE, to become a "hanger-on" of sister company Azupharma when visiting customers. After initial opposition from the GEHE management, all parties were in agreement that Jenapharm should appear in the market with its own identity. In January 1992, the first member of the Jenapharm sales force began visiting gynecologists in West Germany.

But a professional sales team was not enough to secure success. To capture markets, Jenapharm needed an established West German company to take on Jenapharm products. This factor was also one of the motivators for Dr. Taubert in establishing contact with GEHE. Inclusion was extremely important from a medium and long-term perspective. For him, it was also important to secure recognition for Jenapharm as company using its own identity and in turn, to integrate this into GEHE products. The aim was to preserve the "Jenapharm" trademark. After extensive resistance from the GEHE parent company, Jenapharm established its own sales team in West Germany in January 1992.

"I was very lucky that I was able to convince both Boards (that is, the chairmen and the financial board) that I had the correct concept. After a while of putting forward the concept, I was proud that it was endorsed." Dr. Taubert, April 21, 2007.

The original export markets of Central and Eastern Europe had broken away in the process of the Turnaround. The same changes as in East Germany occurred there, meaning that in terms of the Jenapharm market, entirely new marketing and sales organizations had to also be established in these areas.

It was necessary to always be on the ball to find new people for the sales team. In West Germany, this was where one problem always arose: the resentment of potential West German applicants regarding the idea of working for East German companies in the East.

"Particularly nowadays, when I am also responsible for marketing and sales activities, I can see in people who have been working in sales for 25 years that the area of sales ability can still be improved." Dr. Taubert, April 21, 2007.

The spark

Dr. Taubert believed in the company and its potential and wanted it to survive and flourish. He would even have liked to buy Jenapharm himself but could not secure financing from the bank. There was one bank that gave him approval in December 1990. But then the Treuhand came along with its bidding process and the bank withdrew once a certain level was reached (Bank West LB in Düsseldorf, Nordrhein-Westfalen.)

Dr. Taubert soon realized that among the interested parties that applied to the Treuhand, there were various categories: fortune-hunters and very serious people, who were enthusiastic about unification and believed in the potential of the East Germans. And there were also gray areas among the interested parties. Since Dr. Taubert did not possess the minimum financial capacity, he personally was not considered as an interested party. But he invested his commitment and enthusiasm in the company, which was – as already described – decisive for the success story of Jenapharm.

Summary of the crucial success factors for Jenapharm

The following are identified as crucial success factors for Jenapharm:
1. Reorganization of the company and a targeted approach to the requirements of the market economy.
2. Build-up of marketing/sales organization in Germany and the management by this of what remained of the old market. i.e. secure new markets, retain old markets.

3. Building of networks. Establishment of contacts.
4. Through recognition and development of the core area, the creation of prerequisites for new products.
5. Focused generation of growth and exports to ensure medium and long-term success.
6. Reliable human capital and the correct motivation for this.
7. A spark, meaning someone who can enthuse and inspire the employees.

Action and ad-hoc flexibility led to the seven success factors listed above. It makes the Jenapharmian patrisan-strategy, aimed at confronting an external disaster and an internal crisis simultaneously, an ad-hoc strategy for crisis management.

10. Understanding survival

In unified Germany, the survival of East German companies was an unusual and uncommon occurrence, as most East German companies did not survive the transition. In this book, we have concentrated on finding out why and how companies could survive a change as drastic as that from a planned economy to a market economy. The survival of the vast majority of East Germany's companies was threatened with the introduction of the market economy; we set out to describe what managers of the companies that survived did right to fit into a competitive global economy.

When a company's survival is threatened, management that intends to prevail can enter what can be described as "survival mode". Indeed, managers may not necessarily act rationally in a world of uncertainty. This book has looked at various ways of ensuring corporate survival in troubled times. Survival mode can be analysed as encompassing specific skills that managers have or acquire. The contemporary global economy is in many ways more turbulent than at any other time in history. Competitors can emerge from anywhere in the world and rapidly gain competitive advantages. An interpretive approach to the survival strategies employed by East German companies has provided insight into actions taken as a last resort to ensure continued corporate existence.

Survival strategies are important when the existing business model cannot ensure the company's future. How managers deal with difficult circumstances renders insight into their skills. In turbulent markets and hostile business environments, management will have to take drastic measures to ensure continued existence. Interpreting these unique, challenging situations and the specific ways companies deal with them has yielded new and interesting research findings.

It is essential to understand how companies implement strategies to meet and overcome major challenges. Survival strategies can be interpreted in relation to the concrete actions managers take to ensure the continuation of their companies. We have presented numerous examples of how managers have been able to guide their businesses through troubled times; such experiences can be distilled and transferred to other situations in which the existence of the company is at stake.

When facing potential closure, companies resort to actions that are more drastic than those seen in the day-to-day running of a company. Dramatic shifts, such as sudden exposure to global market competition, call for drastic actions. These can be observed in companies that have succeeded, and not in those that have failed. The survivors are the champions of these drastic strategies. The selection of successes from among the failures yields insight into which strategies are successful.

Constructing a new future

A new reality provides opportunities for creating a new future. With the fall of the Berlin Wall, East Germans experienced new freedoms. There were difficulties ahead, and new competition set new requirements on the companies that made it through the initial period of turmoil. A new future could be constructed by combining existing knowledge with the newfound opportunities of the market economy. The companies we studied did not leave the industries they were in. The entrepreneurs we met identified their companies' strengths. These included genuine hand-crafted traditions that had survived in an isolated niche far removed from the laws of profitability, high quality products with value and global reputations, such as Meissen porcelain or Jena glass, and products that, prior to the fall, had provided East Germany with sought-after Western currency. Last but not least, *ostalgia* proved to be a boon for the survival of East German products, particularly at food markets. The most striking lesson from the examples mentioned above has parallels to common advice for surviving an emergency: if you break through the ice and attempt to pull yourself out of the water, you should turn to the direction from which you came, because you know that the ice just held there.

At the same time, these entrepreneurs were willing to adopt new approaches. Old practices were scrapped when they failed in the new economic context; others were kept alive if they were proven to work.

Companies surviving the market economy seldom revolutionised the businesses they were in. Business construction seemed more like an evolution of their past practices. We were surprised to see that a large number of old methods of production could survive. At the same time, the survivors were characterised by quick thinking and rapid adaptability. Factories were reconstructed and rebuilt to be modernised and adapted to new production methods. Few stones were left unturned. The successful part of the reconstruction of East German industry was characterised by rapid development and change. There was little time to spare if companies were to survive the onset of new competition—companies had to be ready to compete from day one. Financial support from western Germany provided a small cushion for a while. In order to survive over the longer time, however, companies had to make successful plans for the future as soon as possible. Survival was a matter of reconstruction. A new future had to be carved out of the old company. Distinguishing workable practices from non-workable practices was a crucial part of ensuring survival in the market economy.

Attracting new investment

The companies making the transition were underfinanced when they were introduced to the market economy, and several investments had to be made to keep up with the West. A major challenge in ensuring survival, therefore, was attracting new investment. New capital could come from private investors, but also from government funding. It was common among surviving companies to receive public funding for the first five years after unification, primarily from regional governments. From our empirical material it is clear that public funding has been essential to survival, although it was not sufficient for ensuring long-term survival. Finding partners or new owners in the West with access to fresh capital was a solution for several (but not all) companies. A number of companies survived on their own without a partner or a "white knight" from the West.

Ensuring a positive cash flow as soon as possible was also central to survival. In our empirical study we see examples of companies loading up lorries full of goods and driving them to open-air markets to find buyers wherever they could be found. In some instances, goods were sold right out of the lorry. We have described this as panic marketing—attempting to find a market at all costs. After all, income from sales could ensure short-term survival and ensure that a minimal staff could be kept working at the company.

Proposing attractive investment opportunities

A survival strategy for East German companies was to present attractive investment opportunities for outside investors. Companies could offer a skilled workforce at slightly lower labour costs. Indeed, wage levels are still lower in eastern Germany, although they have leveled out since unification. East Germans are dedicated and many saw unification as an opportunity to develop new and interesting business opportunities. For example, a company like Freiberger Compound Materials had an interesting technology already developed and was capable of producing vital parts for the computer industry. As a result, Freiberger attracted a new investor who bought part of the company; this had since become a profitable investment and represented a viable new owner for the company.

Other companies have become subsidiaries within a larger enterprise, such as ASS Altenburger, which became a wholly-owned subsidiary after being bought out. This meant that the company had access to fresh capital and new investments from the parent organisation; this was a vital factor behind its long-term survival as a company in eastern Germany. Finding a buyer was also the chosen survival strategy for Jenapharm. We decided to call this a partisan strategy—one where the managers acted in favour of a chosen buyer before the company was put up for sale. The management of Jenapharm was convinced that the organisation that bought the company was important to its own future.

Letting bygones be bygones

The case studies of East German companies render evidence of the suppression of entrepreneurship and free thought under the GDR regime, a dictatorship that attempted to assert political control over capital and production. Management had only limited influence over their own enterprise, since there was political control at every level of production. If a new product would reach the market, for example, it first had to be cleared with political appointees. A company's level of production had to be included in a plan for the economy as a whole.

Surviving companies showed an ability to start fresh and leave the obstacles of the past behind. This was a much-needed ability in the post-GDR era. Many managers felt that they had been subjected to injustices in the past. The most prominent example was Rainer Thiele at the Kathi company, which was founded by Thiele's parents as a family firm. In 1972, however, the company was taken away from the family and put under government control. After an intense struggle, he was able to regain his company in 1990.

The GDR economy was a poor economic performer (despite being the best performing country in the Eastern Bloc) and the country was close to bankrupt in 1989. Entrepreneurship was thwarted by political control and the lack of competition starved innovation. The ability to transition from a planned economy to a market economy was in some instances remarkable. We have studied how managers were able to provide their companies with new beginnings.

Imagining a better future

Carving out a new future for a company after years of central economic planning requires management to imagine a better future for the company. The cases illustrate an ability to envision a new situation and new capabilities. The ability to change the frame of mind from one mindset to another explains why some companies survived. A number of managers undertook periods of intense brainstorming and many other initiatives in support of determining the correct way forward.

Our empirical material shows that anything is possible if managers put their minds to abstract as well as concrete problems. No change has been quite as fundamental as that between a planned and a market economy. Only a few years after the transition, however, some companies were able to become market leaders, first in their home market, and later even in more distant markets. The willingness to change, and an ability to identify the company's own strengths and capabilities had proven essential for ensuring survival.

Creating new value in the market economy

Western markets were beyond reach for most East German products at the time of transition. With average productivity levels one-third of those in the West, East German products typically had little chances of competing, particularly after the introduction of the Deutschmark, which revalued the currency between 300 and 400 per cent and, therefore, overburdened the East German economy. East German producers almost instantly lost their markets (including GDR's own domestic market), which had become hard currency markets overnight.

After years of isolation and lack of competition behind the Iron Curtain, East German products often appeared old fashioned. The producers could be sure of selling most of these products anyway, but only in the GDR or eastern markets within Comecon (the Council for Mutual Economic Assistance). The products were not designed to meet the desires of consumers in a competitive market. Moreover, a developed and expensive system of state subsidies protected them. When more attractive goods were shipped in from the West, the curiosity for something new was greater than consumer loyalty to the old products (it is doubtful whether genuine consumer loyalty had ever even developed during the GDR era). People were left with few alternatives to the products that were offered, and products were often in short supply.

Once an abundance of alternative products came to market, consumers began developing preferences, tastes and loyalties. At this stage, old and, as it turned out, high quality GDR brands came back into fashion, as they represented an identity and continuity that people craved, despite the hardship they had experienced during the GDR era. After all, it was "their" products that were produced locally. This was particularly true with regard to consumer goods such as sparkling wine, chocolate and beer. We followed companies like Halloren and Rhönbrauerei, which managed to maintain substantial market share in face of stiff competition from the West.

Ostalgia in eastern Germany was, first and foremost, an expression of the longing for social stability and order in a turbulent and chaotic new reality. Since the beginning of the 1990s, *ostalgia* has saved thousands of jobs in the region. While western firms with dependencies in the East were successfully leveraging the phenomenon in their marketing, German politicians were condemning those clinging to the values and memories of life in the GDR. It was reactions such as these that made *ostalgia* an active choice—thereby strengthening the self-confidence of many East Germans and establishing an essential precondition for grappling with the challenges of the market economy.

Some companies in eastern Germany made products and services that were undervalued in the market, and neither western nor eastern consumers saw the value of what was produced in the former GDR. Consumers were heavily biased against products that originated from eastern Germany. Companies that could survive this period had a better chance of experiencing brighter days as the dust settled. East German consumers returned to these products, and a number of West German consumers developed a curiosity for what was produced by their Eastern neighbours. More than 20 years after the fall of the Wall, however, prejudice against East German products is still strong in the West, and strategies to overcome this prejudice can be studied in some of our cases.

Utilising existing and new knowledge

The East German companies we analysed had access to a skilled workforce and other means of production that could easily be modernised to meet new standards. Making use of existing intellectual capital and complementing it with market knowledge and new management skills—sometimes imported from western Germany—enabled companies to change rapidly and adjust to new demands. East German companies demonstrated an ability to use their existing knowledge bases to their advantage. Some companies that were considered "high-tech" in previous years, such as the Zeiss company and Jenaerglass, could identify their strengths and their shortcomings.

It was common for East German companies to closely follow western companies within the same industry. As a result, management knew what was necessary to keep up with the competition. The end of the planned economy era also meant access to new machinery and raw materials that could improve products and production techniques. Important to survival was the mindset of the managers and employees—a willingness to change and develop was necessary for ensuring continued production and preventing bankruptcy. The survivors had a strong desire to chase the opportunities that the new times represented.

Experiences of privatisation

As seen in the cases, the role of the Treuhand agency between 1990 and 1994 was different from its traditional role. The more that firms took the initiative and convincingly presented solutions to the Treuhand decision-makers, the less time was lost to bureaucratic struggles. For many other companies, however, this was not possible due to the DM2.17 million in restitution claims, which led to a "paralysing stranglehold" (Rohwedder) on the East German economy. Uncertainty of property ownership in particular was a serious impediment to investment.

Such a statement can be seen in the context of political decisions that were made before Treuhand, in a kind of scapegoat function, was able to act.

The lessons from Treuhand "learning by doing in its purest form" (Breuel) demonstrate that it was right to separate the agency as much as possible from the bureaucratic apparatus of federal ministries. At least one precondition for enabling quicker decision-making was fulfilled through this move. Even the obligation for buyers to present a business concept was an experience worth preserving, although it was not a guarantee of "clean" sales.

In contrast to the business concept, plans for research and development (R&D) were absent. Birgit Breuel, the former chairman of Treuhand, calls this a mistake—the consequences of which continue to be seen today. According to the 2009 Report of the Federal Government on the State of German Unity, "less than five per cent of industrial R&D investments in Germany are made in the new Bundesländer" (Jahresbericht 6)—a clear disadvantage for the future. Most of the companies we visited had fought strongly for keeping at least parts of their R&D units and their leading research personnel. Being able to do so depended on successive products and survival strategies in the very beginning of the 1990s, which was unusual for the overwhelming majority of East German firms in the united Germany, where the research departments were dissolved. The transition from a state-regulated planned economy into a market economy, with the accompanying change of regime, is still a challenge for all those involved.

Corporate survival

Common to all the studied companies was their realisation that a situation they had never planned for had occurred, and that they now desperately needed a plan. They were not paralysed by the crisis, but instead applied ad hoc strategies to survive. They did not hesitate to use temporary measures to keep production running while management pursued future development opportunities. It was essential for management to act instantly, regardless of possible future regulation by the authorities. One conclusion from this is that the companies were active and seized the offensive. Moreover, all of the survivors examined in the present study built their success on their own core competencies.

This research into corporate survival has one central practical implication—to stress the importance of swift and assertive management action when confronted with radically changing conditions. In particular, under no circumstances must production halt, and the company's core competencies must be managed and developed; this can especially be illustrated by the activities of Meissen, Kathi and Jenapharm.

References

Aaker, J., Benet-Martinez, V. and Garolera, J. (2001), Consumption symbols as carriers of culture: a study of Japanese and Spanish brand personality constructs, *Journal of Personality and Social Psychology*, 81, 3, 492-508

Aaker, D.A. and Joachimsthaler, E. (2000), The Brand Relationship Spectrum: The Key to the Brand Architecture Challenge, *California Management Review* 42 (4): 8-23

Aaker, D.A. (1996), *Building Strong Brands*. New York: Free Press

Aaker, D.A., *Keller*, K.L. (*1990*), Consumer evaluations of brand extensions, *Journal of Marketing*, 54, 1, 27-41

Agarwal, M.K. (1995), Review of 40-year debate in international advertising, *International Marketing Review*, 12, 1, 26-48

Ahbe, Thomas (1997), Ostalgie als Selbstermächtigung. Zur produktiven Stabilisierung ostdeutscher Identität. *Deutschlandarchiv*, 1, 614-19

Ahbe, Thomas (2005), Der Osten aus der Sicht des Westens. Die Bilder von den Ostdeutschen und ihre Konstrukteure, in: Bahrmann, Hannes and Christoph Links (ed.), *Am Ziel vorbei. Die deutsche Einheit – Eine Zwischenbilanz*. Berlin: Ch. Links, 268-81

Albright, K.S. (2004), Environmental Scanning: Radar for Success, *Information Management Journal*, 38, 3, 38–45

Anderer, Tatjana (1997), Dahlhoff – Spirituosen für Spaßvögel. *Wirtschaftswoche* no. 38

Andersen, A. (1998), *Knowledge Measurement*, Pittsburg, PA: Next Generation Group, 99-1029

Anderson, Carol H. and Julian W. Vincze (2004), *Strategic Marketing Management*, Boston: Houghton Mifflin

Anderson, James and Narus, James (1999), *Business Market Management*. New Jersey: Prentice Hall

Anderson, J.C., Hakansson, H. and Johanson J. (1994), Dyadic business relationships within a business network context, *Journal of Marketing*, 58, 4, 1–15

Baale, Olaf (2008), *Abbau Ost. Lügen, Vorurteile und sozialistische Schulden*. München: Deutscher Taschenbuch Verlag

Banchelli, Eva (2008), Ostalgie: eine vorläufige Bilanz, in: Cambi, Fabrizio (ed.), *Gedächtnis und Identität*. Würzburg: Königshausen & Neumann, 57-68

Belk, Russel W. Ger, G. L. Askegard, S. (2003), The Fire of Desire: A Multisited Inquiry into Consumer Passion, *Journal of Consumer Research*, 30, 3, 326-351

Berg, Bruce L. (2001), *Qualitative Research Methods for the Social Sciences*, Boston: Allyn and Bacon

Betz, Thomas (2000), 10 Jahre keine Einheit – Ein Kompendium wirtschaftspolitischer Fehler. In: *Zeitschrift für Sozialökonomie*, 127. Folge, 37. Jahrgang. Lütjenburg: Verlag für Sozialökonomie, 2-19

Betz, Thomas G. (2005), Die Eigentumsfrage. Das Prinzip „Rückgabe vor Entschädigung" und seine Folgen. In: Bahrmann, Hannes; Links, Christoph (eds.): *Am Ziel vorbei. Die deutsche Einheit – Eine Zwischenbilanz*. Berlin: Ch. Links Verlag, 107-123

Bisky, Jens (2004), Zonensicht. Kritik der neuen Ostalgie. *Merkur* no. 658

Bjelland, Osvald M. and Robert Chapman Wood 2008. Five ways to transform a business *Strategy and Leadership*, 36, 3, 4-14

Böhmer, Wolfgang (2009), „Gewisse Herzlichkeit statt Besserwisserei". *Volksstimme Magdeburg*, 1 April

Bolin; Göran, Monica Hammer, Frank-Michael Kirsch and Wojciech Szrubka (Ed.) (2005) *The Challenge of the Baltic Sea Region. Culture, Ecosystems, Democracy,* Huddinge: Södertörn Academic Studies 29

Bontis, Nick (1998), Intellectual Capital: an exploratory study that develops measures and models, *Management Decisions*, 36, 2, 63-76

Bontis, Nick (2001), Assessing knowledge assets: A review of the models used to measure intellectual capital, *International Journal of Management Reviews,* 3, 1, 41–60

Borg, Erik A. (2009), The Marketing of Innovation in High-Technology Companies, A Network Approach, *European Journal of Marketing*, 43, 3/4, 364-370

Borg, Erik A.; Kirsch, Frank-Michael and Åkerhielm, Renate (2007), Survivors in the Market Economy. East German Companies after Transition, *The Business Review Cambridge*, 7, 2, 179-188

Borg, Erik A.; F.- M. Kirsch and R. Åkerhielm (2007), *Competent Marketing: Survival stories in Emerging Markets*, Paper presented at the International Business and Management Research Conference June 1-4, 2007, Honolulu, Hawaii, USA

Borg, Erik A.; F.- M. Kirsch and R. Åkerhielm (2007), *Three ways to Survive the Market Economy – A study of East German companies*, Paper presented at the Focal Point Germany conference, Huddinge, Sweden, November 9-10, 2007

Borg, Erik A. (2006), The Latvian Market Constructed: approaches towards independence, consumerism, symbolic leadership and market planning, *Baltic Journal of Management*, 1, 1, 67-81

Borg, Erik A. (Ed) (2006), *Globalisations, Nations and Markets, Challenging issues in current research on Globalisation*, Södertörn Academic Studies, 23

Borg, Erik A. (2001), Knowledge, information and intellectual property: Implications for marketing relationships, *Technovation: The International Journal for Innovation, Entrepreneurship and Technology Management*, 21, 515–24

Borg, Erik A. (1991), Problem shifts and market research: the role of networks in business relationships, *Scandinavian Journal of Management*, 7, 4, 285–295

Borja de Mozota, Brigitte (2003), *Design Management, Using Design to build Brand Value and Corporate Innovation*, New York: Allworth Press

Bornemann, Manfred; Knapp, Adolf; Schneider, Ursula and Sixl, Karin (1999), Holistic measurement of intellectual capital, paper presented at the International Symposium, *Measuring and Reporting Intellectual Capital: Experiences, Issues and Prospects*, 9–10 June, Amsterdam

Bothmann, Jakob (1995), Der Absturz der „Interflug": Krise und Liquidierung der ostdeutschen Fluggesellschaft. In: Dümcke, Wolfgang; Wilmar, Fritz (eds.): *Kolonialisierung der DDR. Kritische Analysen und Alternativen des Einigungsprozesses*. Münster: agenda Verlag, 188-194

Boyer, Dominic (2006), Ostalgie and the Politics of the Future in Eastern Germany. *Public Culture*, 18 (2), 361-81

Breuel, Birgit (2005), Die Treuhandanstalt – Zielvorgaben, Rahmenbedingungen und Ergebnisse. In: Breuel, Birgit; Burda, Michael C. (eds.): *Ohne historisches Vorbild. Die Treuhandanstalt 1990-1994. Eine kritische Würdigung*. Berlin: Bostelmann & Siebenhaar, 13-30

Brooking, Annie (1997), *Intellectual Capital, Core Asset for the Third Millenium Enterprise*, London: Thomson Business Press

Bruce, M.; Daly, L. and Kahn, K-B. (2007), Delineating Design Factors that Influence the Global Product Launch Process, *Journal of Product Innovation Management* 24 (5), 456-470

Bruce, M. and Bessant, J. (2002), *Design in Business – Strategic Innovation Through Design*. Harlow: Pearson Education Limited

Bruce, M. and Cooper, R. (2000), *Creative product design – a practical guide to requirements capture management*. Chicester: Wiley

Bruce, M. and Cooper, R. (1997), *Marketing and Design Management*. London: International Thomson Business Press

Brussig, Thomas (1999), *Am kürzeren Ende der Sonnenallee*. Berlin: Volk & Welt

Bundesministerium für Familie und Senioren (1994), *Familien und Familienpolitik im geeinten Deutschland – Zukunft des Humanvermögens. Fünfter Familienbericht*. Bonn

Burda, Michael C. (2005), Ein Reformschub für ganz Deutschland – Die Treuhandprivatisierung aus nationalökonomischer Sicht. In: Breuel, Birgit; Burda, Michael C. (eds.): *Ohne historisches Vorbild. Die Treuhandanstalt 1990-1994. Eine kritische Würdigung*. Berlin: Bostelmann & Siebenhaar, 176-187

Busch, Ulrich (2005), Die Währungsunion. Politische Weichenstellung für einen ökonomischen Fehlstart. In: Bahrmann, Hannes; Links, Christoph (eds.): *Am Ziel vorbei. Die deutsche Einheit – Eine Zwischenbilanz*. Berlin: Ch. Links Verlag, 75-92

Büttner, Andreas (1995), Die verheerende Wirtschaftsentwicklung in Ostdeutschland in der Zeit von 1990-1994. In: Dümcke, Wolfgang; Wilmar, Fritz (eds.): *Kolonialisierung der DDR. Kritische Analysen und Alternativen des Einigungsprozesses*. Münster: agenda Verlag, 117-129

Catino, Maurizio (2008), A Review of Literature: Individual Blame vs. Organizational Function Logics in Accident Analysis *Journal of Contingencies and Crisis Management* 16 (1), 53–62

Chebat, Jean-Charles (1999), 'Introduction, special issue on strategy implementation and assessment research: Research on implementation deserves as much attention as strategy formulation', *Journal of Business Research* 45: 107–10

Christ, Gerhard (1995), Treuhandanstalt: Privatisierung vor Sanierung? In: Dümcke, Wolfgang; Wilmar, Fritz (eds.): *Kolonialisierung der DDR. Kritische Analysen und Alternativen des Einigungsprozesses*. Münster: agenda Verlag, 154-169

Christodoulides G. (2009), Branding in the post-internet era, *Marketing Theory* 9; 141-144

Collins, J.C. (2001), *Good to Great*, New York: Harper Business

Cooper, R.G. (2008), Perspective: The Stage-Gate Idea-to-Launch Process — Update, What's New, and NexGen Systems *Journal of Product Innovation Management* 25 (3), 213–232

Cooper, R.G. (2004), New Products: *What Separates the Winners from the Losers*. In: The PDMA Handbook of New Product Development, 2d ed., ed Kenneth Kahn. New York: John Wiley & Sons, 3–28

Cravens, David W. and Nigel F. Piercy (2006), *Strategic Marketing*, NY: McGraw Hill Irwin

Curkovic Sime and Robert Handfield, (1996), Use of ISO 9000 and Baldrige Award Criteria in Supplier Quality Evaluation, *International Journal of Purchasing and Material Management*, Spring 1996

Debatte zum Bericht des 2. Untersuchungsausschusses „Treuhandanstalt", 243. Sitzung des Deutschen Bundestages am 21.09.1994. In: *Das Parlament*, Bonn, Nr. 39, 1994-09-30

De Chernatony, Leslie; Harris, Fiona and Riley, Francesca (2000), Added value: Its nature, roles and sustainability, *European Journal of Marketing* 34: 39–56

De Mooij, Marieke (2005), *Global Marketing and Advertising -Understanding Cultural Paradoxes*, Thousand Oaks: Sage Publications

De Mooij, Marieke (2003), *Consumer Behaviour and Culture-Consequences for Global Marketing and Advertising*. Thousand Oaks: Sage Publications

Denzin, Norman K. and Yvonna S. Lincoln, (Eds.), (1998), *The Landscape of Qualitative Research*, Thousand Oaks, Ca.: Sage

Deutscher Bundestag, 11. Wahlperiode, 197. Sitzung, 1990-02-15, Stenographischer Bericht: 15106. Helmut Kohl, Bundeskanzler

Deutscher Bundestag, 11. Wahlperiode, 197. Sitzung, 1990-02-15, Stenographischer Bericht: 15129. Theodor Waigel, Bundesfinanzminister

Dieckmann, Christoph (1997), Mißlingt die Einheit? (lecture), Veranstaltung des Goethe-Instituts Stockholm zum Thema „Die Befindlichkeit nach der Vereinigung". Van der Nootska Palatset, Stockholm, 26 April

Dieckmann, Christoph (2003), Honis heitere Welt. *Die Zeit* no. 37

Dolmetscher der Träume (1999), *Der Spiegel* no. 39

Doole, Isobel and Robin Lowe (2008), *International Marketing Strategy, Analysis development and implementation*, London: South-Western

Drost, Helmar (1993), The Great Depression in East Germany: the Effects of Unification on East Germany's Economy. *East European Politics & Societies* 7, 452-481

Duchessi, Peter, (2002), *Crating Customer Value, The Art and Science*, West Lafayette, Indiana: Purdue University Press

Dumas, Angela and Mintzberg, Henry (1991), Managing the form, function, and fit of design *Design Management Journal*, 2: 26–31

Duysters, G.M. and Hagedoorn J. (1995), Strategic groups and inter-firm networks in international high-tech industries, *Journal of Management Studies*, 32, 3, 361–381

Engler, Wolfgang (1995), *Die ungewollte Moderne*. Frankfurt am Main: Suhrkamp

Financial Times Deutschland (2008), 7 September

Flick, Uwe; Ernst von Kardorff and Ines Seinke (Eds.), (2004), *A Companion to Qualitative Reseach*, London: Sage

Fritze, Lothar (1997), *Die Gegenwart des Vergangenen. Über das Weiterleben der DDR nach ihrem Ende*. Weimar, Köln, Wien: Böhlau

Gale, Bradley T. (1994), *Managing Customer Value: Creating Quality and Service That Customers Can See*, New York: Free Press

Geinitz, Christian, Die Spaltung dauert an. *FAZ*, Frankfurt/Main, 2007-04-05

Geinitz, Christian, Klägliche Einheitsrendite. *FAZ*, Frankfurt/Main, 2007-10-02

Gesetz zur Privatisierung und Reorganisation des volkseigenen Vermögens (Treuhandgesetz), 1990-06-17

Gesetzblatt der Deutschen Demokratischen Republik, (1990), Teil I Nr. 14

Gilmore, J.H. and Pine, J.I. (1997), The four faces of mass customization, *Harvard Business Review*, 75, 1, 91-101

Gorb P. and Dumas A. (1987), Silent Design, *Design Issues*, July, 8, 3, 150-156

Gorka-Reimus, Gudrun (2007), *Hedwig Bollhagen. Ein Leben für die Keramik*. Potsdam: Haus der Brandenburgisch-Preußischen Geschichte, Monumente Publikationen der Deutschen Stiftung Denkmalschutz

Graetz, F. (2000), Strategic Change Leadership, *Management Decision*, 38, 8, 550-564

Green, Deschamps and Paéz (2005), Variation of Individualism and Collectivism within and between 20 Countries *Journal of Cross-Cultural Psychology*, 36, 3, 321-339

Grub, Frank Thomas (2003), *"Wende" und "Einheit" im Spiegel der deutschsprachigen Literatur. Vol. 1: Untersuchungen*. Berlin, New York: Walter de Gruyter

Grönroos, C. (2002), *Service Management och marknadsföring – En CRM Ansats*, Malmö: Liber

Grönroos C. (1990), *Service Management and Marketing. Managing the Moments of Truth in Service Competition* Massachusetts/Toronto: Lexington Books

Hafsi, T. (1997), Le Champ De Recherche En Stratégie: A La Recherche D'un Bâton D'aveugle, *Management International*, 2, 1, 19–26

Hakansson, H. and Snehota, I. (1989), No business is an island: the network concept of business strategy, *Scandinavian Journal of Management*, 4, 3, 187–200

Hakatie, Annaleena; Ryynänen,Toni (2007), Managing Creativity: A Gap Analysis Approach to Identifying Challenges for Industrial Design Consultancy Services *Design Issues*, Winter 2007, 23, 1, 28–46

Hamel, G. and A. Heene (eds) (1994), *Competence-based competition*, Chichester: Wiley & Sons

Härtel, Hans Hagen; Krüger, Reinald; Seeler, Joachim and Marisa Weinhold (1991), *Institutionelle Ursachen von Wettbewerbsverzerrungen in den neuen Bundesländern*. HWWA-Report Nr. 92, 1991-09-01

Haveman, Heather A. 1992. Between a Rock and a Hard Place: Organisational change and performance under conditions of fundamental environmental transformation, *Administrative Science Quarterly*, 37, 48-75

Hein, Christoph (1989), *Der Tangospieler*. Berlin und Weimar: Aufbau

Herrmann, A. Heitmann, M. (2006), Providing more or providing less? Accounting for cultural differences in consumers' preference for variety. *International Marketing Review*, 23, 1, 7-24

Hertle, Hans-Herrmann, and Stefan Wolle (2006), *Damals in der DDR. Der Alltag im Arbeiter- und Bauernstaat*. München: Goldmann

Hofstede, G. (2001), *Culture's Consequences: Comparing Values, Behaviors, Institutions, and Organizations across Nations*. Thousand Oaks, CA: Sage

Hooley, Graham; Nigel F. Piercy and Birgitte Nicoulaud (2008), *Marketing Strategy and Competitive Positioning*, Harlow, Essex: Pearson

Höppner, Reinhard (2000), Sind wir schlechtere Menschen gewesen? *Volksstimme Magdeburg*, 9 March

Houze, Rebecca (2002), Kunst im Hause to the Wiener Werkstätte: Marketing Domesticity With Fashionable Interior Design, *Design Issues*: 18, 1, 3–23

Howard, Jutta E. (2001), *The Treuhandanstalt and Privatisation in the Former East Germany. Stakeholder perspectives*. Burlington: Ashgate

Itami, H. and T. Roehl (1987), *Mobilizing Invisible Assets*, Cambridge MA: Harvard University Press

Jaenecke, Heinrich (2001), Wir sind zwei Völker, *Stern* 33

Jahresbericht der Bundesregierung zum Stand der Deutschen Einheit (2009), Berlin: Bundesministerium für Verkehr, Bau und Stadtentwicklung, 2009-06-10

Janositz, Paul (1990), Ein Ex-Weltmeister im Wiederverwerten. *Stuttgarter Zeitung*, 11 December

Jaworski, Bernard and Kohli, Ajay (1993), Market orientation: Antecedents and consequences, *Journal of Marketing*, 57: 53–70

Jevnaker, Birgit Helene (2005), Vita Activa: On Relationships between Design(ers) and Business *Design Issues:* 21, 3, 25-48

Joiner, B. L. (1994), *Fourth Generation management: The new business consciousness*, New York: McGraw-Hill

Jordan, Lothar (1999), *Mittelstand und Mittelstandspolitik in gesamtwirtschaftlicher Betrachtung. Eine kritische Analyse anhand der Situation in den neuen Bundesländern*. Doctoral thesis, Flensburg

Jordan, Patrick W. (2000), *Designing Pleasurable Products: An Introduction to the New Human Factors*, London: Taylor and Francis

Kanwar, R. (1993), The influence of perceived risk and advertising copy claims on the consumption behavior of Asian Indian consumers, *Journal of International Consumer Marketing*, 5, 4, 7-28

Kapferer, J-N. (2004), *Strategic Brand Management: Creating and Sustaining Brand Equity Long Term*. London: Kogan Page

Kaplan, Robert and Norton, David (2004), *Strategy maps: Converting intangible assets into tangible outcomes*. Boston: Harvard Business School Press

Käppler, Stephan (1995), Alternative Wirtschaftskonzeptionen zur Strategie einer radikalen Privatisierung. In: Dümcke, Wolfgang; Wilmar, Fritz (eds.): *Kolonialisierung der DDR. Kritische Analysen und Alternativen des Einigungsprozesses*. Münster: agenda Verlag, 170-187

Keller, K.L (1998), Strategic Brand Management: Building, Measuring, and Managing Brand Equity, Upper Saddle River, NJ.: Prentice-Hall

Keller, K.L. and Lehmann, D.R. (2006), Brands and Branding: Research Findings and Future Priorities, *Marketing Science* 25 (6): 740–59

Kilmann R.K. (1995), A holistic program and critical success factors of corporate transformation, *European Management Journal*, 13, 2, 175-186

Kirsch, Frank-Michael (1993), Recension of Per Landin: *Sista tangon i DDR. Ett PS.* Stockholm: Symposion. In: *Moderna språk*, Stockholm 1/1993, 108-110

Kirsch, Frank-Michael (1993), Recension of Hans-Joachim Maaz, *Die Entrüstung*, Berlin: Argon. In: *Moderna språk*, Stockholm 2/1993, 228-231

Kirsch, Frank-Michael (1995), Recension of Alexander Osang, *Das Jahr Eins. Berichte aus der neuen Welt der Deutschen / Aufsteiger – Absteiger. Karrieren in Deutschland / Die stumpfe Ecke. Alltag in Deutschland.* Berlin: Links. In: *Moderna språk*, Stockholm 1/1995, 113-116

Kirsch, Frank-Michael; Frisch, Christine & Helmut Müssener (2001), *Nachbarn im Ostseeraum über einander. Wandel der Bilder, Vorurteile und Stereotypen?* Huddinge: Södertörn Academic Studies 6

Kirsch, Frank-Michael, *Willkommen, Herr Doktor Murke! Studien zum Deutschland- und Deutschenbild in Schweden* (2002). Aalborg: Schriften des Zentrums für deutsch-dänischen Kulturtransfer an der Universität Aalborg

Kent, Ray (2007), *Marketing Research: Approaches, Methods and Applications in Europe*, London: Thomson Learning

King, G. (2007), Narcissism and Effective Crisis Management: A Review of Potential Problems and Pitfalls, *Journal of Contingencies and Crisis Management*, 15, 4, 183-193

Klein, N. (2002), *No Logo*. Stockholm: Ordfront

Kodama, Mitsuru (2000), Business Innovation Through Customer-value Creation: Case study of a virtual education business in Japan, *Journal of Management Development*, 19, 1, 40-70

Kogut, Bruce and Udo Zander (2000), Did Socialism Fail to Innovate? A Natural experiment of the Two Zeiss Companies, *American Sociological Review*, 65, 2, 169-190

Köhler, Otto (1994), *Die große Enteignung. Wie die Treuhand eine Volkswirtschaft liquidierte*. München: Knaur

Köhler, Otto (1994), Sterben die Ostdeutschen langsam aus? *Freitag. Die Ost-West-Wochenzeitung*, 33

Kotter, John P. (1996), *Leading Change*, Boston: Harvard Business Press

Königsdorf, Helga (1982), *Der Lauf der Dinge*. Berlin and Weimar: Aufbau

Königsdorf, Helga (1992), Überleben wäre eine prima Alternative. *Berliner Zeitung*, 22 February

Kuczynski, Jürgen (1994), Nachdenken über Ostdeutschland. *Junge Welt*, 30 July

Kurskorrektur im Aufbau Ost. In: Bahrmann, Hannes; Links, Christoph (eds.): *Am Ziel vorbei. Die deutsche Einheit – Eine Zwischenbilanz*. Berlin: Ch. Links Verlag, 317-331

Kurz, Robert (1993), *Potemkins Rückkehr. Attrappen-Kapitalismus und Verteilungskrieg in Deutschland*. Berlin: Tiamat

Kröhnert, Steffen; Klingholz, Reiner (2007), *Not am Mann. Vom Helden der Arbeit zur neuen Unterschicht?* Berlin: Berlin-Institut für Bevölkerung und Entwicklung

Krysmanski, Hans Jürgen (1994), *The Conflict Between the Public and the Private Sector: Developmental Aspects of the German Unification Process and the Treuhand Anstalt*. Korean Sociological Association (ed.), Environment and Development, Seoul: Seoul Press

Lalonde, Carole (2007), The Potential Contribution of the Field of Organizational Development to Crisis Management' *Journal of Contingencies and Cri-*

sis Management, 15, 2, 95–104

Lalonde, Carole (2004), In Search of Archetypes in Crisis Management *Journal of Contingencies and Crisis Management*, 12, 2, 76–88

Land, Rainer; Willisch, Andreas (2005), Ostdeutschland – Ein Umbruchsszenario. Warum der Aufbau Ost als Nachbau West nicht gelingen konnte. In: Bahrmann, Hannes; Links, Christoph (eds.): *Am Ziel vorbei. Die deutsche Einheit – Eine Zwischenbilanz*. Berlin: Ch. Links Verlag, 11-33

Lapierre, Jozée (2000), Customer-perceived value in industrial contexts, *Journal of Business and Industrial Marketing* 15: 122–40

Latour B. (1998), *Artefaktens Återkomst*. Nerenius & Santérus Förlag: Stockholm

Lay, Conrad (1997), *Der Siegeszug der Ostprodukte. Zur Mentalitäts- und Produktgeschichte der deutschen Vereinigung* http://www.oeko-net.de/Kommune/kommunel-97/tlay197.html

Leenders R. Th. A. J; van Engelen Jo M. L; Jan Kratzer J. (2007), Systematic Design Methods and the Creative Performance of New Product Teams: Do They Contradict or Complement Each Other? *Journal of Product Innovation Management* 24 (2), 166–179

Levitt, T. (1983), The globalization of markets, *Harvard Business Review*, 61, 3, 92-102.

Leysen, André (2005), Ein Europäer im Verwaltungsrat der Treuhand. In: Breuel, Birgit; Burda, Michael C. (eds.): *Ohne historisches Vorbild. Die Treuhandanstalt 1990-1994. Eine kritische Würdigung*. Berlin: Bostelmann & Siebenhaar, 48-58

Luft, Christa (1992), *Treuhandreport. Werden, Wachsen und Vergehen einer deutschen Behörde*. Berlin und Weimar: Aufbau-Verlag

Maaz, Hans-Joachim (1991), *Das gestürzte Volk oder Die verunglückte Einheit*.

Berlin: Argon

Maaz, Hans-Joachim (1992), *Die Entrüstung*. Berlin: Argon

Maier, Harry (1991), Integrieren statt zerstören. Für eine gemischtwirtschaftliche Strategie in den neuen Bundesländern. In: *Aus Politik und Zeitgeschichte. Beilage zur Wochenzeitung „Das Parlament"*, Bonn, 29, 1991-07-12

Maier, Harry (1997), *Mittelstand in den neuen Bundesländern. Expertise für die Enquete-Kommission „Überwindung der Folgen der SED-Diktatur" des Deutschen Bundestages*, Flensburg

Malhotra, Naresh K. and David F. Birks (2007), *Marketing Research, An Applied Approach*, Essex. England: Pearson Eucation

Matheson Connell, Carol (2004), Transformation of "a business in risk": knowledge and learning for reinvention, *Management Decision*, 42, 9, 1178-1196

Marschall, Birgit (1997), Von Hilflosigkeit und Gedankenlosigkeit. Bei einer Podiumsdiskussion in Hamburg gingen Birgit Breuel, Gregor Gysi und andere der Geschichte der Treuhandanstalt nach. *Berliner Zeitung*, Berlin, 1997-03-04

Martinet, A.C. (1996), Pensée Stratégique Et Rationalités: Un Examen Epistémologique Working paper No. 23, Institut d'administration des entreprises, Lyon

Minol-Werbung (1993), *Volksstimme Magdeburg*, 17 December

Mintzberg, H., Ahlstrand, B. and Lampel, J.(1999), *Safari En Pays Stratégie*. Paris: Editions Village Mondial

Mintzberg H. (1987), Five P's for Strategy, *California Management Review*, 30, 11-24

Mitroff, I. (2004), *Crisis Leadership: Planning for the Unthinkable* New York: John Wiley & Sons

Moeller, Michael Lukas & Hans-Joachim Maaz (1991), *Die Einheit beginnt zu zweit. Ein deutsch-deutsches Zwiegespräch.* Berlin: Rowohlt

Moultrie, J.P.; Clarkson J. and Probert D (2007), Development of a Design Audit Tool for SMEs *Journal of Product Innovation Management* 24, 4, 335–368

Morgan, Robert E.; Carolyn A. Strong and Tony McGuinness (2003), Product-Market Positioning and Prospector Strategy: an analysis of strategic patterns from the resource-based perspective, *European Journal of Marketing*, 37, 10, 1409-1442

Mühlberg, Dietrich (2001), Beobachtete Tendenzen zur Ausbildung einer ostdeutschen Teilkultur http://www.bpb.de/publikationen/GQL7SA.html

Müssener, Helmut & Frank-Michael Kirsch in Zusammenarbeit mit Charlotta Brylla und Ursula Naeve-Bucher (2000), *Nachbarn im Ostseeraum unter sich. Vorurteile, Klischees und Stereotypen in Texten.* Stockholm: Södertörn Academic Studies 1

Muzellec, L. and Lambkin, M.C. (2009), Corporate branding and brand architecture: a conceptual framework, *Marketing Theory,* 9, 39-54

Naumann, Earl (1995), *Creating Customer Value: The Path to Sustainable Competitive Advantage, Cincinnati*, Ohio: Thomson Executive Press

Neue Ostalgie-Welle rollt (2003), *Stuttgarter Zeitung*, 6 March

Noble, Charles (1999), The eclectic roots of strategy implementation research, *Journal of Business Research* 45, 119–35

Normann, R. (2001), *När kartan förändrar affärslandskapet, Rethinking Business*. Malmö: Liber, (English version printed by Chichester: Wiley)

Onkvisit, S. and Shaw, J.J. (1999), Standardized international advertising: some research issues and implications, *Journal of Advertising Research*, 39, 6, 19-24

Ouedraogo, Alidou (2007), Crisis Management and Corporate Strategy in African Firms: Towards a Contingency Approach *Journal of Contingencies and Crisis Management,* Vol. 15, No. 4, December, 220-231

O'Reilly, C.A. and M.L. Tushman 2004. The ambidexterous organization, Harvard Business Review, 82, 4, 74-82

Palmer, Adrian and Bob Hartley (2002), *The Business Environment*, Maidenhead, Birkshire: McGraw-Hill

Parasuraman, A.; Dhruv Grewal and R. Krishnan (2004), *Marketing Research*, Boston: Houghton Mifflin

Petty, Richard and James Guthrie (2000), Intellectual capital literature review, Measurement, reporting and management, *Journal of Intellectual Capital*, 1, 2, 155-176

Pettigrew, A., Ferlie, E. and McKee, L. (1992), *Shaping Strategic Change*. London: Sage.

Pine, J; Gilmore, J. (1999), The Experience Economy, *Harvard Business School Press*, Boston

Pinkert, Ernst-Ullrich (ed.) (1998), *Deutschlands „innere Einheit". Traum oder Alptraum, Ziel oder Zwangsvorstellung?* Text und Kontext, Sonderreihe, Bd. 40. München: Wilhelm Fink Verlag

Post, James E.; Anne L. Lawrence and James Weber (2002), *Business and Society: Corporate Strategy, Public Policy and Ethics*, New York: McGraw Hill

Priewe, Jan (1993), Privatisation of the industrial sector: the function and activities of the Treuhandanstalt, *Cambridge Journal of Economics,* 17, 333-348

Priewe, Jan (2001), Ostdeutschland 1990-2010 – Bilanz und Perspektive. In: *Ostdeutschland – eine abgehängte Region?* Dresden: Junius-Verlag

Reißig, Rolf (2005), Anspruch und Realität der deutschen Einheit. Das Transformations- und Vereinigungsmodell und seine Ergebnisse. In: Bahrmann, Hannes; Links, Christoph (eds.): *Am Ziel vorbei. Die deutsche Einheit – Eine Zwischenbilanz*. Berlin: Ch. Links Verlag, 293-316

Roesler, Jörg (2005), Die Treuhandpolitik. Verkauf und Abwicklung statt Sanierung und Umwandlung mit dem Ergebnis einer weitgehenden Deindustrialisierung des Ostens. In: Bahrmann, Hannes; Links, Christoph (eds.): *Am Ziel vorbei. Die deutsche Einheit – Eine Zwischenbilanz*. Berlin: Ch. Links Verlag, 93-106

Roos, Johan, Göran Roos, Nicola Carlo Dragonetti and Leif Edvinsson (1997), *Intellectual Capital, Navigating the New Business Landscape*, London: MacMillan Press

Ryans, J.K., Griffith, D.A. and White, S.D. (2003), Standardization/adaptation of international marketing strategy, *International Marketing Review*, 20, 6, 588-603

Sachse, Carola (2002), *Der Hausarbeitstag. Gerechtigkeit und Gleichberechtigung in Ost und West 1939-1994*. Göttingen: Wallstein

Salem Khalifa, Azaddin (2004), Customer Value: A review of recent literature and an integrative configuration, *Management Decision*, 42, 5, 645-666

Schachtschneider, Karl Albrecht (1996), *Sozialistische Schulden nach der Revolution. Kritik der Altschuldenpolitik. Ein Beitrag zur Lehre von Recht und Unrecht*. Berlin: Duncker & Humblot

Schipanski, Dagmar (2008), „Für Ostalgie besteht kein Anlaß", *Focus* 3 December

Schmidt, Helmut (1993), *Handeln für Deutschland. Wege aus der Krise*. Berlin: Rowohlt

Schmidt, Michael (2008), Die offenen Adern Ostdeutschlands. *Der Tagesspiegel*, Berlin, 2008-04-24

Schroeder, Jonathan E. (2009), The cultural codes of branding, *Marketing Theory,* 9; 123-126

Schroeder, J.E. and Salzer-Mörling, M. (eds) (2006), *Brand Culture*. London: Routledge

Schröder, Richard (2005), Die schnelle staatliche Einheit. Wirtschaftliche und politische Gründe für den eingeschlagenen Weg. In: Bahrmann, Hannes; Links, Christoph (eds.): *Am Ziel vorbei. Die deutsche Einheit – Eine Zwischenbilanz*. Berlin: Ch. Links Verlag, 34-47

Schürer, Gerhard (1992), Analyse der ökonomischen Lage der DDR mit Schlußfolgerungen. Vorlage für das Politbüro des Zentralkomitees der SED. Geheime Verschlußsache b5 1158/89. In: *Deutschland-Archiv* 10/1992, 1112-1120

Scott, W.R. (2001), *Institutions and Organizations*. London: Sage Publication

Sebastian, R. (2005), The Interface between Design and Management *Design Issues*, 21, 1, 81-93

Seibel, Wolfgang (2005), *Verwaltete Illusionen. Die Privatisierung der DDR-Wirtschaft durch die Treuhandanstalt und ihre Nachfolger 1990-2000*. Frankfurt/Main: Campus Verlag

Senge, P. (1990), *The Fifth Discipline* London: Random House

Simon H. (1981), *The Sciences of the Artificial* Cambridge MA: MIT Press

Sinn, Gerlinde and Sinn, Hans-Werner (1992), *Jumpstart. The Economic Unification of Germany*. Cambridge, Massachusetts: The MIT-Press

Sinn, Gerlinde, and Hans-Werner Sinn (1993), *Kaltstart. Volkswirtschaftliche Effekte der deutschen Vereinigung*. München: C. H. Beck

Sinn, Hans-Werner (2005), *Ist Deutschland noch zu retten?* 2nd ed., Berlin: Ullstein

Sirisagul, K. (2000), Global advertising practices: a comparative study, *Journal of Global Marketing*, 14, 3, 77-97

Skandia, (1995), Supplement to Skandia's 1995 Annual Report Stockholm: Skandia

Skandia, (1996), Supplement to Skandia's 1996 Annual Report Stockholm: Skandia

Slappendel, C. (1996), *Perspectives on Innovation in Organizations: Power, Meaning and Design*, London: Routledge

Solberg, C.A.(2000), Standardization or adaptation of the international marketing mix: the role of the local subsidiary/representative, *Journal of International Marketing*, 8, 1, 78-98

Späth, Lothar (2005), Jenoptik – Die wahre Geschichte eines erfolgreichen Unternehmens. In: Breuel, Birgit; Burda, Michael C. (eds.): *Ohne historisches Vorbild. Die Treuhandanstalt 1990-1994. Eine kritische Würdigung*. Berlin: Bostelmann & Siebenhaar, 97-113

Spiegel, Hubert (2008), Ein Verleger unter Räubern. *FAZ*, Frankfurt/Main, 2008-04-02

Steimle, Uwe (2006), Kein geschichtlicher Alzheimer. *Freitag. Die Ost-West-Wochenzeitung*, 35

Steinitz, Klaus (1998), *Die Wirtschaft in den neuen Ländern nach der Wende*, www.memo.uni-bremen.de/docs/steinitz98.pdf

Steiner, Jürgen; Dieter Kappler and Herman-Josef Berg (2003), *From Jena to Mainz - and Back Again*, Mainz: Schott

Stewart, Thomas (1997), *Intellectual capital: The new wealth of organizations*. New York: Doubleday Currency

Stewart, Thomas A. (2001), *The Wealth of Knowledge, Intellectual Capital and the Twenty-first Century Organization*, New York: Doubleday

Stokes, Robyn (2006), Network-based strategy making for event tourism, *European Journal of Marketing* 40, 682–95

Stolz aufs eigene Leben (1995), *Der Spiegel* no. 27

Suárez, Fernando and Utterback, James (1995), 'Dominant designs and the survival of firms', *Strategic Management Journal* 16, 415–30

Sveiby K.E. (1997), The New Organizational Wealth: Managing and Measuring Knowledge-based Assets, San Francisco, Ca.: Berrett-Koehler

Svengren, L. (1995), *Industriell design som strategisk resurs – en studie av designprocessens metoder och synsätt som del av företagets strategiska utveckling*. Lund: Lund Univ. Press

Swan, Jacky; Sue Newell; Harry Scarborough and Donald Hislop, (1999), Knowledge Management and Innovation: Networks and Networking, *Journal of Knowledge Management*, 3, 4, 262-275

Sylvester, Regine (2003), Ich habe so Freudenmomente. *Berliner Zeitung*, 1 March

Szymanski, D.M., Bharadwaj, S.G. Varadarajan, R.P. (1993), Standardization versus adaption of international marketing strategy: an empirical investigation *Journal of Marketing*, 57, 4, 1-17

Tagesspiegel, (2009), *In Schweden ist Erziehung nicht nur Frauenthema*, Berlin, 25 February 2009

Tellkamp, Uwe (2008), *Der Turm. Geschichte aus einem versunkenen Land*. Frankfurt am Main: Suhrkamp

Thierse, Wolfgang (2001), Fünf Thesen zur Vorbereitung eines Aktionsprogramms für Ostdeutschland. www.ZEIT.DE, 3 January

Thompson, H. (1998), What Do Customers Really Want? *Journal of Business Strategy*, July-August, 17-21

Thorpe, Eleri and Morgan, Robert (2007), 'In pursuit of the 'Ideal Approach' to successful marketing strategy implementation', *European Journal of Marketing* 41, 659–77

Thompson James D. (1967), *Organizations in action: social science bases of administrative theory,* New York : Mc Graw-Hill

Tiger, Lionel (1992), *The Pursuit of Pleasure*, Boston: Little, Brown and Company

Tippach-Schneider, Simone (2004), *Tausend Tele-Tips. Das Werbefernsehen in der DDR*. Berlin: Schwarzkopf & Schwarzkopf

Tollhagen-Åkerhielm, R. (2003), *Skräddare utan tråd: en illustration av fyra företag i klädbranschen*. Stockholm: Dokusys

Tollhagen, R. (1994), *A History of Work Environment Innovation. Sweden*, Dublin: European Foundation for the Improvment of Living and Working Conditions, Working Paper No.: WP/95/02/EN (EPOC Publications)

Treuhand intern. Tagebuch. (1993), *Herausgegeben von Birgit Breuel*. Berlin: Ullstein

Urde, Mats (1994), Brand orientation – a strategy for survival, *Journal of Consumer Marketing* 11, 18–32

Van de Ven, A.H. (1986), Central Problems in the Management of Innovation, *Management Science*, 32, 590-607

Varadarajan et al., (2006), Brand Portfolio, Corporate Image, and Reputation: Managing Brand Deletions *Journal of the Academy of Marketing Science*, 34, 2, 195-205

Varadarajan, P. Rajan and Satish Jayachandran (1999), Marketing Strategy: An

Assessment of the State of the Field and Outlook, *Journal of the Academy of Marketing Science*, 27, 2, 120-143

Vehse, Wolfgang (1994), Privatization German Style. A Look inside the Practices and Policies of the Treuhandanstalt. Colloquium "Privatization in NACC Countries", Brussels: http://www.nato.int/docu/colloq/1994/eco947.txt

Verganti, R; Buganza, T. (2005), Design Inertia: Designing for Life-Cycle Flexibility in Internet-Based Services, *Journal of Product Innovation Management* 22 (3), 223–237

Veryzer, Robert; Borja de Mozota, Brigitte (2005), The Impact of User-Oriented Design on New Product Development: An Examination of Fundamental Relationships *The Journal of Product Innovation Management* 22: 128–143

Volkskammer der Deutschen Demokratischen Republik (1990), 10. Wahlperiode, 35. Tagung, 1990-09-13. Stenographische Niederschrift 1680

von Dohnanyi, Klaus (2005), Der "Markt" allein konnte es nicht richten. Plädoyer für eine Kurskorrektur im Aufbau Ost. In: Bahrmann, Hannes; Links, Christoph (eds.): *Am Ziel vorbei. Die deutsche Einheit – Eine Zwischenbilanz.* Berlin: Ch. Links Verlag, 317-331

von Stamm, Bettina (2004), Innovation: What's Design Got to Do with It? *Design Management Review,* Winter: 10–19

Waigel, Theo (2005), Die finanzpolitischen Rahmenbedingungen des Treuhand-Modells. In: Breuel, Birgit; Burda, Michael C. (eds.): *Ohne historisches Vorbild. Die Treuhandanstalt 1990-1994. Eine kritische Würdigung.* Berlin: Bostelmann & Siebenhaar, 59-72

Walker, Orville C.; Harper W. Boyd and Jean-Claude Larréché (1992), *Marketing Strategy*, Homewood IL: Richard D. Irwin

Walter, Norbert; Quitzau, Jörn (2005), Gab es marktwirtschaftliche Alternativen zur Treuhandprivatisierung? In: Breuel, Birgit; Burda, Michael C. (eds.): *Ohne historisches Vorbild. Die Treuhandanstalt 1990-1994. Eine kritische*

Würdigung. Berlin: Bostelmann & Siebenhaar, 160-175

Weick, Karl E, (2001), *Making sense of the organization.* Oxford: Blackwell Business

Weinstein, Art and William C. Johnson (1999), *Designing and Delivering Superior customer Value: Concepts, Cases and Applications*, New York: St. Lucie Press

Wendel, Kay (1995), Die Treuhandanstalt und die Deindustrialisierung Ostdeutschlands. In: Dümcke, Wolfgang; Wilmar, Fritz (eds.): *Kolonialisierung der DDR. Kritische Analysen und Alternativen des Einigungsprozesses.* Münster: agenda Verlag, 142-153

Wenzel, Siegfried (2006), *Was war die DDR wert? Und wo ist dieser Wert geblieben? Versuch einer Abschlußbilanz.* 7th edition. Berlin: Das neue Berlin

Werbung in der DDR (2004), Gespräch mit Gottfried Scheffler, DEWAG-Experte http://www.mdr.de/damals/lexikon/1593647.html

Whitelock, J. Rey, J.C. (1998), Cross-cultural advertising in Europe, *International Marketing Review.* 15, 4, 257-276

Wickström, S. et.al (1998), *Det interaktiva företaget - med kunden som största resurs.* Stockholm: Svenska Förlaget

Wiersema, Frederik and Treacy, Michael (1993), Customer intimacy and other value disciplines, *Harvard Business Review,* Jan–Feb: 84–93

Wiesenthal, Helmut (1999), *Die Transformation der DDR. Verfahren und Resultate.* Gütersloh: Bertelsmann

Wie Konzerne aus dem Westen mit ostdeutschen Traditionsmarken von der DDR-Nostalgie profitieren (2003), *Wirtschaftswoche,* no. 41

Wiig, Karl M. (1997a), Integrating Intellectual Capital and Knowledge Management, *Long Range Planning,* 30, 3, 399-405

Wiig, Karl M. (1997b), Knowledge Management: where did it come from and were will it go?, *Journal of Expert Systems with Application*, Special issue on knowledge management, Autumn 1997

Witzel, Holger (2003), Das Märchen von der Ostalgie. *Stern*, no. 37

Wolfe, R.A. (1994), Organizational Innovation: Review, Critique and Suggested Research Directions, *Journal of Management Studies*, 31, 357-81

Wolfgang; Wilmar, Fritz (eds.): *Kolonialisierung der DDR. Kritische Analysen und Alternativen des Einigungsprozesses*. Münster: Agenda Verlag, 154-169

Wolle, Stefan (1998), *Die heile Welt der Diktatur. Alltag und Herrschaft in der DDR 1971-1989*. Berlin: Ch. Links

Wood, R.C. (2007) How Strategic Innovation Really Gets Started, Strategy and Leadership, 35, 1, 21-29

Yavas, U. Verhage, B.J. Green, R.T. (1992), Global segmentation versus local market orientation: empirical findings, *Management International Review*, 32, 3, 265-72

Zou, S. Tamer, C.S. (2002), The GMS: a broad conceptualization of global marketing strategy and its effect on firm performance, *Journal of Marketing*, .66, 4, 40-56